COMMUNITY IN A CROWD

Egalitarianism

General Editor:
Bruce Kapferer, *Professor Emeritus of Anthropology, University of Bergen, and Honorary Professor, University College London*

Although frequently understood as having originated in the European Enlightenment and discussed as a key concept of a Western modernity, egalitarianism is conceived here as an energy underpinning most human action when confronted with forms of oppression that deny, destroy, inhibit or limit the achievement of human potential. The volumes in this series contribute to the general understanding of egalitarian processes and the barriers to their realization.

Volume 3
Community in a Crowd: Bitcoin and the Quest for Liberty in Tel Aviv
Matan Shapiro

Volume 2
Egalitarian Dynamics: Liminality and Victor Turner's Contribution to the Understanding of Socio-historical Process
Edited by Bruce Kapferer and Marina Gold

Volume 1
After the Pink Tide: Corporate State Formation and New Egalitarianisms in Latin America
Edited by Marina Gold and Alessandro Zagato

COMMUNITY IN A CROWD

Bitcoin and the Quest for Liberty in Tel Aviv

Matan Shapiro

berghahn
NEW YORK • OXFORD
www.berghahnbooks.com

First published in 2026 by
Berghahn Books
www.berghahnbooks.com

Library of Congress Cataloging-in-Publication Data
A C.I.P. cataloging record is available from the Library of Congress
Library of Congress Cataloging in Publication Control Number: 2025038611

British Library Cataloguing in Publication Data
A catalogue record for this book is available from the British Library

EU GPSR Authorized Representative
LOGOS EUROPE, 9 rue Nicolas Poussin, 17000, LA ROCHELLE, France
Email: Contact@logoseurope.eu

ISBN 978-1-83695-299-2 hardback
ISBN 978-1-83695-300-5 epub
ISBN 978-1-83695-301-2 web pdf

https://doi.org/10.3167/9781836952992

This open access edition of *Community in a Crowd: Bitcoin and the Quest for Liberty in Tel Aviv* has been funded by the University of Bergen.

This book is dedicated to the memory of my father,
David Shapiro (1954–2021)
A man bigger than life, who stood out in the crowd.

CONTENTS

ILLUSTRATIONS

ACKNOWLEDGEMENTS

This book is the result of ethnographic fieldwork I carried out intermittently between July 2017 and June 2019 in Tel Aviv as part of Professor Bruce Kapferer's ERC Advanced Grant project, titled 'Egalitarianism: Forms, Processes, Comparisons'. Based at the Department of Anthropology, University of Bergen (UiT), Norway, the project was jointly financed by grants from the European Research Council (ERC), the University of Bergen and the Norwegian Research Council (NRC). I thank all these academic organizations for having provided the opportunity to conduct this study and bring it to a successful conclusion.

I extend my everlasting gratitude to Bruce Kapferer and Don Handelman for their uncompromising support along the way. I consider Don and Bruce's extensive scholarly enterprises as principal sources of intellectual inspiration that have informed much of the analysis presented in this book. I will never find enough words to convey my gratitude to both.

I am indebted to the members of the Bitcoin Embassy in Tel Aviv for enabling me to take part in their everyday activities. I am particularly grateful to Noa Mashiah, Meni Rosenfeld, Ayal (Yona) Segev, Shmuel Dreilinger, Maya Dreilinger, Assaf Bahat, Jonathan Rouach, Bar X., Yossi Y., Amos Z., Nadav A., Uriyah B. and Sarah Wisner; all of whom have contributed enormously to this manuscript with their knowledge of Bitcoin, kindness and great humour. There are many other good people I could have mentioned but the page is short, and some of them would surely wish to remain anonymous. I thank everyone profoundly and I hope we shall one day meet again.

Sadly, a key research interlocutor had passed away from an illness several years after I concluded my fieldwork in Tel Aviv. I refer to him in this book as Nissim (pseudonym). I send my sincere condolences to his family and friends. Nissim's views on technological utopias and egalitarian sociality were eye-opening, and they helped understand the project of the Embassy at a more profound level. I hope this book will contribute to spreading some of Nissim's insights and to popularising his dreams of a better world, adding his name to the small but prestigious list of Bitcoin true-believer Hall of Famers, where he no doubt belongs.

I profoundly thank Dr. Janine Su, who helped edit the final draft of this manuscript. Her suggestions were priceless. I also thank several other scholars who have provided useful comments on earlier drafts or have critically discussed my ideas during seminars. These include Diana Espírito Santo, Hanna Skartveit, Martin Holbraad, Allen Abramson, Roland Kapferer, Kirsten Bell, Andrew Lattas, Filipe Calvão, Valerio Simoni, Bjørn Enge Bertelsen, and Knut Rio. Colleagues from the Egalitarianism Project at the University of Bergen likewise have made a difference during many brainstorming sessions. Thanks so much!

Finally, I am grateful to early-access readers who have already sent their voluntary support. For those who wish to send their contributions in the future, I can be reached at this address: bc1qazm553nr9pr57gqrvxw0f83klxxmta36kvpjxj. Or through this QR code:

Matan Shapiro, 2025

INTRODUCTION

Origins

In 2013, Yoni Shemesh converted his small architecture studio at the heart of Tel Aviv into what at the time was one of the first Bitcoin meetup centres in the world. He cleared the 15 sqm ground floor, leaving there only one sofa, a few shelves and a big LED screen. He also smashed the front wall and replaced it with a huge glass. In a country where armed guards control the entrance to nearly every public institution, the message was clear: *everybody is welcome* (see Figure 0.1.). Alluding to the pioneering 'Bitcoin Centre' trading floor in New York – but going a step further by self-styling the space as a sort of diplomatic hub – Shemesh dubbed it *The Bitcoin Embassy in Tel Aviv*.

As the story goes, it all began after a night of heavy drinking dedicated to what Embassy associate Uri described to me in 2018 as 'the most hallucinated ideas on how to advance mass adoption of Bitcoin'. The next morning, in a cloudy hangover, Shemesh decided to act on one of these hallucinations. By that afternoon he had already produced silver badges with the Bitcoin symbol and the inscription 'Ambassador'. The core group of Embassy associates held another meeting that same week, this time over coffee. They decided that each would volunteer for one or two shifts per week to provide information about Bitcoin to anyone who dropped in. Although no template was used, the way shifts tended to be structured consisted of occasional information sharing with random visitors, focusing on either Bitcoin ideology or its financial benefits relative to fiat (i.e. state-backed) currencies. This also included the provision of practical technical advice to newcomers, such as how to install a cryptocurrency wallet, the pragmatic meaning of central concepts and investment strategies in the world of Bitcoin, and how to send and receive money via the Bitcoin

Figure 0.1. The entrance to the Bitcoin Embassy in Tel Aviv. Credit: Matan Shapiro.

network. These voluntary shifts in turn entitled each Ambassador to take part in the decision-making process. They would meet roughly every two weeks to 'decide things in a decentralized way', as Shemesh described this in an interview, alluding to their reliance on a flat social structure.

I first heard of the Embassy in September 2017. I had just begun research on egalitarian impulses in the emergent Israeli cryptocurrency scene and was exploring potential sites for fieldwork. I initially attended meetups organized by different Israeli startup ventures, which were ideal spaces for networking. During one of these meetups I met an investor called Gur. It was a sweltering day, and we both sipped from half-frozen beer bottles on the twenty-sixth floor of a luxurious office building in north Tel Aviv, where the startup that had organized the meeting rented an entire floor. When Gur heard I was looking for a suitable site for fieldwork, he insisted that I visit the Embassy. 'It is the real thing', he assured me, 'a real crypto community [in Hebrew: *Kehila*]'. I asked if I needed to make an appointment in advance, as was the norm for other such meetups. Gur laughed to signal I was way off track. He then raised his beer and declared, 'To the revolution!' I smiled faintly and toasted. *This feels promising*, I remember thinking as I marked in my diary a visit to the Embassy for the following Sunday.[1]

Welcome to the New Economy

The Embassy occupied the unimpressive tiny ground floor of an old five-storey residential building on Ahuzat Bayit Street in Tel Aviv, part of a wider area that tour guides call 'The White City' due to the now-crumbling white façades of Bauhaus buildings constructed there between the 1920s and 1940s. To the left of the Embassy entrance was the door leading to the upper floors of the rundown building, protected by a heavy lock and an intercom. To the right stood a small shop selling designer furniture. The building shared a wall with the one next to it, creating an uninterrupted structure stretching between Montefiore and Ahad Ha'am Streets. Around the corner there was a café, and on the pavement in front of the Embassy next to motorcycle railings was a wooden bench. Later during fieldwork I discovered that the bench effectively extended the Embassy into the street, as Ambassadors often sat there to smoke, drink beer, talk or just enjoy the evening breeze coming from the magnificent Mediterranean coast down the hill.

Across the street stood a massive building that was the home of the Tel Aviv Stock Exchange. It occupied most of that side of the street, its windows gleaming and its outdoor ticker displaying the changing values of Israeli stocks in flickering red and green lights.[2] The building cast a permanent shadow along the street, an advantage in a city where summer temperatures can easily reach 35 degrees Celsius, and the humidity is at times unbearable.

I stood outside for a while, taking it all in. I then inhaled deeply and stepped through the glass door. The first thing I saw was an inscription on the wall in Hebrew and English with the Embassy logo on top (see Figure 0.2). It read:

'Welcome to the New Economy! Here you can ask, share and talk [about] new decentralized cryptocurrency (sic). This is an open source community. Bitcoin accepted.'

Figure 0.2. Welcome inscription on the wall at the Embassy. Credit: Matan Shapiro.

A hoarse 'shalom' came from the old sofa in the centre of the room. A man with a snow-white ponytail sat there by himself, examining something on his mobile phone.

'Shalom', I mumbled, not sure if this man was the same one who greeted me.

'Are you the guy who called yesterday and wanted to sell?' The man with the ponytail stared at me.

'Sell what?'

'Bitcoin, what else!?'

'No, it's my first time here.' I smiled faintly.

'Ahh', he nodded. 'Sit then, we'll talk.' He stood up, reached his hand out to shake mine and gestured towards the chair in front of the sofa. 'Nissim. Nice to meet you.'

'Matan. Likewise.' I sat down. 'I am doing anthropological research on Bitcoin, and I'd like to write everything you say.'

'Yes, of course, you came to the right place.' Nissim checked his phone again. 'So, let's begin with that guy that called here yesterday. I answered the phone. The guy said he had seen the slow rise in the value of bitcoin in the last year and he believes that it will crash down soon. So he asked if he could come over to sell his bitcoin holdings. Everything! What do you think I said?'

'No idea . . . I heard that investing in bitcoin can be dangerous.' I was asking more than asserting, while casually taking my notebook out of my bag.

'Wrong answer', Nissim nodded energetically. 'You should never sell everything at once! Bitcoin is iron-strong [*barzel*]; if it crashes it will rise again. It is unbeatable, and that is the reason that here at the Embassy we believe that Bitcoin is your only insurance policy against financial meltdown. And it will come; there is no doubt about it.'

I nodded. That was exactly what I expected to hear in an 'embassy' dedicated to promoting what at the time I perceived merely as just another profit-making device in the incessant sprawling of capital. But the rest of Nissim's enthusiastic monologue sparked my curiosity:

> Remember what I am telling you; in Bitcoin it is not enough to have money, you need to know what you are doing [with the money] and understand what *liberty* is. Every step you take in the world of Bitcoin, you discover yourself; it is a process of internal revelation, like peeling an onion. You are all the time in a continuous lesson. Bitcoin makes your brain active. When you begin investing you find yourself thinking how to upgrade your life to the level you want to reach. It is like a spiritual doctrine that also has a material side to it.

'Spiritual?' I was genuinely surprised. 'What you call "the material side" surely is the main incentive', I insisted.

'Not at all. The number one mistake people make is to think that Bitcoin is all about getting rich. But Bitcoin is in fact *opposed to* all the other capitalistic systems!' He continued:

> In our world people only know how to take – the municipality takes, the government takes, and for what? For security. '*We guarantee your security with ballistic missiles so they don't attack us from Iran.*' Well, they can't even deal with flimsy

> kites.[3] . . . They just exploit the person, and I don't blame them. The bankers have the *freedom* to decide for us. The system gives them that freedom, which comes at our expense. They don't give us the freedom to decide for our own sake. And Bitcoin gives us the ability to take that freedom [into our own hands], which they don't allow us, and endow ourselves with it, merely by purchasing the correct coin, the right way, which doesn't tell you what to do, do this or that . . . [but rather] be free, be whoever you want, do whatever you want . . .

'How is that different from any other money system, or investment in stocks?' I asked.

'The difference is that here you have a community.' Nissim spoke as if this was obvious:

> Bitcoin, since it is decentralized, and since it is not controlled by a central body or a superpower, can create a community which is homogenous in the sense that it takes care of its own needs with its own means. Today you can't do this [in the normative economy] because you cannot change [policy] priorities or decide that one service is more important than the other. But in our community [i.e. in the Bitcoin Embassy], things are decided for the benefit of everyone. For example, although it's a bit banal, we always bring pizzas for the open meetings we hold. What, are we going to tell each person [present] to pay for their share of the pizza? I can buy pizza for ten people; I have the ability so I will do it. There is collaboration and sharing here that is not pre-calculated. Nobody comes and says, 'Today I am buying pizza for everyone, remember that'.

'Well, you can say the same thing about any other group of people that decide to take things into their own hands', I charged. 'What would be the difference between the Bitcoin community and a group of colleagues who started a business together in an office building?'

Nissim stared at me obliquely, his chin almost touching his chest. He then typed something on his mobile and handed it over to me. 'Have a look', he said. 'This is Yaron, he is one of the Ambassadors here. Some years ago, he did an interview with a vlogger. He explains very well how Bitcoin can make a difference in the world. It's not long.'

I pressed PLAY and Yaron's head appeared on the screen. He said:

> Why is Bitcoin good as a substitute for money and gold? Let's start with the fact that it doesn't have a Sovereign – [President] Obama, for example, who now [in 2014] needs 2.5 trillion dollars for health care, or Bush Senior and Bush Junior [who needed money] to finance wars in Iraq and Afghanistan – if [they] need it, the Federal Reserve will print it. There is no such thing in Bitcoin! There isn't any sinful centralized body – an insane mechanism . . . [instead] there is . . . a wonderful internet *ore*, an international freedom language that *overrides boundaries and shatters the Sovereign*, the Prophet Moses of the Third Millennium, who will

> undoubtedly liberate us from the Pharaoh . . . The revolution of Bitcoin [will be] greater than anything that ever happened in the history of mankind . . . Bitcoin will be bigger than the internet, than Google, than Facebook, than the wheel, than $E=mc^2$. Satoshi Nakamoto [the still-anonymous inventor of Bitcoin] will be more famous than Michael Jordan and Jesus. *Bitcoin will be the backbone of human society in the world for everything: money, real estate, language, propriety, voting, organization, communities, stock-exchange platforms – everything will be [based] on Bitcoin . . .*[4]

'Unbelievable!', I whispered. Initially I had expected to find at the Embassy radical capitalists devoted to financial profiteering. Instead, I encountered a self-proclaimed community of social reformers. I remembered Gur's promise that Embassy personnel were 'a *real* crypto community' and felt a sort of anthropological eureka moment. Do all Embassy members perceive Bitcoin as a revolutionary project, which is 'not only about money' but rather a 'language of freedom' that would destroy 'the Sovereign'? To find out, I sought permission from Embassy associates to conduct ethnographic fieldwork with them, ending up accompanying Embassy activities and key research interlocutors for a period of nearly two years.

The Analytical Problem

Although Embassy members held broadly divergent sociopolitical convictions, and even sometimes differed on economic issues, they agreed on one fundamental principle – that Bitcoin was a tool of personal liberation. Their argument was simple: in the hegemonic or 'centralized' financial system, as they labelled it, social relations were overly regulated by 'third parties', such as banks, financial corporations, SWIFT services and credit card companies. Due to their intermediary role, these institutions also wielded enormous political and economic powers, which Embassy members claimed would always be detrimental to individual freedoms. Mass adoption of Bitcoin, in turn, will eliminate the current dependency on these institutions, enabling instead peer-to-peer (P2P) cash transactions at a global scale unfettered by fiscal protectionism. Expanding this notion from finance to societal structures at large, Embassy associates argued that Bitcoin could therefore also eliminate most forms of top-down regulation, thus bringing into existence a truly egalitarian society of economically autonomous peers.

The main idioms interlocutors used to justify the feasibility of this vision were 'decentralization' (*bîzúr*) and 'trustlessness' (often pronounced in English).[5] Both these terms were derived from the quasi-mythical *White Paper* published in 2008 by Satoshi Nakamoto, the pseudonymous inventor(s) of Bitcoin.[6] The paper describes the functionality of what quickly thereafter became known as '*the blockchain*' – an open-source ledger, which uses algorithmic calculations to regulate the exchange of money between individuals (Greenfield 2018: 123–25). The White Paper transparently included the codes required to set up the blockchain on any odd computer, and it was published in an email-distribution listserv that at the time was regularly accessed by hundreds of subscribers. These codes have remained open to public scrutiny ever since, thereby permanently *decentralizing* control of the ledger across the entire network of users. Every attempt to defraud someone should thus immediately be identified and thwarted by multiple unrelated auditors. Decentralization prevents any single stakeholder from changing the algorithms without the consent of other users, and as a result it enables the safe exchange of money directly between stakeholders at an exceptionally large scale. As a key concept and mode of action, 'decentralization' enables every bitcoin holder to send their coins across the network securely, without anybody being able to stop or modify the transaction.

This last feature also makes *trustless money transactions* possible (Greenfield 2018: 122–23). Satoshi, as Bitcoiners around the world usually call them, described this feature in the White Paper (2008) as a 'reduction' of the level of trust required to send and receive cash online. Empirically this means that Bitcoin adopters do not have to trust neither human nor corporate intermediaries (i.e. third parties). In contrast, all peers can trust the mechanical system that regulates transactions in real time because its cryptographic formulas are open for all to see, thereby allowing users to verify on their own that the blockchain is functioning well. At least in theory, every Bitcoin adopter should gain in this way absolute certainty about the validity of their transactions. Embassy associates described this feature as an effective 'automation of trust', which they argued discarded human moral weaknesses (like the temptation to defraud or steal) and faulty sensory faculties (like occasional typing errors) from financial relationships.

But here lies an intricate problem. Anthropologist Viviana Zelizer (2005) argued that trust is an *ethical contingency* of close relationships. As such, trust is fundamental to the exchange of money, favours, goods, etc., insofar as it implies emotional dependency on or a measure of deference to meaningful others; especially in a context of long-term reciprocity that is not strictly commercial (see Richard and Rudnyckyj 2009). Anthropologist David Graeber (2011) later complemented this stance, arguing that ethical contingency itself is endemic to *debt relationships*, which require a horizon of future exchange and therefore at least a measure of commitment from reciprocating sides.

When combined, these arguments then challenge Embassy associates' ambitions to establish a small-scale community based on the exchange of trustless money, let alone their aspiration to build an egalitarian society of fully autonomous peers. That is so because these perspectives suggest that trustless technology would necessarily *cut* any emotional contingency between peers on the network (see Strathern 1996), thus dissolving the fabric of human community that is essential to conducting any economic reciprocity over time. The pretension to decentralize power through trustless technology threatens communitarian cohesion at the level of grassroots activity because it radically fragments trust-based societal institutions into a variety of ad hoc, instrumental, dyadic arrangements; which, according to Zelizer (2005) and Graeber (2011), could hardly *replace* trust-based collaborative agreements. This prism thus associates Bitcoin with market-driven economic models (namely Hayek 1958[1948]; Menger 2009[1892]), which diminish the scope of trust-based, community-oriented economic activities as it substitutes them with a set of individuated mechanical exchanges.

This critique could apply to some Bitcoiners, no doubt. But it could not explicate the attitudes and actions at the Embassy, wherein interlocutors *did* in fact value meaningful intimate relationships. For example, Ambassadors often expressed unflinching ethical commitment to majority rule, voluntarism, coordinated direct action, transparency, communal responsibility, and the maintenance of protocol; all of which are features of collective organization that require collaboration, mutuality and trust. Relationships cultivated at the Embassy, in other words, sometimes paradoxically curtailed individual dependency on trustless exchange, which interlocutors otherwise kept praising as near-spiritual gateways to freedom.

Although they were unable to solve this apparent conundrum – wherein methodological individualism is paradoxically mobilized to induce collective affinity, and vice versa – interlocutors at the Embassy generated an innovative ethnographic theory that partially mitigated the tension. As I quickly learned, at the heart of Embassy sociality was the desire to create a network of people who would be ethically indebted to each other as members of a community but economically indebted only to themselves. Individual autonomy is here measured by the ability to remain debtless in an economy heavily reliant on credit, while moral cohesion is sought through the successful maintenance of a flat (or 'decentralised') community organization. Interlocutors unsurprisingly thus used such notions as 'social equality' and 'distributive justice' to articulate the power of collective action in transforming human worlds. An ethos of collective affinity at the Embassy suggested that individual units and social wholes were *not* antimonious.

To work through this vernacular view, I realized, it would be crucial to go beyond the dialectic deadlock that portrays rational choice and societal intimacy as irreconcilable. I thus found myself asking: What does it even mean to take part in an 'open-source, community'? How is membership in this community, which requires some measure of collective cohesion to advance its stated objectives, reconciled with the libertarian ideals of total individual autonomy and trustless reciprocity? And even more broadly, what does this counterintuitive notion of communalist individualism (or individual communalism) tell us about emergent forms of social organization in a rapidly digitalizing world?

The Argument

Building on these questions, this book advances two interconnected arguments. First, I argue that Embassy associates were able to imagine themselves as both devoted communalists *and* committed individualists because the Embassy itself was a liminal space within which it was possible to bridge these usually opposed imaginaries. Liminal spaces and situations, being existentially neither 'here' nor 'there', at times serve to successfully mitigate paradoxes precisely because they are at least partially withdrawn from mundane routines while also simultaneously enhancing aspects of everyday dilemmas (Turner 1969, 1974; cf. Kapferer 2024). Ambassadors embraced the liminality of the Embassy, in other words, by continuously mixing 'centralized' and 'decentralized' organizational modalities in their everyday practice. The credibility of their project indeed *depended on* this fusion, which annulled the purported distance between enclosed (or centralized) models of social interaction and open-ended (or decentralized) ones (see Hayes 2019; Swartz 2018; Tuddenham 2024). Going beyond the moneyness of Bitcoin – that is, its market liquidity as a store of value and its reliability as a unit of exchange – this argument seeks to explain how interlocutors in Tel Aviv turned a heterodox debate on economic decentralization into an ambitious experimental project, whose acuity they used to challenge the hegemonic relationship between autonomy and indebtedness in contemporary Israel.

The second argument will focus on Bitcoin crowds. I here rely mainly on the work of Christian Borch (2007, 2009, 2012), who demonstrated how fluctuating stock prices in financial markets funnel masses of individual traders into synchronic – yet temporary and continuously changing – trading positions. To describe this phenomenon, Borch (2007) used the term 'crowd syndrome' – a tendency to be swept away with others in a mass gathering, or, alternatively, in designated digital spaces – and act like them; whether this manifests economically, politically, judicially or otherwise. 'Syndrome' encompasses both the tendency of investors to follow the actions of informal industry leaders, who are perceived to be more knowledgeable or as having sufficient economic influence on trends; and the tendency to get caught up emotionally in the seductive allure of the market, as boom-and-bust cycles intermittently consolidate or disperse buyers and sellers at a global scale, thereby inspiring intense emotional amalgamations of anticipation, thrill and gloom. These two factors might at time demolish the perceived boundaries between peers, turning them into a single mass of people who seemingly act synonymously and synchronically *as a sprawling crowd.*

This analytical direction also owes to Elias Canetti's (1984[1960]) fantastic analysis of the power of crowds. Canetti contends that a crowd comes into being when an emotional 'discharge' occurs, a sensory reaction he understands as a sudden loss of personal boundaries, which breeds unity with those around oneself. He calls this 'the loss of the fear of being touched' (ibid.: 17), which, he argues, makes us oblivious to interpersonal distance both spatially and affectively. It is not enough for people to gather around a leader who promotes this or that idea to make them a crowd, in other words. Rank and personal, 1974 charisma alone are seldom enough to mobilize people into mass action. Something must synergize some kind of deeper unity between people who assemble together in order to transform a multitude of strangers into a cohesive crowd. No matter how ephemeral this unity may be, Canetti argues, discharge is essential to generating a sense of collective empowerment by which crowds operate. Such discharge causes people who had never met before to feel closer, as a sudden affective flare passes *through* them. To be effective, Canetti insists, discharge must be unpredictable; even carefully arranged ritual settings, which are specifically designed to spark an emotional response, cannot guarantee the mobilization of untamed and previously unrelated groups of people into coordinated mass action.

In Bitcoin, rapid and often extreme value fluctuations against fiat currencies – especially the US dollar, euros and pounds sterling – directly influence trade volumes and wealth liquidity, intermittently consolidating and dispersing masses of unrelated traders across the cybernetic 'trading floor' on the blockchain. I will show that this dynamic institutes crowding at a global scale, demonstrating that synchronized yet arbitrary formation into groups of sellers and buyers become a key aspect of Bitcoin sociality especially during periodic cycles of boom and bust, which pull holders into mutual engagement at a hectic pace.

To link these two arguments together I will demonstrate ethnographically that the Embassy spontaneously became an intermediary or 'liminal' (Turner 1969) space for alternative sociality, which enabled people to experience their membership in the Bitcoin movement as *extremely decentralized* online but *highly concentrated* offline. Understanding the social dynamic of this reality, as I will show, can help theorize contemporary techno-utopian conceptions of society even beyond the specific case of Bitcoin.

Methodological Notes

I decided to focus my research on the Embassy and its people primarily because it was a dynamic social club and a vibrant meeting space. Although there were other such social clubs around the world, Bitcoin-related activities at the time were still mostly taking place online across social media outlets and virtual exchange platforms. Much of the global conversation also focused on money rather than societal reorganization (Dodd 2018). Taking part in Embassy routines was therefore a striking opportunity to immerse myself among people who pragmatically implemented 'Bitcoin values' in their lives, and who explicitly saw themselves as a 'community'. Fieldwork enabled me to reconceptualize Bitcoin, whose materiality I was now able to turn from a spectral abstraction into a tangible human reality. To protect the privacy of main protagonists, in the book I anonymized or pseudonymized some aspects of that reality.

During fieldwork I visited the Embassy frequently, often several times a week, usually just hanging out with whoever happened to be there and occasionally also helping with administrative tasks. I regularly attended meetings organized at the Embassy or at nearby venues, including cryptocurrency conferences, lectures, drinking events, hackathons, chess competitions and parties commemorating Bitcoin milestones or Jewish/Israeli holidays. During these events, interlocutors sometimes engaged in public storytelling of Bitcoin myths, which differed from the open lectures for disseminating professional knowledge about it. I also accompanied the meetings of the Israeli Bitcoin Association (hereafter IBA), where Embassy members had a significant presence, and which often physically took place at the Embassy. In parallel I also conducted fieldwork online, paying special attention to ongoing debates on the 'Israeli Bitcoin' Facebook group, which became a major ethnographic venue. Initiated by Embassy members in 2013 as a platform to exchange ideas, by 2018 the page following had grown to include about 30,000 members. Most were silent observers, but others engaged in lively and often heated daily discussions. In addition, I followed discussions on Signal, Telegram and WhatsApp groups used by Embassy members and among wider circles of cryptocurrency adopters in Israel. On these platforms I learned the elaborate slang that Embassy members have developed over the years. Further data was collected during many unstructured conversations with Embassy and IBA members – which I transcribed with consent – as well as dozens of semi-structured life-history interviews with key interlocutors who kindly agreed to take part in the research.

Embassy members certainly developed a distinctly *Israeli* style as they integrated the principles of the New Economy in their everyday activities. Yet, this style included few references to the wider context of power relations in

Israel, including the complex political struggle between left and right over social and security issues, and the ongoing occupation of the Palestinian territories. Shirly, a veteran Ambassador, once told me that she believed Bitcoin would be accepted widely in Israel because it resonated well with three main processes in contemporary Israeli society: (1) disillusionment with collective forms of protest; (2) inflation of available vectors of belonging formed around gender, religious and political identities (e.g. veganism, the settlement colonial project); and (3) individuation of consumerist lifestyle choices, or the idea that one is autonomous and in control of his or her own aesthetic expression.

Each of these cases included an implicit perspectival stance, wherein collective processes were condensed into particularized forms, thus replacing the hegemonic imaginary of a national and harmonious 'Jewish Community' in Israel with the allure of post-national citizenship in a globalized, yet politically fragmented, world. Nissim had once defined this same tendency as 'tribalism', referring specifically to the fact that most of the people he knew, young and old, identified with their friends on WhatsApp and Facebook more than they did with the broader Israeli society and its mainstream values. This stance recognized and effectively legitimized the accelerated dispersal of mutually exclusive value systems and moral expectations in the Israeli public sphere. It associated Bitcoin with the continuing fragmentation and impending collapse of a Jewish-Israeli national community, whose foundational ethos had once adhered to the myth of unending solidarity derived from a shared history of persecution (Anderson 2016[1983]).

I concluded my fieldwork several months before Israel entered into a period of unprecedented political instability, which continues to this day. Beginning in 2019, the country held five successive election campaigns lasting well into 2021, each ending in a hung parliament. The government that was finally formed in 2021 collapsed a year and a half later, and the country held another election, wherein Benjamin Netanyahu's far-right political block had gained majority. Netanyahu formed a new government and subsequently launched in early 2023 a coordinated attack on the Israeli judicial system. Widely perceived as undermining the strength of Israeli democracy, this motion was then followed by a massive civil disobedience campaign during most of 2023, wherein hundreds of thousands of demonstrators took part in massive outdoor protests against the government.[7]

And then came the 7 October 2023 terror attack. Hamas terrorists had massacred in that day more than a thousand Israelis – most of them innocent civilians – and kidnapped several hundreds more. This was the catalyst for an all-out regional war which, apart from Israel and Hamas, included the Iran-backed Lebanese organization Hezbollah and the Yemenite Houthi militants. These armed conflicts later also included a direct military confrontation between Israel and Iran itself. The war, which at the time of writing is still going on, resulted in a devastating human atrocity in Gaza. Major NGOs and Western States' officials have accused both Israel and Hamas of committing crimes against humanity[8].

During my fieldwork in 2018–19, the occurrence of such a disaster was quite literally unimaginable, and consequently it was largely absent from mundane conversations. Most Ambassadors cared little whether one held right-wing or left-wing views, or whether anybody defined themselves as Jewish, Arab, Israeli, Palestinian, gay, straight, orthodox, atheist, libertarian, Socialist, liberal, conservative or any other conceivable vector of identity. The issue of Palestinian independence and the ongoing occupation of the West Bank were treated as mere background noise – when they were discussed at all – and my impression was that Embassy associates did not think that these issues were relevant to Bitcoin at all. In retrospect, I realize that their aversion to the topic merely reflected a general sense of indifference and a burdening fatigue among Jewish Israelis regarding the accumulating implications of the Israeli-Palestinian conflict on civilian life. Like most people around me at the time, then, I did not identify the thickening clouds. Refraining from collecting more data on power, politics and militarism in Israel was ultimately the result of my own inability to realize that Israel was entering an entirely new – and very dark – stage in its history. I encourage colleagues to cover these lacunas in future research, providing new insights on how the historical events of the last few years have impacted Israeli Bitcoiners as well as the wider crowd of Bitcoin supporters across the globe.

Another important issue that I could not cover in this book concerns the over-representation of men at the Embassy. In an interview with Shlomit, one of the few women who was part of the core group of Ambassadors, I enquired why that was so. She responded that most of the time she did not pay attention to the low number of women in the scene, as she was used to it from her time as a computer science undergraduate. She said that increasingly women were signing up for technology studies and mentioned that 'generally women are less inclined to take the quick, aggressive financial decisions that you have to make with Bitcoin'. She did not relate to my further query about whether it was emblematic of other gender imbalances in society. Since this issue hardly ever came up – and when I did bring it up, interlocutors simply agreed that there should be more space for women in the world of Bitcoin – I will not elaborate on gender in the Israeli Bitcoin ecosystem. As with the political sphere, however, it is an important issue that merits a focused ethnographic study of its own.

Bitcoin is notoriously divisive, even when it comes to aesthetics. I decided to transcribe 'Bitcoin' with a capital 'B' because Bitcoiners themselves, in Israel and beyond, tend to use this form to describe their movement. When 'bitcoin' is written with a lowercase 'b' it usually relates to the currency itself in the context of being treated as a unit of exchange, much like 'dollars' or 'euros'. Bitcoin with a capital 'B', then, implies a wider framework that Bitcoiners understand at a moral rather than an economic register. My usage in this book reflects Bitcoiners' self-understanding as a distinct group united by common beliefs and a set of shared practices. Capital 'B' here acknowledges and denotes my interlocutors' intent to take part in a transnational Bitcoin orthodoxy. This was reinforced by the theatrical performances sometimes staged at the Embassy (see Chapter 5), presenting semi-spiritual allegories that associated Bitcoiners with post-apocalyptic salvation, and occasionally portraying Bitcoin myths; all of these were emergent forms of social distinction. I capitalize 'Embassy' for the same reason, as a meaningful space for the cultivation of communalist boundaries, and which interlocutors conceptualized as a cultural institution rather than a business centre.

The Book

Techno-utopian ideas are as old as Noah and his ark, and it seems reasonable to argue that they are intrinsic to social experiences of time and materiality. Similarly, as Norman Cohn (2001[1993], 2004[1957]) has shown, notions of equality, submission, individualism, communalism and domination have for centuries been explored in different combinations as part of myths and cosmological theories. Even P2P cash transactions were practised long before neoliberalism emerged as a political-economic force (Graeber 2011; Ingham 2004; Simmel 2004[1990]). Hierarchical and egalitarian experimentations with money technologies, in short, are by no means distinctly modern, and their philosophical implications often turn out to be broader than the political-economic framework promoted by champions of decentralized markets (Shapiro and Skartveit 2025; Swartz 2020).

The technological novelty of Bitcoin, as I see it, therefore goes beyond politics and the economy. Its social impact mostly lies in successfully linking virtual and actual realities into a single moral-economic frame of reference, from which heterogenic crowds of adopters could construe or contest different forms of alterity at both global and local registers (Shapiro 2022, 2024). Focusing on the intrinsic paradoxes and local complexities that the 'Bitcoin community' acquired in Israel, the book methodically develops this assertion over seven chapters.

Chapter 1 provides the necessary historical, technical and theoretical background about the growth of the Bitcoin phenomenon over the previous decade. I will locate the genealogy of the Embassy in a specific sociocultural process that began in the 1960s in the US and culminated in the globalization of P2P modalities of exchange in the sharing economy of the early 2000s. This will be followed by in-depth explanations of technical, political and philosophical terms that are used widely among Bitcoiners around the world. This chapter should serve as an introduction to Bitcoin sociality, which will be useful also for those readers who are already well versed in it, as the discussion also explicates the cultural undercurrents of techno-libertarian politics and their growing influence on contemporary mass movements around the globe.

Chapter 2 describes how Embassy associates organized their community. What constituted the boundaries of this community, I suggest, was not merely the possession of or trading in bitcoin; but active participation in a conversation about the moral scope of techno-cryptographic interactions, both virtual and actual. Rather than conformity to a core ideology, pertinence to the community was based on people's differential subject positions in an ongoing moral debate on freedom, money and individual agency. For that reason, I will emphasize, Embassy members could segment rapidly into a multiplicity of smaller groups while still supporting the community at large and contributing to the Embassy's primary proselytizing role. They enacted the principle of 'decentralization' at the very basis of their collaborative efforts to advance Bitcoin, claiming that their success should serve as real-world example for sceptics and critics.

Chapter 3 builds a case for individualism within Bitcoin, analysing how interlocutors cultivated personality traits that they assumed were necessary for survival in the upcoming New Economy. Strategies that marked this process included embracing the idea of becoming 'your own bank'; fostering a 'HODL' philosophy (a deliberate misrepresentation of the verb 'to hold') as a key investment precept; propagating the values associated with patience, humility and spiritual self-development; accepting the libertarian axiom that personal responsibility is a path to freedom; and recognizing the importance of the wider Bitcoin global community in supplying a stable base of support for these perspectives. Engaging with Margaret Thatcher's infamous dictum 'there is no such thing as society' – while contrasting it with Ayn Rand's Objectivist ideas – this chapter demonstrates how a *mass society* of 'individual men and women' does in fact emerge in the context of Bitcoin sociality.

Chapter 4 explores the liminality of the Embassy as a space located 'in between' centralized and decentralized imaginaries of social organization. I will show empirically that Ambassadors switched back and forth between their bank accounts and their digital wallets, each being the material embodiment of what they imagined as mutually exclusive value systems. Partaking from Victor Turner's (1974) notion of the liminoid – a specific form of liminality that is conducive to creative action – I analyse the Embassy space as 'middle ground' or a meeting point between centralized and decentralized political-philosophical frameworks. I speculate that this was a decisive factor in the making of the Embassy into a cultural centre from which associates could preach for a radical reorganization of social institutions. I will argue that intrinsic to this liminality was the ongoing tension between communitarian and individualized definitions of freedom, which interlocutors continuously negotiated.

Chapter 5 examines the millenarian views shared by Embassy members, who developed a theory of space and time regarding the expected emergence of a new world order following the inevitable collapse of the fractional-reserve banking system. I analyse the cosmogonic implications of this expectation, which, as opposed to some recent critiques, I argue should not be understood as indicative to the emergence of a 'financial religion' (see Faustino, Faria and Marques 2022; Golumbia 2018). Rejecting the idea that Bitcoin sociality may somehow be compared with religious lifestyles, this chapter explicates why many Embassy members saw eschatological crisis in a positive light, its rapturous powers thus feeding the ideal of trustless sociality along with its aspired triumph (cf. Shapiro and Skartveit 2025).

Chapter 6 focuses on crowding in the world of Bitcoin. I show how value fluctuations on the blockchain regularly establish a curious topology that impacts traders' decisions as they engage with other traders online. Developing this spatial dimension, I claim that Bitcoiners the world over respectively become 'closer' or 'more distant' from one another when they sell or buy bitcoin, especially when a sudden rush takes place due to Fears of Missing Out (FOMOs). Crowding is continuously produced as a byproduct of this dynamic (Shapiro 2024). The bitcoin blockchain is in that sense an interface, whose automated self-referential dynamic and intrinsic instability work to disperse money and affect across cyberspace. Even though crowding phenomenality on the blockchain is often unpredictable – a result of sudden emotional 'discharge' (Canetti 1984[1960]) that literally 'pushes' people into selling and buying positions – the dynamics of commerce within the Bitcoin ecosystem are contingent on such bursts.

Chapter 7 focuses on the potentially destructive force of crowds that remain entirely dependent on random value fluctuations. I show that the growth of a global Bitcoin crowd could destroy the spirit of Bitcoin communitarianism, especially as it concerns the collaboration that interlocutors at the Embassy relished. Following on from discussions on Italian Futurism and Guy Debord's *The Society of the Spectacle* (1994[1967]), I will ask whether the liberating qualities of crowd dynamics might also isolate individuals and engender a more despotic political order; as was the case with Futurists a century before. Precisely those aspects of Bitcoin sociality that Embassy members claimed united them in exploring new forms of liberty could thus lead to a concentration of power in the hands of the few. This chapter critically explores one of the darker turns that a wide-ranging adoption of decentralized sociality could take.

The Conclusion summarizes the methodological and theoretical implications of this study. I will emphasize again that Bitcoin is a cosmological artefact as much as it is a money technology (see Brunton 2019), whose *dynamic circulation* enables postmodern crowds of autonomous individuals to feel they are rising together from the sands of history to storm a metaphorical Bastille of omnipotent power; at once enforcing imaginaries of heroic individualism and a righteous collective struggle. I speculate that this dynamic is already becoming an important social phenomenon, and that it will likely be shaping our shared social space both online and offline in the coming decades.

In this book I ultimately venture to achieve three main objectives. First, I will describe in its full complexity the social life at the Embassy and its vicinity, representing Ambassadors' techno-utopian ideals as accurately and empathetically as possible. The book thus intends to tell the story of Bitcoiners in Israel from a heuristic subject-position that has so far received little public attention, partially because media coverage on Bitcoin to date has tended to focus on its financial aspects rather than its political-philosophy and cosmogonic features. Second, I will connect analytically local convictions and beliefs – as well as the grassroots activities I observed and took part in – with crowding phenomenality online. I do that by linking the dynamics of community building among Israeli Bitcoiners with the dynamics of trading on the blockchain. And third, I will offer critical insights on my interlocutors' own search for personal and collective liberty, which defined both their emotional togetherness and community structure. Taken together, the book thus advances the assumption that the growing popular involvement in cryptocurrency sociality necessitates a heightened public conversation on techno-utopian ideals, one that goes beyond utilitarian discussions on risk and financialization to engage instead with the emergent construction of postmodern mythical frameworks in a time of rapid digitalization. I invite you to slide with me down the rabbit hole.

NOTES

1. In Israel, Sunday is the first day of the week and a regular work day.
2. Months later, I asked and learned that the proximity between the embassy and the stock exchange was a total coincidence – a poetic juxtaposition of arch-nemeses, nonetheless.
3. This refers to kites loaded with explosives that at the time were occasionally being sent from Gaza, which Israel seemed unable to intercept and destroy.
4. To protect Yaron's identity I am not providing the link.

5. To describe 'centre-less-ness', Embassy members conjugated the Hebrew verb *lê'-vá-zer* (from the root *b.z.r*), meaning both 'decentralization' and 'distribution'. They thus implied the lack of a centre-periphery relationship and a dynamic dispersal through space. To describe 'trust', they used the Hebrew word *emun*, an adjective derived from the root *a.m.n*. To convey trustlessness, interlocutors either used the combination 'lack of trust', or the original English term. Note that *a.m.n* is also the root for *emunah*, which means 'belief'.
6. In 2016, an Australian computer engineer named Craig Wright claimed he was in fact Satoshi Nakamoto. This claim was dismissed by figures of authority in the world of Bitcoin. Wright later made this claim again in court. At the time of writing, the bulk of Bitcoin adopters still treat his claims with dire scepticism.
7. During this period, a profound transformation of the Israeli political landscape has taken place. By 2025, the ongoing crisis had effectively accelerated the destruction of an already crumbling ethos of conviviality between Jewish and Arab citizens of Israel, also magnifying in the process the increasingly violent clash between right-wing and left-wing Jewish-Israeli political factions over the direction that Zionist ideology should take in the coming decades. This struggle has escalated to the point it threatened to shatter whatever was left of the consensus among different segments of the Jewish People, in Israel and in the diaspora, concerning their presupposed shared destiny as a united 'People of Israel' (*Am Yisrael*).
8. Israel withdrew from the Gaza Strip unilaterally in 2005. In 2018–2019 liberal Israelis generally believed that Gaza no longer posed an existential threat to the State of Israel. That was so despite the recurrence over the years of several 'rounds' of armed conflict, as they are called in Israeli popular discourse, between Israel and Hamas. Following the 7 October attack in 2023, however, the IDF reoccupied the Gaza Strip as part of its military campaign against Hamas, obliterating nearly everything in its path and causing unprecedented destruction.

CHAPTER 1

ROOTS

Communalist Visions

Cybernetic innovation occupies a ubiquitous sociotechnical space in the contemporary world. It has effectively inspired the thorough digitalization of everyday life over the last fifty years. Although for many nowadays this process seems natural – even deterministically predictable, given the perceived advantages of computation for nearly any field of human activity – it in fact represents a significant transformation in ways of thinking and doing since at least the Enlightenment, replacing a tendency to map a*ctual* physical and social realities with a drive to invent and then realize *potential* technological and human worlds (Pickering 2011). In his work on the sociocultural origins of Silicon Valley, Fred Turner (2006) argued that this process represents a radical shift in priorities, not only at the level of governmental spending and other macro-level policies, but also on the slippery terrain of 'public opinion'. During the 1960s, Turner (2006: 12) argues, most Americans perceived computers as a tool used primarily by technocrats in the so-called 'military-industrial complex' to wage 'machinic' wars. By the mid-1980s, though, computers were already widely seen as tools of self-expression (ibid.: 14–16). Cybernetic imaginaries thus became powerful metaphors for social connectivity, leading early adopters of digital technologies to think of themselves as a political, cultural and spiritual avant-garde.

Turner focuses on the New Communalists in the US, a branch of the hippie movement that in the 1960s set out to the woods to try to establish social utopias. Disappointed with the failure of the counterculture to transform mainstream dogmas, communalists organized settlements in remote areas to practise egalitarian values, search for meaningful existence and live in harmony with nature. They relied on small-scale DIY materialism to gain independence from centralized services. As opposed to mainstream countercultural activists and politicians, who tried to advance societal-scale reform at the heart of urban America (e.g. the Civil Rights Movement and opposition to the Vietnam War), New Communalists retired to the margins of society to create their aspirational utopias of democratic self-governance, ecological sustainability and spiritual holism. They imagined a society based on such communes as a self-sustaining superorganism with a shared consciousness and distributed intelligence.

These experiments, Turner argues convincingly, were not naïve rebellions squashed by the aggressive expansion of capital in the 1980s and 1990s. Neither were they heroic 'last stands' against the globalization of commodities and labour, or the expansion of corporate powers that took place in the early 2000s. To the contrary, communalist ideas and values merged into the newly distributed form of American capitalism, eventually becoming one of its most powerful driving forces. Ideas about the liberating potential at the species-wide scale of cybernetic systems, networked organization of work, an ethos of informality and horizontal or distributed authority have all become catalysts for Silicon Valley entrepreneurial revisionism, which in the 2020s remains one of the most dominant business models for the hi-tech and related industries everywhere (see Turner 2006: 175ff.).

Sociologists Richard Barbrook and Andy Cameron (1996) have dubbed this business model – including the lifestyle habits that it inspired and supported economically – 'the Californian Ideology'. 'Promoted in magazines, books, TV programmes, Web sites, newsgroups, and Net conferences', they observed, 'the Californian Ideology promiscuously combines the freewheeling spirit of the hippies and the entrepreneurial zeal of the yuppies' (ibid.: 45). By fusing hippie ideas about collective emancipation with libertarian ideas about individualism and free choice, Barbrook and Cameron (1996: 63) claim, Californian 'ideologues' coproduced a seductive 'zeitgeist' for a new 'virtual class', consisting mainly of what Kroker and Weinstein (1994: 15) described as 'the techno-intelligentsia of cognitive scientists, engineers, computer scientists, video-game developers and all the other communications specialists'. Endorsing dialectical materialism, Barbrook and Cameron (1996: 49–50) argue:

> Over the last few decades, the pioneering work of the community media activists has been largely recuperated by the hi-tech and media industries. Although companies in these sectors can mechanise and subcontract much of their labour needs, they remain dependent on key people who can research and create original products, from software programs and computer chips to books and TV programmes. Along with some hi-tech entrepreneurs, these skilled workers form the so-called 'virtual class' ... Unable to subject them to the discipline of the assembly line

> or replace them by machines, managers have organised such intellectual workers through fixed-term contracts. Like the 'labour aristocracy' of the last century [i.e. the nineteenth century], core personnel in the media, computing and telecoms industries experience the rewards and insecurities of the marketplace. On the one hand, these digital artisans not only tend to be well-paid, but also have considerable autonomy over their pace of work and place of employment. As a result, the cultural divide between the hippie and the 'organisation man' has now become rather fuzzy. Yet, on the other hand, these workers are tied by the terms of their contracts and have no guarantee of continued employment. Lacking the free time of the hippies, work itself has become the main route of self-fulfilment for much of the 'virtual class.'

The strange-sounding 'Whole Earth 'Lectronic Link' network – popularly known as 'the WELL' – was an important milestone in the emergent construction and ultimate triumph of this new class. One of the earliest online communities, established in the early 1980s, WELL members exchanged messages with one another on various forums, some open to all subscribers and some designated as private chatrooms. The network cofounders, the biologist-artist-entrepreneur Stewart Brand and the epidemiologist Larry Brilliant, were both veterans of the 1970s communalist movement. Brand, in fact, held celebrity status among communalists and tech entrepreneurs alike, since he was the founder and main editor of *The Whole Earth Catalogue*, a magazine that he distributed between the communes of California from 1968 until 1972. Inspired by a famous picture of Earth as seen from space, which NASA shared with the media partly because Brand himself publicly campaigned for them to do so, Brand established the *Catalogue* to disseminate and promote eco-libertarianism of the Murray Bookchin school (see Bookchin 1982). This was a vision of a world populated by self-sustaining communities that were integrated into their natural habitat, and which reciprocated with each other based on their own needs rather than macro-level considerations, large-scale centralized planning policies or imposed sociocultural hierarchies. Like Bookchin, Brand focused on such organizational ideals as heterarchy and distributed management – that is, the setting up of flexible organizational networks that could easily be adapted to changing political situations, and which had no fixed hierarchical structures – while also emphasizing holism and open dialogue as elemental to the economic success of the communes.

Addressing common material needs while maintaining the DIY ethos that was at the core of these eco-libertarian experimentations, the *Catalogue* provided communalists with access to cheap tools, which included 'agricultural equipment, weaving kits, mechanical devices, books like *Kibbutz: Venture in Utopia*, and digital technologies and related theoretical texts, such as Norbert Wiener's *Cybernetics* and the Hewlett-Packard 9100A, a programmable calculator' (Wiener 2018). This blend of texts, tools, and other material resources enabled communalists to use technology both as a medium to achieve economic independence in the isolated communes and to cultivate spiritual awakening necessary for sustaining their utopian goals.[1]

Brand, Brilliant and their associates realized in the early 1980s that the internet was likely to succeed previous media in the distribution of such ideas, so they adapted the original *Catalogue* into this exciting new tool. The 'WELL' was the result. Established in 1985, the WELL was nonetheless designed to be more than just a vehicle to transmit information. Rather, it was supposed to function as a *dynamic* channel that could enable individuals to fully express themselves while also amalgamating between them a collective existence. As Turner (2006: 142–48) put it, the WELL merged communalism with cybernetics. Communalism manifested in transparent dialogue between users, who could comment publicly on every post. The cybernetic aspect was inscribed in the software regulating the interactions between members, which functioned like a self-referential system in the sense that it was constantly being reshaped by users. Turner (2006: 146) summarizes these two structural aspects by comparing the WELL to a 'homeostat':

> Like a communard of the late 1960s, [Stewart Brand] was working to establish a forum in which individuals could express themselves and form an alternative community of kindred of soul. Like a cybernetician, however, he was also designing a recursive, self-sustaining experiment. The WELL was to be the socio-technical equivalent of a homeostat. Once set in motion by its creators, it was to learn as it went, to find its ideal temperature, so to speak, through the actions of its constituent parts. In this sense . . . the users of the WELL were to become simultaneously themselves and circuits in a self-regulating biotechnological system. Machine and man would evolve, to the benefit of each and of the system as a whole. That coevolution would take place simultaneously in the interpersonal, electronic, and economic realms. At the social and electronic levels, the system itself would be part of the circuit. That is, archived in bits, arrayed in conferences and discussion threads, the WELL, like the *Whole Earth Catalogue*, would serve as a record and a map of community interactions. Like elements of a homeostat, individuals could monitor that text and reshape it by means of future interactions.

Unlike commercial companies of the time, which copyrighted textual information and limited its use, WELL members owned the content they produced and were allowed to market it back to the community, thus using the platform to disseminate and even sell ideas, inventions, software or other products (Turner 2006: 144). Although members did occasionally meet, they mostly communicated virtually, networking on 'conferences' and 'discussion threads', as they were called, to extend communalist sociality from its land-based naturalist origins to the vast territories of cyberspace.

However heterogeneous the sociocultural orientations and sociodemographic backgrounds of WELL members, their online conversations created a shared textual database. For Brand and Brilliant, these texts reflected both individual interests and the *shared consciousness or knowledge base* of the community as a whole. The skills communalists in the 1970s acquired to cultivate vegetables and build ecological domes thus evolved by the mid-1980s into full-scale digital literacy, which was now required to create computer-communities on the emergent internet. By using these skills to produce, exchange and disseminate information online, WELL members established a new kind of communalist zeitgeist, generating what Brand and his partners understood as a fascinating new type of *distributed cognition.* They were in that sense articulating keen interest in the potential realization of virtual utopias, to which I now turn.

Virtual Minds

Rather than coming full-circle to 1970s communalism, then, WELL subscribers developed their original vision in new directions. The growth of the information industries in the 1980s not only gave them tools to advance their spiritual convictions, but it also inspired them to commercialize their ideas. Business ventures set up by such people as Kevin Kelly (a communalist and associate of Stewart Brand, who later co-established *Wired Magazine*), Steve Jobs (who was an avid reader of the *Whole Earth Catalogue* in his youth) and Stewart Brand himself were influential in the development of Silicon Valley (Turner 2006). By the mid-1990s, communal lifestyles at the social, spatial and economic margins could be reinvented – or rebranded, given Brand's direct involvement – as *collaborative networks.* Here, *rational individuals* rather than cohesive communes would work together to shapeshift society. Barbrook and Cameron (1996: 56) identified (and criticized) the power of this syncretic approach, which creatively combined left and right ideologies, arguing:

> By mixing New Left and New Right, the Californian Ideology provides a mystical resolution of the contradictory attitudes held by members of the 'virtual class'. Crucially, anti-statism provides the means to reconcile radical and reactionary ideas about technological progress. While the New Left resents the government for funding the military-industrial complex, the New Right attacks the state for interfering with the spontaneous dissemination of new technologies by market competition. Despite the central role played by public intervention in developing hypermedia, the Californian ideologues preach an anti-statist gospel of hi-tech libertarianism: a bizarre mishmash of hippie anarchism and economic liberalism beefed up with lots of technological determinism.

At least until the bursting of the dotcom bubble, however, those who were living this 'bizarre mishmash' defended its internal coherence as a holistic and authentic endeavour to make the world a better place. Take for example John Perry Barlow, who was a farmer, a WELL subscriber and a songwriter who worked extensively with the Grateful Dead – an engagement that granted him celebrity status in the 1970s and 1980s. A mythical countercultural figure during his own lifetime, Barlow wrote in 1996 a manifesto he titled *A Declaration of the Independence of Cyberspace*. In this document, which was as brilliant and poetic as most of his other texts, Barlow illustrated a powerful mystical perception of the internet as a free, unregulated, open territory that would enable new forms of societal arrangements untethered from the hegemonic political system and its norms or demands. After disavowing the right of governments to sanction their populations, Barlow promulgates his belief in new forms of disembodied freedom that he claimed could be gained only in cyberspace:

> Governments of the Industrial World, you weary giants of flesh and steel, I come from Cyberspace, the new home of Mind . . . You have no sovereignty where we gather . . . Cyberspace does not lie within your borders. Do not think that you can build it, as though it were a public construction project. You cannot. It is an act of nature and it grows itself through our collective actions . . . Cyberspace consists of transactions, relationships, and thought itself, arrayed like a standing wave in the web of our communications. Ours is a world that is both everywhere and nowhere, but it is not where bodies live . . . Our identities have no bodies, so, unlike you [nation states], we cannot obtain order by physical coercion. We believe that from ethics, enlightened self-interest, and the commonweal *[sic]*, our governance will emerge . . . In our world, all the sentiments and expressions of humanity, from the debasing to the angelic, are parts of a seamless whole, the global conversation of bits. We cannot separate the air that chokes from the air upon which wings beat . . . We will create a civilization of the Mind in Cyberspace. May it be more humane and fair than the world your governments have made before. (Barlow 1996: n.p.)

Preserving the flair of the communards, who rejected the utility of conventional politics in significantly changing societal power imbalances, Barlow here turns to mind experiences as the real space for the acquisition of freedom. Roaming in cyberspace with the like-minded is here compared to the isolated woods of the 1970s, where communards could avoid the monitoring gaze of the authorities. Barlow thus associated cyberspace with Gnosticism, that is, the idea that personal enlightenment could only be achieved through mystical experiences rather than by accepting the inherited wisdom of mainstream values. Barlow's underlying notion was that cyberspace served as the only safe place for people to escape the omnipotence and omniscience of authoritative and domineering moral powers (see also Barlow 1990). The role that psychology and spiritualism played for hippies and WELL members in the 1980s – enabling them to explore personal and collective minds – has now migrated to 'the conversation of bits . . . upon which wings beat' (Barlow 1996). While highlighting the crucial position of individualism in the imminent information era, Barlow nonetheless also called for a *mutualistic collective presence online*, which he had experienced as a WELL subscriber in the 1980s (Turner 2006).

In the case of WELL activities, two main factors distinguished *mutualism* from earlier communalist traditions. First, the boundaries of the community were protected by personal passwords and a paid membership, thus encouraging the creation of an idiosyncratic organizational culture which was nevertheless free from spatial considerations. Rather than isolate themselves in remote forests, communalists could now communicate from the comfort of their urban flats, practising a disembodied experience of the kind Barlow (1996) later promoted. Second, interaction between members could be done both publicly (open for all to read) and privately (by invitation), thus enabling members to exchange ideas and services inclusively or exclusively at will. The lack of formal leadership meant that every idea could be heard and debated, while confidential personal conversations could take place uninterrupted in parallel threads. The WELL also avoided ponderous voting mechanisms, rulebooks and other cumbersome bureaucratic procedures that had characterized the communes of the 1970s. The immediacy and directness of textual interaction enabled new kinds of computer-mediated intimacies, relinquishing the possibility of public scrutiny that accompanied face-to-face encounters in the communes. The WELL was groundbreaking even during its own time, although it remained a fringe subculture until internet access became common in the 1990s.

One of the consequences of WELL experimentalism was the reframing of mutualist political activism in the 1990s as a struggle to ensure civil liberties online. John Perry Barlow's relentless activism was pivotal to the success of that movement. In 1990, he teamed with famed software engineer and entrepreneur Mitch Kapor, as well as the already-legendary cryptographer and computer scientist John Gilmore. Together, they cofounded a network of activists who worked towards the establishment of a free internet. They called it, in the fashion of leftist guerrilla movements in the 1960s, the Electronic Frontier Foundation (EFF). Barlow, Kapor and Gilmore secured funds to establish the EFF from Steve Wozniak, a hacker-turned-entrepreneur who cofounded Apple with Steve Jobs in 1975. In that sense, the EFF embodied from its inception a 'Californian' entrepreneurship ethos, which unlike mainstream digital industries promoted an organizational critique of Silicon Valley corporate culture.[2]

Although other processes were also at play, the 'bizarre' emergence of a hippie-liberal ideology in the 1980s and 1990s (Barbrook and Cameron 1996) established the discursive foundation for the techno-libertarian subcultures of the 2000s. Critics correctly claim that the root metaphor of 'making the world a better place', by the 2020s a battered cliché, was a thinly veiled self-aggrandizing mantra that coated aggressive market-making strategies in a countercultural rhetoric of egalitarian harmony. As such, it promoted new forms of personal freedoms and advocated for greater individual expression offline (Wiener 2020), rather than merely strengthening virtual communities or producing a virtual mind. But this cliché also reflected a tenacious belief in the emancipatory power of technology, which in a way laid the groundwork for the establishment of crypto communities a decade later. This process, as I will now show, was tightly connected to the newfound mystique of heterarchic P2P modes of interaction; that is, assemblages of entities (such as nodes or peers) that can be organized either sporadically or purposefully, but which are never ranked in hierarchical order.

Heterarchy in Cyberspace

A makeshift group of mathematicians, computer engineers, yuppies and tech entrepreneurs – most of them living on the American west coast – popularized in the 1990s the idea that the nascent internet was a space of struggle and conflict around issues of privacy and copyright laws (Turner 2006). Three of the informal leaders of that loosely organized civil-society movement – Eric Hughes, John Gilmore and Timothy May – dubbed themselves 'Cypherpunks' (Hayes 2019).[3] All three were later portrayed wearing masks on the cover of *Wired Magazine*, which published in that volume a long and flattering article on the movement and its goals (Levy 1993). Attacking corporate and state surveillance online, the Cypherpunks focused their activism on cryptography, the mathematics of encryption (Swartz 2018). They campaigned to remove limitations on civilian uses of encryption, which in the US were still partially classified as a military-grade weapon (Levy 1993). In his now canonical 'A Cypherpunk's Manifesto', Eric Hughes (1993) wrote:

> We must defend our own privacy if we expect to have any. We must come together and create systems which allow anonymous transactions to take place. People have been defending their own privacy for centuries with whispers, darkness, envelopes, closed doors, secret handshakes, and couriers. The technologies of the past did not allow for strong privacy, but electronic technologies do . . . [This is why] Cypherpunks write code. We know that someone has to write software to defend privacy, and since we can't get privacy unless we all do, we're going to write it. We publish our code so that our fellow Cypherpunks may practice and

> play with it. Our code is free for all to use, worldwide . . . We know that software can't be destroyed and that a widely dispersed system can't be shut down . . . The Cypherpunks are actively engaged in making the networks safer for privacy. Let us proceed together apace.

Hughes associated Cypherpunk activism with a new social order, which he insisted should be premised on the anonymous exchange of information. This drive to enhance privacy through anonymity included a deeply rooted belief in the redemptive power of 'code', which Cypherpunks saw as the infrastructure to ensure radical cultural change. Cypherpunk activism thus entailed a defiant stance, pushing for formal legislation that would protect freedom of speech in cyberspace while also supporting personal initiatives and a DIY attitude that reflected both the countercultural communalist ethos of the 1970s (Turner 2006) and the spirit of entrepreneurship inscribed in the Californian Ideology (Barbrook and Cameron 1996). In a 499-word call to arms, titled 'The Crypto Anarchist Manifesto', Timothy May (1988: n.p.) poetically described this techno-libertarian *Geist*:

> Computer technology is on the verge of providing the ability for individuals and groups to communicate and interact with each other in a totally anonymous manner. Two persons may exchange messages, conduct business, and negotiate electronic contracts without ever knowing the True Name, or legal identity, of the other. Interactions over networks will be untraceable, via extensive re-routing of encrypted packets and tamper-proof boxes which implement cryptographic protocols with nearly perfect assurance against any tampering . . . These developments will alter completely the nature of government regulation, the ability to tax and control economic interactions, the ability to keep information secret, and will even alter the nature of trust and reputation . . .
>
> Just as the technology of printing altered and reduced the power of medieval guilds and the social power structure, so too will cryptologic methods fundamentally alter the nature of corporations and of government interference in economic transactions. Combined with emerging information markets, crypto anarchy will create a liquid market for any and all material which can be put into words and pictures. And just as a seemingly minor invention like barbed wire made possible the fencing-off of vast ranches and farms, thus altering forever the concepts of land and property rights in the frontier West, so too will the seemingly minor discovery out of an arcane branch of mathematics come to be the wire clippers which dismantle the barbed wire around intellectual property.
>
> Arise, you have nothing to lose but your barbed wire fences!

Most of May's predictions turned out to be accurate; some were realized during the 1990s, and some, like Bitcoin, in the first and second decades of the twenty-first century. Encryption technologies have existed on the market since the mid-1970s, but May was one of the first experts to formulate its utility in political terms. He did not treat anonymity as a goal in itself, but as a means of supporting new collaborative associations online, which in turn could change power imbalances between governments and citizens. May envisioned a fully encrypted sociality that disregarded any normative convention, legal or otherwise. He compared direct exchange protected by encryption with ancient royal seals, although its power was used in the opposite direction; if seals were an important administrative tool for power centralization in the ancient world (Pittman 2018), they could now be used not only to decentralize control of the flow of information across society, but in fact to *individualize* it.

P2P Business Models

In cybernetics and systems research, 'peer' is a technical concept used to describe a node linked with other nodes as part of a network (Taddeo and Vaccaro 2011). Cypherpunks used it mainly in this sense (Hayes 2019). The term was nonetheless popularized with the success of Napster – one of the first commercial file-sharing programs, which nineteen-year-old American university student Shawn Fanning released in 1999 (Strahilevitz 2002). Napster provided a shared database for all the MP3 music files its users made available from their own hard drives. This enabled users anywhere in the world to search for and download music directly from any other individual user. Lior Strahilevitz (2002: 6–7) surveyed the types of reciprocity and community spirit that this form of direct interaction generated:

> After conducting an initial search, the user had several search options. She could search for another artist or song. Or she could examine the file directory of a particular user who showed files satisfying the first search criteria to see what other files that user had made available for downloading. For example, a user interested in expanding her jazz horizons might have searched for files containing music by a well-known artist such as Miles Davis or Louis Armstrong and subsequently looked at the directories belonging to users who have extensive collections of Davis or Armstrong recordings. In that way, users found high-quality music made by an artist of whom they had never previously heard. Napster users occasionally engaged in virtual conversations with the users who were supplying them with music files . . . The user began to download the music and, at the same time, paged the uploading user to see if he was interested in exchanging instant messages about the artist. Napster also hosted chat rooms that involved many users simultaneously. Napster thereby permitted music lovers to share information and conversation with others who had similar tastes.

Fanning defined the system as a 'peer-to-peer file sharing model' (Greenfeld 2000) because Napster itself – a registered commercial company – did not centrally host the MP3 files on its own servers at any stage. P2P file transfer was unmediated, digitally mimicking the real-world practice of friends sharing music with each other. Napster merely provided a centralized index of songs and artists as a means of connecting 'peers' to one another, as Strahilevitz (2002) explains. Writing in *Time* magazine, Karl Greenfeld (2000) explained just how disruptive P2P connectivity was at the time:

> In creating Napster, Fanning not only transformed the music business, but he also helped launch a new programming movement – and a whole wave of start-ups dedicated to what has become known as P2P, or peer-to-peer, client-based Internet software. Among Napster's revolutionary qualities is that it allows computer users to exchange files directly, avoiding server bottlenecks and, Fanning once hoped, legal problems . . . There are myriad – and totally legal – possibilities for P2P applications, from swapping dense technical files through a local-area network (something scientists at the Centers for Disease Control are looking into) to replacing corporate servers with P2P systems for business applications.

Giesler and Pohlmann (2003b) created the neologism 'emancipative consumption scape' to describe the phenomenological (rather than merely technological or economic) impact of disintermediation in Napster. They defined this as a closed system separated from its external social or technical environment. Separation means near-total technical and human self-reliance, which becomes possible because the 'scape' produces a self-referential or autopoietic dynamic; its code infrastructure and human operations would never be dependent on external manipulation. If Napster self-regenerated the exchange of music files between subscribers, its 'emancipative consumption scape' demonstrated the remarkable economic and logistical utility of an interconnected network of peers (see also Benkler and Nissenbaum 2006).

Giesler and Pohlmann (2003a, 2003b) argued that the dynamic of sharing in such 'emancipatory' space mitigated tensions between exclusivity and altruism (see Stage 2013). By this they referred to a sense of personal and collaborative emancipation between Napster subscribers – who would send each other files for free and engage in conversations on music and art, either directly or in chat rooms (see Strahilevitz 2002). Napster's P2P model thus enabled subscribers to enter long-term gift-exchange relationships that included an ethical commitment to reciprocate, share and collaborate (namely, Mauss 1990[1925]).

Benkler and Nissenbaum (2006) likewise argue that the 'open-access' software industry of the early 2000s (which they call 'commons-based peer production') structurally encouraged virtuous behaviour. P2P sociality became a big hit, they claim, primarily because it inspired a sense of community and an experience of liberation from hyper-consumerism, thus also reinforcing a personal commitment to practising and promoting such virtues as generosity, honesty, mutuality, etc. (Benkler and Nissenbaum 2006: 404–5). The ethereal existence of the 'community' became dependent on these virtues, which in their cumulative force were seen to overcome and displace the interests of music industry gatekeepers (Giesler and Pohlmann 2003a; Strahilevitz 2002; see also Lazarus 2022: 154).

In parallel, Cypherpunk attempts to create P2P money systems were taking place in the backwaters of designated libertarian forums and cryptography academic conferences (Popper 2015). Building off the 1976 introduction of the 'Diffie-Hellman protocol' – a method of exchanging information between peers over an unsecured public platform that nevertheless protects the exclusivity of a 'private' key known only to the peer with access to it (Diffie and Hellman 1976) – attempts to produce digital money began to accelerate by the mid-1980s (Chaum 1985). Repeated communication on the matter between programmers and cryptographers also took place throughout the 1990s in Cypherpunk channels. Satoshi was a regular contributor in at least one famous forum, as I noted, and they must have read (or even written) pre-Bitcoin papers on the theme (e.g. Szabo 1997). In fact, some of these early papers appeared in the bibliography of the 2008 White Paper (for example Dai 1998), to which I now turn.

The White Paper

In October 2008, Satoshi Nakamoto disseminated a document titled 'Bitcoin: A Peer-to-Peer Electronic Cash System' (2008a) on an email-distribution listserv that was connected to the original (and by then mythical among those involved) Cypherpunk mailing list. While explicating in depth the functioning of this 'electronic peer-to-peer money system', the paper also included an important, if tacit, libertarian political element (Dodd 2018; Golumbia 2016; Nelms et al. 2018; Scott 2014; Swartz 2020); as it clearly promoted peer networking to bypass and thereby oppose governmental censorship over the production, distribution and control of money. From its inception, then, Bitcoin was not equivalent to other contemporary financial assets such as stocks or bonds, or indeed fiat money, because unlike these, it was explicitly created to avoid and even subvert normative economic regulation. To understand how this is done, I must describe the functioning of the entire system in some detail.

As I began to explain in the Introduction, Bitcoin is a decentralized money system that successfully and reliably regulates itself, thus making obsolete the need for an external auditing body that would supervise the legality of transactions between users. To do this, the system produces a public digital ledger that enables every single user to download a continuously updating copy of the entire history of transactions. In the White Paper Satoshi had used the term 'chain of blocks' to describe the ledger, but it soon became known among early adopters as 'the blockchain'. This name refers to the fact that, roughly every ten minutes, the system seals all the data it had registered in a virtual 'block', which thus contains a detailed record of all the transactions registered during that time period. Every such block would then be sealed with a timestamp and immediately linked to the block that preceded it. Data could not be altered retroactively, both because it would never be stored on one central hub and because every blocks is protected by a cryptographic formula that makes it effectively tamperproof (Antonopolous 2015). This process thereby generates a 'chain of blocks' that stretches back in time to the first-ever 'Genesis Block' produced by Satoshi themselves on 3 January 2009 (see below).

Based on previous attempts to create digital money (Back 2002[1997]; Dai 1998) but going beyond them, the blockchain fulfils two main roles. First, it monitors and registers all transactions in real time, thus making it possible to verify automatically whether any of the connected nodes had tried to fraudulently send the same bitcoin twice; a trick called 'double spending', which had to be avoided in order for the system to become reliable (Greenfield 2018). The fact that each computer/node that runs the blockchain constantly monitors all the transactions sustains the decentralized design of the blockchain, ensuring that no single entity can control the register or change it. Second, and at the same time, each block contains a cryptographic code that conceals a set number of bitcoins. For a chance to own these coins, every computer/node that runs the blockchain can perform a series of complex mathematical calculations that would eventually decrypt the code and unlock the bitcoins it conceals. The node that would ultimately spend more computation power will necessarily also decrypt the code faster. Satoshi described this process as 'proof' that the actual machine participating in the competition has also actively and simultaneously been 'working' to register transactions during the time period that preceded the sealing of each block. 'Proof of work' thus entitles each node the right to make part of the competition to be the first who would decrypt the code that protects the concealed Bitcoin that come with each new block.[4]

Satoshi (Nakamoto 2008a: 4) compared this process of verification and 'extraction' of bitcoins to gold mining, an analogy which highlights the increasing rarity of the coin as its main source of value generation (Zimmer 2017). Designed to produce exactly 21,000,000 coins overall, the coins released into the world with every signed block are preprogrammed to reduce by half every four years. It began with fifty coins per block and diminished as time passed. The last remaining bitcoin would thus be extracted from the blockchain sometime in the early 2140s. Given the public and open-ended nature of the blockchain, Satoshi implied that any additional layer of coding (or the creation of collateral systems) that might be needed in the future would require majority decision and a consequent consensus among nodes.[5]

Satoshi originally assumed that every node would be able to *individually* mine bitcoin. Yet, since 2013, this operation had grown into a multimillion-dollar industry, comprised of mining 'pools' that combine enormous computation power (Dodd 2018; Calvão 2018). It quickly became unsustainable for individual users to mine coins privately because, given their tiny computational power, they would spend more on electricity consumption than they could cover. Lone miners, therefore, would rarely if ever be able to extract any bitcoins from the system (DuPont 2019). Individual users would gain some political power in the bitcoin blockchain if they became 'full nodes', as opposed to 'light nodes' – the former keep a complete copy of the blockchain on their device and can thus personally verify every transaction ever made, while the latter only participate in verifying *ongoing* transactions (because they have not downloaded the entire history of the blockchain into their computers). Anybody could become a full node, and serious investors generally apply full-node capacities because it maximizes both their capacity to empirically 'verify' that the blockchain has not been compromised by an attacker and their ability to mind new coins (for further explanations on this feature see Antonopoulos and Harding 2024).[6]

The blockchain consequently automates large-scale *mathematical consensus* (Greenfield 2018). So long as it remains economically viable (i.e. miners and nodes earn more than what they spend), the system will continue to distribute auditing responsibilities between nodes, effectively creating a heterarchic digital territory that enables all nodes to 'see' each other all the time (Hayes 2019; but cf. Schneider 2019: 271–72). The novelty of the blockchain, then, is that it dramatically reduces the power of any single entity to issue money while relocating this power ('back', as some Bitcoiners in Israel would have it) into the hands of a multiplicity of users. This also guarantees that no single entity could alter the ongoing process of verification and extraction, thus obviating the need to trust other users. The final paragraph in the White Paper (Nakamoto 2008a: 8) emphasized this property as the crux of the invention:

> We have proposed a system for electronic transactions without relying on trust. We started with the usual framework of coins made from digital signatures, which provides strong control of ownership, but is incomplete without a way to prevent double-spending. To solve this, we proposed a peer-to-peer network using

> proof-of-work to record a public history of transactions that quickly becomes computationally impractical for an attacker to change if honest nodes control a majority of CPU power. The network is robust in its unstructured simplicity. Nodes work all at once with little coordination. They do not need to be identified, since messages are not routed to any particular place and only need to be delivered on a best effort basis. Nodes can leave and rejoin the network at will, accepting the proof-of-work chain as proof of what happened while they were gone. They vote with their CPU power, expressing their acceptance of valid blocks by working on extending them and rejecting invalid blocks by refusing to work on them. Any needed rules and incentives can be enforced with this consensus mechanism.

Bitcoin, it seems fair to argue, was to defy the global financial order from the very beginning. Satoshi probably chose to remain anonymous because they were aware of the potentially iconoclastic impact of their invention, which could be weaponized by those seeking to destroy hegemonic power structures. Although there is nothing violent or revolutionary in the White Paper itself, it did provide the blueprint for an alternative economic system that could potentially attract and affect every single person on the planet. Deferring responsibility over money production and distribution from governments and commercial banks to individual stakeholders and private companies, Bitcoin has quickly been framed by early adopters as the gnostic enabler of a new era of financial liberation.

Genesis

Satoshi mined the first bitcoin on the blockchain on 3 January 2009, following several months of intensive debates on the mailing list where they had earlier posted the White Paper. That first block has since acquired a mythical status and iconized as 'The Genesis Block'. Not only was it the technological beginning of what came to be a global social movement, but it also tacitly promoted the political message previously advanced by veteran Cypherpunks and techno-libertarians. The mention of the term 'peer-to-peer' in the title of the White Paper itself suggests that the ghosts of Cypherpunk texts and ideas were at the centre of Satoshi's project.

The Genesis Block included an encryption concealing that day's headline of the British newspaper, *The Times*. The decrypted timestamp read: '*The Times* 03/Jan/2009 Chancellor on brink of second bailout for banks.'[7] More than a mere technical proof that the blockchain could not have been operational before 3 January 2009, this message implicitly rebuked the occasional crashes and resulting governmental bailouts intrinsic to the dominant fractional-reserve banking system. After all, Satoshi could have chosen other signs, symbols, or references to timestamp their invention, including the encryption of a different title from the same first page of *The Times* or even a random title from an odd sport magazine. The mention of UK bail-outs is therefore likely to be deliberate, and for all it matters it indicates a strong libertarian bias.

Satoshi had sent the first-ever transaction on 12 January 2009 to Harold Thomas 'Hal' Finney II, a known computer scientist, techno-libertarian and Cypherpunk activist, who in that sense materialized the connection between the old guard of Cypherpunks with the emergent new Bitcoin avant-garde (Hayes 2019). Satoshi also regularly exchanged emails with several other Cypherpunk subscribers both before the publication of the paper and for about two years afterwards, extensively debating P2P sociality correspondents and often expressing strong techno-libertarian views. On 7 November 2008, for example, Satoshi responded to a critical email, whose author exclaimed that 'You [i.e. Satoshi] will not find a solution to political problems in cryptography.' Satoshi, in response, mentioned Napster (Nakamoto 2008b):

> Yes, but we *can* win a major battle in the arms race and *gain a new territory of freedom* for several years. Governments are good at cutting off the heads of a centrally controlled networks *[sic]* like Napster, but pure P2P networks like Gnutella and Tor seem to be holding their own. [italics added][8]

'A new territory of freedom' rhetorically resembles the 'emancipative consumption scape' highlighted by Giesler and Pohlmann (2003b) when analysing the emergence of P2P sociality in the early 2000s. Satoshi thus established a kinship genealogy for Bitcoin, which led from Hughes, Gilmore, May and many others who exchanged ideas on the Cypherpunk mailing list to the rise of the 'sharing economy' that was based on decentralized P2P computing architecture in the early 2000s. In Napster, P2P relations empirically consolidated what Dick Hebdige (1979: 58) called years earlier a 'community of outsiders', who defined themselves as a community through their rejection of 'centralized' copyright law (Giesler and Pohlmann 2003b). In Bitcoin, P2P relations consolidated a community defined by its rejection of financial regulatory policies and institutional monitoring power. Bitcoin early adopters in fact took this dynamic of distancing and consolidation of boundaries a step further, because transactions required paying small fees to the miners who sustained the blockchain. Reciprocity between peers has thereby become monetized as a structural condition of the operation of the network. The result was a plurality of P2P relations, which functioned both as an alternative to mainstream market dynamics, *and as a new dynamic in its own right*, which did not directly confront State-controlled markets (Taddeo and Vaccaro 2011: 109).

Turning P2P sociality from a means to an end enabled the decentralization of money exchange at scale, ensuring there would be no 'single points of failure' that could bring the system down. It thus became a key element in Bitcoin's famed resilience to external disruption. Bitcoin's release was in that sense a material realization of Cypherpunk political advocacy, which promoted literacy in software coding as means of resisting State and big-tech corporate power (May 1992, 1994), and a watershed moment in the genealogy of techno-utopian financial activism. The Genesis, which Bitcoiners in Israel and beyond still commemorate (see Chapter 5) must therefore be understood as an actualization of multiple sets of interactions in the world, a tangible reality, rather than as a metaphor or a fantastic-symbolic utterance relished by 'true believers'. It is not surprising that an original copy of the front page of *The Times* from 3 January 2009, together with a printed inscription of the code of the Genesis Block and its decrypted message, were honourably framed in a wooden casing and hung on the wall at the Embassy (see Figure 1.1)[9].

The creation of Bitcoin might have taken years, but once it became operational it migrated quickly from the subcultural Cypherpunk fringes into the mainstream of cryptographic production; developing eventually in the early 2020s into an entire industry popularly called 'Decentralized Finance' (DeFi). In the mid-2020s, thousands of other blockchain-based cryptocurrencies exist on the market, many of them accompanied by passionate ideological avowals to protect such values as individual freedom, decentralization, trustlessness, and deregulation. Recognizing the primacy of Bitcoin, however, proponents of most other cryptocurrencies have accepted the term 'altcoins' (derived from 'alternative coins') to describe this secondary class of cryptographic money forms. Before I explain how these are different from Bitcoin – at least as true believers at the Embassy perceived it – I will briefly analyse two well-researched examples.

Altcoins

BitNation-Pangea was established in 2014 (Faria 2019) as an online 'nation' consisting of several 'borderless communities'. It issued a decentralized token mischievously called 'XPAT' (Atzori 2017: 48), which was explicitly designed to function as an arbitrage and reputation mechanism (Faria 2019). XPAT was distributed to users by an AI named Lucy in exchange for points for 'good behaviour' that users accumulated through their interaction with others on the platform (Faria 2022: 86–88). XPAT was supposed to energize and support in this way a decentralized autonomous organization (DAO), an online legal entity governed by algorithmic smart contacts (Buterin

Figure 1.1. A framed issue of *The Times* from 3 January 2009, including the code of the Genesis Block and its decrypted message. The frame hung on the wall of the Embassy for several years and later moved to Shemesh's new business venture in Tel Aviv several streets away. Credit: Matan Shapiro.

2015a). This enabled users to upscale their 'communitarian' initiatives far beyond the borders of the states they lived in (De Filippi 2018), and set up political structures of their own creation. BitNation members deliberately turned to the exchange of money in cyberspace as a form of *refuge* from state jurisdiction. Inês Faria (2022: 86–87) analyses the project objectives as both communitarian and anarcho-libertarian:

> In a rather immediate manner, the project found its manifesto in the idea that markets are decentralised, and that if they represent fluid networks adaptable to the everyday life management strategies that people employ, then they would also provide the solution to all the problems facing current democratic governance – cryptocurrencies and blockchain would facilitate these markets, mobilised by the decentralisation narratives they support ... Inspired by this belief on the generative power of money, the platform establishes a digital jurisdiction governed by a tokenised reputational system in which people interact through smart contracts. In this jurisdiction, anyone can create their own virtual nation with its own constitution, become a citizen of other virtual nations, acquire services online, and contribute to improving the legal codes for smart contracts ... The tale here endorses competitive libertarian governance through a system whereby people do not have to trust each other, since their interactions are mediated by algorithms perceived as less biased than humans. Cryptocurrencies as money thus serve as a means to realise a project, and as a measure of social control through an incentive-based reputation system established by algorithmically made evaluations.

The project nonetheless failed, and in 2022 its website was bought by a cryptocurrency news agent using the brand name 'Bitnation'. Faria (2022) attributes the collapse to two main reasons. First, the aspired-to close-knit, ideologically committed 'community of trust' never actually materialized. This was partly due to the 'crypto-winter' of 2020 and 2021 – the prolonged devaluation of the entire cryptocurrency market, which was accompanied by sellouts – and partly because the project remained completely open source. Structural 'openness' enabled people from across the globe to freely join in, but Faria (ibid.: 88) argues that this also made it difficult to establish sustainable social ties between them over time. Second, Faria identifies a tension between the libertarian narrative that infused the project with an ideological fervour and the concrete economic conditions that decentralized borderless communities required if they wished to thrive (see Schneider 2019). While the project vocally advertised the importance of generic communities, it did not supply the economic infrastructure, nor the moral commitment required for its pragmatic realization. Faria writes (2022: 90):

> Despite the radical proposals to change the world based on cryptocurrencies as monies, the social and political ties needed for such transforming endeavours are nonetheless the same as the ones binding communities of users of other [fiat] currencies: social need or demand; social relations that are already there or are forming; trust; and/or the dynamics of power structures embedded in a currency's widespread use. These entanglements between proposed and mainstream

economies, and the conditions of money to exist as a social technology affect blockchain projects no matter how radical their tales are [references removed].

Another reason for the decline of BitNation-Pangea was, however, more prosaic; namely, the increasing rumours online that the project was not in fact genuine. A crypto tracking site called CryptoSwede published articles in 2018 and 2019 that cast doubt on the level of ideological commitment in the BitNation project. The article from 2019 even cites a Telegram conversation with the project's main organizer, who stated that further development could not proceed before BitNation was financially profitable.[10] Although the organizer later divided the project into a 'decentralized movement' and a separate profit-oriented startup, both eventually collapsed (Faria 2022: 89). In a competitive environment that was rapidly changing, and that was soaked in scepticism or even outright paranoia, too many potential supporters might have just lost faith. Rather than a community, in short, BitNation became a prototypical mass of unrelated strangers, which eventually dispersed.

A second example demonstrates the opposite social morphology, as it consisted of an unrelated mass of crypto supporters that crystallized into something resembling a 'community of trust'. Dogecoin is a decentralized digital currency created in 2013 by software engineers Billy Markus and Jackson Palmer as a joke. Modelling their coin on the 'Doge' meme that went viral in 2013 – and playfully choosing as their logo a picture of the Shibe-Inu pedigree dog featured in the original meme – Markus and Palmer explicitly sought to satirize the cryptocurrency market, but nonetheless immediately attracted online crypto-enthusiasts completely unrelated to the two main developers. These new crypto-curious adopters thus began exchanging Dogecoin between them. Soon, they established independent Dogecoin blogs and flooded the internet with Dogecoin-related humorous tweets, memes and photos. Stunned by this unexpected popular interest, the Dogecoin development team established in 2014 a nonprofit foundation, whose short manifesto reads as follows:[11]

> We are Dogecoin, the accidental crypto-movement that makes people smile. We are developing a currency for the people, and we strive to do only good everyday. Through this work we have come to value: Being **useful**, we value *utility* over *technical brilliance*. Being **personable**, we value *individuals and interactions* over *profit-driven economics*. Being **welcoming**, we value *collaboration and trust* over *competition and exclusivity*. Being **reliable**, we value *working solutions* over *speed of delivery* [emphases in original].

The community avoided centralization by using Twitter, Reddit and recently also Discord accounts, all of which still publish millions of posts annually. The ethos of unseriousness evolved with time to include direct moral imperatives, although no sanction mechanism was enforced. Dogecoin supporters thus associated *play* with the expectation to spread *good vibes* online and offline. The developers supported this ethos and turned it into a quasi-spiritual goal. The official Dogecoin site states: 'The Dogecoin community cares about supporting each other, being kind, teaching people about cryptocurrency, fundraising, having fun, making memes, and being absurd. This is nicely captured by Dogecoin's unofficial tagline: **D**o **O**nly **G**ood **E**veryday', which constitutes the common ground of a global 'Doge' political-philosophical operational framework.[12]

Online forums influenced demand for the coin, which in turn contributed to price fluctuations during tides of highs and lows on exchange platforms. Unstructured and apolitical, community members have thus been purchasing Dogecoin and exchanging it between them as a manifestation of their appreciation for the absurd. This was also economically feasible because the coin was produced in enormous quantities to deliberately guarantee a low monetary value against fiat currencies.[13] Many crypto investors at some stage or another have bought Dogecoin. Beginning with a minimal value of US$0.0001 per DOGE, increasing demand inflated its price over time, reaching about 0.09 DOGE per dollar in early 2023. This meant that those who bought enough DOGE in the early years could cash out significant profits, a bonus that quantified their initially innocent or whimsical involvement in a community dedicated to generating 'goodness'. The Dogecoin market capitalization volume in early 2023, which was the last time I checked, revolved around the US$12 billion mark, at the time ranking it ninth in overall trade volume on coinmarketcap.com. The online community of users, in short, with their special visual style, feel-good discourse and quirky humour, steadily raised the financial value of Dogecoin as a byproduct of their ongoing interactions.

The case of Dogecoin demonstrates how heuristic references to community, while loosely defined, can survive and flourish over time. Dogecoin in the early 2020s had become the closest thing to a truly global currency that is cheap to hold and easy to exchange. Unlike XPAT, Dogecoin supporters also promoted fairness and a collaborative spirit as values that should precede competition, efficiency and profit making. The community could represent a self-sustaining digital/cybernetic system *and* a stable social ground for economic reciprocity. Use of the term 'community' as a frame of reference ultimately turned Dogecoin forums into a collective symbol of faith, harmony, collaboration and growth.

Bitcoiners observed the rise of such collaborative communities with mixed feelings. On one hand, communities like Dogecoin contributed to the intention of many Bitcoiners to revolutionize not only markets but also minds. In doing so, they expanded the market capitalization of the crypto economy, increasingly turning it into a global force that could no longer be ignored. On the other hand, communities like BitNation-Pangea gave a bad name to the entire scene while also diverting funds that could be used productively to develop further P2P economic infrastructures out and away from the market; as profiteers would typically convert most of their crypto earning back into fiat in order to maximize their real-world use value. As a result, many Bitcoiners would qualitatively distinguish Bitcoin itself from most other cryptocurrencies, asserting that these in fact replicated economic and political structures that characterized the fractional-reserve banking system. Although the politically correct term for new cryptocurrencies in the emergent blockchain industry was 'altcoins', interlocutors in Tel Aviv thus often mockingly called them 'shitcoins'. They thus exposed a crucial epistemic tension among cryptocurrency adopters regarding the utility and use-value of the blockchain.

Bitcoin vs Blockchain

Faustino, Faria and Marques (2022) contributed a thoughtful analysis of the enchanting aspects of blockchain technology, which they argue were developed as a reaction to the 2008 subprime meltdown. In a time of radical change, they claim, the role of the 'blockchain community' – perceived broadly as encompassing all cryptocurrency adopters across the world, including Bitcoin – was to stabilize a chaotic economic reality. In this reading, the emergence of a so-called global 'blockchain community' is premised on the sharing of myths and the enacting of rituals, which they argue have repelled the instability produced by the collapse of banks, the volatility of commercial networks and the fragility of supply chains. The authors reference *cargo cults* to describe this form of enchantment, employing functional-psychological terms to suggest that cryptocurrency adoption signals a need for comfort and safety:

> When confronted with military technology which they could not fully understand, Melanesians started to enact rituals where they would simulate certain conditions – an airplane landing on an airstrip, for example – in the hope of being rewarded with an abundance of goods from the coloniser. Just as the mock airstrips in this example failed to produce airplanes, western techno-scientific marketing similarly sometimes fails to produce the announced results in what has been named 'cargo cult science'. (Faustino, Faria and Marques 2022: 69)

This analysis nonetheless misrepresents two epistemic notions, which at least for Embassy associates in Tel Aviv were essential markers of their self-identification as Bitcoiners. First, Embassy associates claimed that blockchain technology was far from an 'enchanting' technology. Ambassador Yoav once told me, for example, that 'blockchain is just a trade-off we [Bitcoiners] are willing to tolerate because it enables us to be free'. Maintaining P2P communication, as Yoav explained it, required compromise. For him, the blockchain itself was not a wonderful invention that was going to disrupt industries in fantastical ways, but rather a *price* that Bitcoiners must currently pay to be able to exchange money between them without having to go through banks and credit card companies. Yoav further argued that from the outset 'anybody who understood this technology realized that blockchain was inefficient and primitive', especially as it was 'incapable of dealing with mass transactions that centralized credit card companies could process easily'. The blockchain was thus employed by default for lack of better options, not because of its alleged enchanting power.

As opposed to 'blockchain', Yoav claimed, it was Bitcoin itself that was valuable; by solving the problem of 'double spending' (see above and Faustino, Faria and Marques 2022: 72), Satoshi had enabled the reorganization of entire societies into a multiplicity of P2P relationships (should Bitcoin be adopted at a massive scale). What distinguished Bitcoin from blockchain was the fact that the technicalities of Bitcoin were maintained and debated openly by a multitude of unrelated individuals across the globe. The cryptocurrencies that followed Bitcoin, Yoav claimed, were centrally or semi-centrally controlled; and therefore they were not fully trustless. Rami, an Ambassador and a key interlocutor who took part in this conversation, went further to argue that there was no such thing as blockchain without Bitcoin. He showed us on his phone a banner that he had created to explicate how clever branding nonetheless increasingly naturalized the alleged distinction, turning Bitcoin into 'just another blockchain product'. On the banner he depicted side by side a bright-red logo bearing the term 'Blockchain' with a capital 'B', and a McDonald's logo with its famous rounded capital 'M'. 'Blockchain is pure branding', he said, pointing out how the 'B' produced a tacit image of success and sophistication. 'Hi-tech entrepreneurs think they can get rid of the ideology and promote the technology as if these were two different things. But they can't because these things can't be separated.'

Other interlocutors likewise emphasized the disruption of hierarchical power relations and the ability to reorganize grassroots economy as Bitcoin's main advantages. It is the discursive framework and communalist spirit that was the revolutionary aspect of Bitcoin, rather than its underlying technology; which in fact was partially functional already back in the mid-1980s. New blockchains that relied on new discursive contexts for the use of cryptocurrencies were therefore seen as either useless or degradable; and Ambassadors consequently tended to treat blockchain technology dismissively, at times even with contempt. Once, for example, I asked Daniel (AKA Dani) Bloom, one of the informal leaders at the Embassy and a key research interlocutor, what distinguished Bitcoin from blockchain. He responded swiftly:

> Let's put it this way: in the 'blockchain-blockchain' industry there is also a kind of community spirit, but it is not the same community that Bitcoin has, which is more about *values*. Blockchain is more commercial [in its orientation], and it's more industrial; the conferences are usually about money and commercialization, and they are not talking about advancing something out of faith. That is why the community is so important to everything we [in Bitcoin] do.

Bloom's distinction between faith-based and commercialized or alienated communities leads to the second disputed heuristic, which revolves around ideological commitment to social change. Not only that 'blockchain-blockchain' applications were slow and user unfriendly, but they were also seen as perverse, a case of throwing the baby out with the bathwater. Bitcoin differed from blockchain, true believers like Bloom claimed, because on top of decentralization, trustlessness and secure P2P exchange, it also included a vision of *social change*, a belief in egalitarian communities, a vision of reorganization of existing institutions and the pretension to establish a 'new economy'. The wider blockchain industry lacked these values, at least as most interlocutors understood it. Reiterating precisely the same comparison used by Faustino, Faria and Marques (2022), Bloom thus referred to other blockchain projects as 'cargo cults':

> Much of the blockchain industry is just 'copy-paste' of big words and technical concepts. But they are not really decentralized, and they cannot help with personal development. People who don't understand [Bitcoin] might think that these [blockchain] endeavours are real, but they are not; only from the outside this looks like Bitcoin, but inside it is something completely different, exactly like these wooden airplanes that from the outside look like an airplane but inside they do not have the things that turn them into an [real] airplane.

Bloom regarded the fetishization of the blockchain in the 'decentralized financial industries' simply as a big Ponzi scheme. He argued that, unlike Bitcoin, which did not and would never belong to anyone, blockchain-based applications (e.g. cryptographic coins, crowdfunding schemes, prediction markets, etc.) were for the most part created by centralized for-profit businesses, and thus were not able to 'advance a solution' – a term interlocutors used frequently during my fieldwork to suggest that some of the so-called revolutionary crypto inventions were in fact only reproducing old problems that Bitcoin would, in contrast, resolve. He thus perceived non-Bitcoin cryptographic assets as replicas, which used the *image* of Bitcoin but discarded its value-content. Incorporating blockchain applications into existing industries (e.g. the supply chain) was thus understood as taking the Bitcoin operational system out of context and even distorting the original instructions that appeared in Satoshi's original 'manual'. 'Blockchain-blockchain' industries, Bloom ultimately claimed, were a *setback* rather than an incentive for mass adoption of Bitcoin (see also Antonopoulos and Harding 2024).

In their uses of the term 'cargo cult', Faustino, Faria and Marques (2022) erase the crucial differentiation that Bloom makes, positioning all crypto-asset holders in a single, unified, category.[14] As Bloom's critique of the hollowness of cryptoassets other than Bitcoin suggested, however, Israeli Bitcoiners drew a thick line between 'blockchain-blockchain' enterprises and the Bitcoin project. This coincided with ideas that *only* Bitcoin was sufficiently revisionist to successfully challenge common mainstream financial aphorisms; for example, that SWIFT services should monitor cash transactions, or that corporations and states must survey financial transactions online to keep society safe. In Chapter 5, I will elaborate on the millenarian/utopian edge of this faith in the singularity of Bitcoin, which thereby present Bloom's recruitment of cargo cults in a different light. For now, it is enough to highlight that much of interlocutors' revolutionary fervour was derived from the ideology of *Bitcoin distinction* to the exclusion of all other experiments in decentralization.

Conclusion

As I will demonstrate in the remainder of the book, interlocutors in Israel commonly constructed a direct semantic link between Cypherpunk militancy, the commercialization of encryption tools, the rise of P2P sociality online, and the emergence of a decentralized global community of bitcoin users. Ambassadors were not, however, necessarily referring to themselves or other human users when describing P2P transactions as foundational to their participation in a designated 'community'. A peer could be a real person, of course, but in reality, the term referred to any entity behind a transaction on the blockchain, including a bot programmed to buy and sell bitcoin online according to market dynamics, for example. Every bitcoin holder could consequently operate many different cryptocurrency wallets at once, each assigned with a unique identifying address, which turned each address into a singular 'peer' when a transaction was made. A peer could even be a *group*, as Tim May had suggested thirty years earlier, if an arrangement was made for several people to jointly own and operate one or more cryptocurrency wallets (popularly known today as a 'multi-sig' or multiple-signature cryptocurrency wallet). That was in fact the case with the management of a shared digital wallet at the Embassy, whose internal organization and fund distribution techniques will feature in the next chapter. As will become clear, their community indeed depended on the autonomy of peerage – personal or collective – but it was also premised on the power of collective gatherings of the communalist kind.

Acknowledging the historicity of P2P modalities, Embassy associates were not oblivious to the fact that decentralized peerage could also be done successfully with other coins. As I elaborate in Chapter 3, some of the Ambassadors explicitly recognized the two examples of cryptocurrency communities I surveyed above, which represented divergent directions that Bitcoin could also take. Initiatives such as BitNation-Pangea, which used the term 'community' strategically, generated the mystique of a romantic *Gemeinschaft* to connect personal and collective freedom with the material pursuit of financial independence. They produced a libertarian metaphysics more than grassroots intimacies, however, using the term 'community' so abstractly that it was difficult to identify its 'communalist' content. The resulting dynamic was that of distancing, rather than cohesion. Even though people attempted to practise their community, they stretched its boundaries so much that they dissipated entirely, turning community members into a mere mass of unrelated, detached individuals.

Dogecoin, in contrast, became increasingly cohesive despite a lack of ideological commitment to political causes because it singularized the interest of the collective into a 'good vibes' attitude. A sense of companionship emerged spontaneously, attracting more fans that mimetically acquired some habits, idioms and other features of Dogecoin communication online. The undefined collective, most of it composed of people who have never met each other, quickly began describing themselves as a 'community for good'. When people at the Embassy spoke of their community, they directly emphasized this type of relationship as a preferred modality, although it was not framed as necessarily good or bad. The dynamic of enclosure, seen as the tightening of intimate relationships between colleagues and friends who shared a passion, was seen as a crucial element in any successful dispersion of the Bitcoin message and consequent mass adoption. In the next chapter, I will begin exploring how this emphasis on friendship became dominant in the Israeli Bitcoin scene, gradually turning a group of fringe investors into a formalized 'community'.

NOTES

1. After 1972, the *Catalogue* continued to be published sporadically until its final dissolution in 1998. For the full list of the Whole Earth issues and the magazine's various offshoots see *Whole Earth Index*: https://wholeearth.info/ (accessed 29 July 2025).
2. Still active in the 2020s, the EFF is at the forefront of global civil society organizations promoting the distribution of encryption tools and the development of open-source information industries. Since 2011, the organization has also been supporting the use of cryptocurrencies. See: https://www.eff.org/ (accessed 29 July 2025).
3. 'Cypherpunk' is a deliberate misspelling that mischievously combines 'cipher' and 'punk' with a twist alluding to the 'cyberpunk' sci-fi subgenre of the 1980s.
4. An alternative block production system is called 'proof of stake'. It is based on 'staking' wealth in a common pool and receiving rewards relative to the amount committed. It does not demand a high expenditure of energy, but at the time of writing, staking has not yet been incorporated into Bitcoin.
5. In 2011, British Anonymous activist Amir Takki proposed a mechanism that enabled the global community to discuss and implement changes to the blockchain. It included a dataset called Bitcoin Improvement Proposals (BIP), which followed a standard peer-review protocol. Upon posting new proposals they would be subject to public discussion, followed by a voting procedure. Anybody could generate a BIP entry by sending their proposal to a designated open-source listserv. To be implemented, a BIP must be accepted by a decisive 'economic majority' of 95 per cent of registered nodes.
6. An open-access Bitcoin dictionary provides this definition: 'Full nodes download every block and transaction and check them against Bitcoin's consensus rules . . . [such as, among others]: (1) Blocks may only create a certain number of bitcoins; (2) Transactions must have correct signatures for the bitcoins being spent; (3) Transactions/blocks must be in the correct data format' (https://en.bitcoin.it/wiki/Full_node (accessed 14 July 2024).
7. The cypher is: 000000000019d6689c085ae165831e934ff763ae46a2a6c172b3f1b60a8ce26f. Commercial entities have since produced themed paraphernalia bearing this long alphanumeric figure, especially black T-shirts.
8. Gnutella is an early decentralized P2P protocol. Tor is a P2P-based software that enables users to explore the internet anonymously. The 'decapitation' of Napster refers to a series of lawsuits filed against the company by major music-industry actors and artists, which resulted in the termination of the company's activities on one hand, and the commercial endorsement of the P2P-sharing model in that industry on the other hand.
9. Shemesh, the architect who initially opened the Embassy, moved his private business to another location and took the frame with him. I photographed it at this new location. During fieldwork a homemade copy of the original newspaper was hung on the wall at the Embassy along with a metal plate bearing the block cypher and its decrypted message.
10. https://www.cryptoswede.com/bitnation-founder-tarkowski-admits-profit-motive/ (accessed 22 January 2023).
11. See https://foundation.dogecoin.com/manifesto/ (accessed 23 January 2023).

12. See https://www.dogecoin.com (accessed 23 January 2023).
13. Rarity preserves value, as in the case of expensive metals (see Zimmer 2017).
14. The issue of cargo cults is fascinating, but I am unable to analyse it here in depth. I only wish to note that both Faustino et al. (2022) and Bloom in fact employed an outdated view of this phenomenon. Rather than merely exposing a native ignorance of technology, cargo cults were contextual frameworks for local political action, which usually took the form of re-establishing kinship relations with both peers and ancestors, thereby strengthening such connection as authoritative moral institutions. I here follow Andrew Lattas (2007: 151), who argued convincingly that anthropologists have been using the term 'cargo cult' uncritically to encompass diverse movements 'that are better understood as millenarian or utopian'. Lattas analysed cargo-related symbolism as a point of conflict, a contextual social struggle over the ability of dead ancestors to shape modern life, and the ways such categories as race, colour, class and wealth took part in the construction of political imaginaries in Papua New Guinea.

CHAPTER 2

THE COMMUNITY

First Encounters

Dani Bloom came across Bitcoin accidentally in 2011 during a conversation with colleagues online. The conversation dealt with MIRI, a nonprofit 'trying to develop AI that will operate in accordance with human values and not against them, because otherwise humanity will be destroyed', as Bloom explained to me in 2019.[1] He then elaborated:

> So, MIRI began accepting donations in bitcoin at some stage in 2011, and of course we are talking about people who are progressive and who adopt new inventions relatively easily, so they gave it a chance. There was a post on this in Less Wrong,[2] and I read it, and I began thinking, 'What is this, is it like PayPal?' So, I started reading on it and became really intrigued. At that time, I was the head of research at a startup, responsible for developing algorithms to measure similarity and difference between internet sites. It was just after I completed my master's degree in maths. At that point I understood that Bitcoin was a bit more interesting than what I was doing [at the startup], so I began a process of phasing out of that job.

Bloom downloaded Satoshi's White Paper and was captivated by its mathematical beauty, especially the elegant solution to the problem of 'double spending'. As a brilliant mathematician and a gifted computer scientist, Bloom was interested initially in the technical aspects of Bitcoin. To see how the system worked he purchased several central processing units (CPUs) and assembled them into a homemade mining machine. He then opened an exchange platform and began trading online.[3] About a month later, impressed, he decided he must talk with other Israelis about his new passion:

> Then, in August 2011 the community began – people began to approach me by mail to ask things, and I began to know many people. Someone also opened a

> Facebook page, and on this page there were early discussions on this [Bitcoin]. At some stage I suggested that we meet, and I made an event [on Facebook], to which eight people confirmed they would come, and only three arrived. That was right after the first international conference in New York for Bitcoin. That conference was the first Bitcoin conference in history, which seemed important, so I flew there. At the next meeting [in Tel Aviv] I met Ronen, who was interested in Bitcoin as much as I was.

Ronen, who at the time was studying for his BA in computer science, subsequently joined Bloom as a meetup group leader. They initially used Facebook to coordinate these meetings, and later moved to the Meetup application, which had become a popular professional networking platform. They soon began to attract people in the dozens. Many of those who attended meetups continued to do so throughout 2012, forming relationships and building trust. A fraternal sense of partnership began to sink in. Bloom explained that this was a spontaneous process, much in the same way that the consolidation of a distinct 'community' in Israel emerged out of the combined interests and curiosities of its future members:

> I didn't think of a community back then, but there was an international community online, which was basically a forum that later became the 'Bitcoin Talk' forum. The community there included people who knew each other more or less, or knew *of* each other, so it was not just talking with strangers. By participating in this forum, I learned that any community is eventually based on two things – familiarity with others and the collective understanding or common language that people share. Only then comes a shared goal and a shared vision. [Bitcoin] conferences were essential for this at the beginning because you wanted to know personally people who, beforehand, you only knew as text on a screen.

Bloom used the term 'community' (*kehila*) both to describe the amorphous global mass of Bitcoin investors and the smaller-scale group that was beginning to form in Tel Aviv. This reference to community implied an empathetic reading of in-group alterity that included companionship, mutualism, equality and a shared belief in the future of Bitcoin, which also galvanized a spirit of rebellion. Bloom thus believed from the outset that face-to-face interaction was critical for advancing the goal of mass adoption. Friendships made during these early meetings among enthusiasts inspired him to establish the Israeli Bitcoin Association (IBA), which he and his colleagues registered as a non-governmental organization (NGO) early in 2014, shortly after the establishment of the Embassy. A new phase in the development of the community thus began. As Bloom put it:

> In 2013 things began to get more serious. The value of bitcoin went up [passing the US$1,000 mark] and more people around the world heard of it. In Israel, a major financial paper made an article on this, and then a financial TV programme

made an item on this. In our meetups we began to count 120, 160 people, and so on, and volumes of commerce went up. At that time, I closed my [bitcoin exchange] business and I needed to find something to direct my energies into. That is when we decided to institutionalize this as an association, which could advance the issues of Bitcoin in Israel . . . at the time I thought I would dedicate about 50% of my time to the association, and I ended up dedicating 100%, depending on how you count.

When Shemesh opened the Embassy in 2013, a collective of Bitcoin aficionados had already been meeting regularly for approximately two years. Shemesh took part of this collective, and the decision to establish the Embassy was thus taken in collaboration with colleagues who sought a venue to proselytize the message alongside establishing a legal entity that would lobby for support from higher up and serve as a consulting authority on taxation and other legal issues. Separation between the Embassy and the Association was important for them because it enabled flexibility. The Embassy would sustain a decentralized social organization aimed at challenging contemporary sociocultural patterns in education, personal relationships, citizenship and financial markets. The IBA, meanwhile, would function as a formal representative of the community, speaking a language of regulation, anti-money laundering and technological progress. Bloom explained how community members collaborated across these organizations:

Let's say that the embassy is closer to the original vision of Bitcoin and the Association is closer to more traditional ways of doing things. You need both – you cannot influence the world if you are not behaving in a complicit manner. You need both a body that will be open source, and another body that works with the current rules, and you need a lobbying body that will consult the authorities, and you need to challenge the authorities in a way that influences the way policy makers think, if we hope to change their minds about this [Bitcoin].

This strategic division proved crucial in the consequent growth of the community from 2014 onwards. Initially, IBA members shared a similar sociodemographic profile. Apart from Nissim, who was approaching his seventieth birthday at the time, and who had been working most of his life in construction, they were mostly young (mid-twenties to mid-thirties), middle-class, secular and university educated. Most of them also had some background in computer science or economics, and they shared an interest in disruptive technological gadgets. With the opening of the Embassy, they were nonetheless joined by more heterogeneous crowds, including sporadic visits by Palestinian residents of East Jerusalem, Bedouin money launderers from the Negev Desert and several Orthodox Jews – one of whom in fact later became Ambassador. As I elaborate below, the Embassy thus became a focal point of synergetic action aimed at bringing the 'crypto revolution' into full grassroots visibility.

The Embassy

I once asked Yoni Shemesh what distinguished the Embassy from any other bitcoin trading centre in the world. He answered, characteristically, that the Embassy was never meant to be a mere trading centre, but rather, a *community centre* for those wishing to contribute to the emergence of the New Economy. Consequently, he explained, unlike a functional trading centre, the Embassy was built as an exemplary organization where people would practise the moral principles undergirding the New Economy, thereby integrating them empirically into their everyday lives. These principles were *egalitarianism, consensus* and *transparency*. For the first, Shemesh explained, 'egalitarianism' meant that Embassy members would not use any formal designation of hierarchy, and that responsibility for Embassy activities would be distributed on a voluntary basis, rather than allocated by leaders. He admitted that when some of the business ventures that were set up by Embassy associates began to flourish, several local figures did assume informal leadership roles. These roles extended from personality, however, rather than rank, and they were never institutionalized. Charisma, devotion to proselytizing activities (which implied an ideological commitment) and good organizational skills could all become a pretext for leadership, as would long-term involvement with the Bitcoin global community, 'deep' knowledge of blockchain, high-level technical expertise, etc.

The second principle – consensus – meant expressive reliance on collective decision-making as a replacement for coercion. During my fieldwork this included open debates, sometimes during meetings and sometimes on WhatsApp or Facebook, wherein different views were heard and considered. When possible, decisions would be taken unanimously, while more intractable disagreements would be decided by a majority vote. Disagreements did appear, as I detail below, but these were not mitigated formally, as there was no organizational enforcement mechanism that could intervene. Rather, tentative collusion was always preferred as a political arbitrage mechanism. When negotiations failed, the tendency was to let things be and move on.

The third principle – transparency – was a statement on honesty, as some described it. Shemesh decided to install a glass front wall, as I mentioned in the Introduction, precisely because he believed it would convey a strong message to visitors. As he told me during an interview: 'The transparent front makes it impossible for us to count money in a back room and become hustlers. It forces us to position our values out in the open, in front of everybody, so people can inspect us and decide for themselves if we are true to our word or not.' Ambassadors also avoided hushed conversations when visitors were around, maintaining an environment premised on openness. Even formal Embassy meetings were open to outsiders, including those held in conjunction with the IBA board. They were usually also filmed by Embassy personnel and later published unedited online. IBA resolutions would later appear on the Embassy website, in addition to being added to the IBA's own website. Transparency was therefore mostly associated with the performance of a 'clean', honest and critically exposed *public sphere.*

Ambassadors obviously did have secrets, as well as personal disagreements, business interests they wanted to keep private, and other sensitive matters that they preferred treating tactically rather than ideologically. For now, suffice it to say that in most cases I have come across, these would fall under the rubric of normative gossip rather than conspiratorial undercurrents representing hidden motives or political power struggles between individuals. For example, rumours would at times circulate about fraud or dishonesty enacted by celebrity-status Israeli crypto-entrepreneurs who were not directly related to the Embassy. Or at other times people might share with close friends their speculative market analyses, which always also included implicit investment strategies.

One reason that such issues remained in the background, beyond their intrinsic sensitivity, was Embassy members' prudence regarding anything that could sound like investment advice. Often, even during public talks and personal conversations with newcomers, they would add the proviso 'this is not an investment advice' when sharing their personal opinions on crypto, fiat and the future of money. They did not want to take responsibility for other people's monetary decisions, but, more importantly, wished to avoid the possibility of being sued. These ethical standards, then, boiled down to five main 'values' that all Ambassadors would explicitly highlight in various occasions as the informal (however unwritten) *constitution* of the community. These values were, as Shemesh framed them:

(1) sharing (*shituf*);
(2) transparency (*shkifut*);
(3) meritocracy (*meritokratia*, as this term has been localized into mundane Hebrew. By this, as Shemesh further explained, he referred to incentivizing deeds, not ideas);
(4) personal responsibility (*akhrayut*); and
(5) voluntarism (Shemesh switched between *bkhira hofshit*, which means 'free choice', and *hitnadvut*, which means voluntarism. In both cases the

emphasis is on lack of external coercion as well as the conscious relinquishing of the codes that undergird normative manager-worker relationships in the centralized economy).

Emphasis on these values (or, I prefer, virtues) at the personal level inspired organizational principles at the collective level. Take, for example, the fruitful collaboration between the Ambassadors and Bits of Gold, at the time the only registered cryptocurrency exchange agency (and thus a for-profit organization) in Israel. Established in 2014 by Embassy veterans Jeremy and Guy, the company began paying the rent for the entire space in 2016 while using the tiny mezzanine on the second floor as an office.[4] To make this possible economically they imported, together with Shemesh, an automatic teller machine, which they called 'Bitcoin ATM' (using the generic Hebrew neologism *kaspomat*, slang for 'automatic money extraction'). The machine could convert new Israeli shekels (ISO code: ILS, but unofficially abbreviated as NIS), though not the other way around, into bitcoin or Ethereum; a cryptocurrency which by 2017 had already become a trusted asset and the second-most-valued coin in the emergent cryptocurrency market. Jeremy, Guy and Shemesh installed the machine on the ground floor of the Embassy with the intention of using the commissions earned on every purchase to cover the high rent. The machine soon became an attraction for new adopters who would come from across the country to purchase bitcoin (see Figure 2.1).

Figure 2.1. The Bitcoin cash machine at the Embassy, 2018. Credit: Matan Shapiro.

Ambassadors, for their part, used the machine mostly for practical demonstrations, encouraging newcomers to purchase insignificant amounts of bitcoin (around US$2 or US$3) so they could learn how to exchange funds on the blockchain. Until 2018, the machine was the centre of the economic infrastructure that controlled cash flow at the Embassy. The Embassy did not, however, become a 'centralized' working environment. Rather, as Shemesh conveyed during a lengthy interview, the ATM in fact strengthened the voluntary organizational structure of the Embassy, while also increasing its collective economic power. His explanation will lead me to the next section:

> Even our economic structure is decentralized. When we started, we opened a bitcoin wallet and rotated the password between us on a voluntary basis, so that at any given moment nobody would know who was holding it. We earned money by selling products such as beers or snacks or hot soups in the winter. We charged people not in Israeli shekel, but in bitcoin. When you opened the fridge and took a beer, you had to send bitcoin fragments to the Embassy wallet. Since we never converted this treasury to fiat, and since the value of bitcoin only went up, we accumulated a lot of money. The account now holds the bitcoin equivalent of hundreds of thousands of shekels, which are not owned by a single owner but by all of us collectively; and when we hold meetings, we decide together how to distribute the money. I had 'a say' in these meetings because [until 2016] I paid the rent, but the decision-making mechanism we built was completely decentralized and voluntary . . . The Embassy was both a society and an economic structure that was ex-territorial, and its governance was completely decentralized!

Work and Play

Embassy members treated their shifts and other knowledge-sharing engagements as forms of *work,* albeit voluntary. Their 'job' was simply to speak about Bitcoin with whomever happened to come in, explain the basic technicalities, and generally 'evangelize' the good tidings of the New Economy. This amounted to the task of 'spreading the Bitcoin vision', as Roy, a new Ambassador at the time of fieldwork, described it. Indeed, at the Embassy there had always been a stock of Bitcoin stickers, shirts, newsletters, hats and other gadgets, all of which presented on shelves at the bottom floor, which Ambassadors sometimes gave out as souvenirs to visitors (see Figure 2.2 and Figure 2.3).

Side by side with these informal efforts, however, Ambassadors regularly also organized Bitcoin workshops and professional lectures, mostly carried out by prominent figures in the Israeli Bitcoin scene but occasionally also featuring some of the most influential persons in the cryptocurrency world, including Jimmy Song, Vitalik Buterin, Joseph Lubin, David Chaum

Figure 2.2. Bitcoin-themed stickers at the Embassy, 2018. Credit: Matan Shapiro.

Figure 2.3. Shelves at the Embassy with Bitcoin regalia, including the Bitcoin cash machine and a public billboard, 2017. Credit: Matan Shapiro.

and many others. As I will further exemplify in Chapter 4, several of these celebrities later visited the Embassy to network or hang out, further establishing its prestige as the centre of the community in Israel. Another important activity included the hosting of an annual Bitcoin hackathon, partly subsidized by the IBA. In later years the hackathon grew to the extent that it had to be moved out of the small Embassy compound to bigger venues, while also inspiring several technology firms in Tel Aviv to organize their own cryptocurrency-related hackathons. With time, 'the Embassy developed into an ecosystem in its own right', as Dani Bloom phrased it during a conversation. He then added:

> A community forms out of acquaintances. Because when you meet someone, and then you read his posts, you already have a more personal approach to what he says. When I write something, and people understand what I meant – especially if I use slang like 'let's advance a solution' (*léKadem pîtaron*) or HODL [slang for 'don't spend your bitcoins'; see Chapter 3] – this makes a community.

One of the most striking forms that the localized character of the community took was indeed the spontaneous emergence of slang, jokes and neologisms, which community members began to use daily. This went beyond such terms as HODL – a deliberate misrepresentation of the verb 'hold' that I will analyse at length in the next chapter – which they used to distinguish those who invested in Bitcoin for ideological reasons from those who traded in it for money. An important local idiom, for example, was 'advancing a solution' (*léKadem pitarôn*), as Bloom phrased it above, which implied that the old/centralized economic system was full of problems that needed to be resolved in a decentralized fashion. In one of our conversations, Bloom directly connected this with a collective sense of togetherness:

> One person alone cannot advance a solution. You need many people who collaborate and work together, and this is why the physical meetings and the ceremonies (*tkasim*) are so important . . . When a person knows he is a part of something more or less cohesive, he gets the motivation to give more of himself to it. I see it on me, and on other people, when you give from your money or time, you do it because you believe in this, *and you would not believe in it if you were the only one who does it*. So, when you work together – and there is also a measure of mutual expectation, as if we are all looking at each other to see that everyone shares the burden – this is how you can advance things [towards a solution].

Another common slang term used by Embassy personnel was *Tkhina* – or tahini, the liquid sesame paste – which implied that other cryptocurrencies likewise lacked substantial cohesion or form. In contrast, Bitcoin itself was described as being like 'iron' (*barzel*): firm, robust, unbendable, hard to break and durable.[5] 'Harry-Pottering' was used to describe blocking other Bitcoiners on Facebook, the imagery of which was derived from the 'invisibility cloak' sometimes worn by Harry Potter in J.K. Rolling's magical-realism book series.

Humour was probably the most important local aspect of such slang, developed ad hoc, occasionally catching fire and used broadly, but sometimes disappearing after an idiom, act, icon or punchline would lose its effectivity. One such humorous linguistic feature, for example, which faded away after several months, was adding an 'h' to the beginning of certain words, thus distorting their usual sense and suggest fakery. Instead of saying 'altcoins', for example, one could say 'haltcoins', which conveyed the implicit message that other cryptocurrencies could not be trusted and should not be purchased. These techniques were also applied to terms that were not supposed to be used at all, as they were seen to represent concepts or values that community members would regard as contrary to the spirit of Bitcoin mutualism. That was the case, for example, of then-fashionable shortening of Bitcoin into the mnemonic 'bit', mostly used by seasoned traders to convey that they were 'in the thick of things'. Embassy personnel, however, regarded this idiom as cheap and even derogatory, as they strove to distinguish themselves from professional traders interested in money more than social reform. These linguistic features, among others, thus mediated intimate familiarity, creating a world of meanings understood internally between community members and a shared heritage, while distinguishing those who practised and developed it from outsiders. During a public lecture that he titled 'Bitcoin: Parties and Social Life', Bloom explained why such a distinction was important:

> We, in the community, organize many professional meetups, where people can learn about Bitcoin. But there are also events at which there are no lectures and no agenda, events at which people just come together to have fun, talk, drink and play Swedish Chess[6] . . . I think that one of the main reasons that Bitcoin has survived and achieved success in the last ten years . . . is that there is a cohesive community that advances it [the Bitcoin cause]; it is not as if each person [in the community] only took care of professional issues, or commercial ventures, or their individual economic interests. On the contrary, the community is really about people who spend time together and work together towards a common goal.

The idea that the community is an assemblage of people who 'spend time together and work towards a common goal' was in fact the only delineation anybody ever provided at the Embassy for a provisional boundary that separated insiders from outsiders. Within this framework, communitarian relations were not, however, seen as a collective means towards the goal of mass adoption. Rather, Bloom and his colleagues believed that this goal could only be achieved if their community first became cohesive organically – a true grassroots organization premised on personal ties and an internal division of labour – on which all else can be built later. Precisely for that reason, Embassy associates sought to live out a dynamic community life that included events and hangouts as a means of collectively defying 'centralized' financial conduct.

These meetups were also different from the semi-ritualized (and usually hilarious) commemorations of Jewish as well as Bitcoin-specific holidays, which I analyse in Chapter 5 as expressions of millenarian attitudes. These ceremonies consolidated intimacies 'inside' the community, while positively representing the material scope of such intimate familiarity to the world beyond it in a theatrical and often exaggerated fashion. Mundane meetups, however, were less ceremonial, and thus better categorized as play-zones (see Shapiro 2019).

Take Sunday night Satoshi Square meetups as a prominent example. These meetups quickly turned from events focused on selling and buying bitcoin into spaces for fellow travellers to socialize. Bloom smiled when he recounted that with time people had in fact forgotten the original commercial intention of these meetings, which were initially established in New York as platforms for face-to-face stock exchanges in the early 2010s. In Tel Aviv, Satoshi Square nights were an *agora*, or perhaps a tribal bonfire of sorts, which lacked any form of orchestration or even rules (as opposed to trading grounds; see Smith 2005). 'The major force behind the growth of the community is the gatherings and the parties', Nissim once told me. Friendships that were developed during mundane gatherings, he said, were lasting because they were spontaneous. Evidently, as both Nissim and Bloom commented in different occasions, people would begin showing up at the Embassy spontaneously, even if they just so happened to be in the neighbourhood.

To strengthen the impact of these informal spaces of sociability, Bloom had set up a separate meetup slot on Wednesday evenings, which he named Finney Square, after the late computer scientist who was the first person to receive a bitcoin transaction, in 2009, from Satoshi Nakamoto (see Chapter 1). Since Bloom was a high-level chess player, he initiated in 2018 a routine of Chess and Go board game competitions during these Wednesday night events, with what he called 'Swedish Chess' format being the highlight of the evening. Before and after games people would drink, smoke and talk about the cryptocurrency market or raise questions about morality, authority and trust, always meeting new people in the process (see Figure 2.4). Bloom told me in an interview that the very existence of these forms of playful interactions would serve as proof for sceptics that decentralized social organization could encourage the forming of trust relationships, which he regarded as the basis of every community:

> When you meet a person, it increases your trust in them. You can philosophize if this is justified, because after all people can cheat you after you've met, but psychologically it is less difficult to swindle someone online because there is no

Figure 2.4. Chess competition during a Finney Square meetup in Tel Aviv, 2018. Credit: Matan Shapiro.

> personal connection at all, and you can do it at a huge scale by sending mass phishing emails, for example. I learned at [Bitcoin] conferences that there are many honest people, and many scammers too, but also people who are in the middle, who generally are not looking to cheat or defraud you but *could* do it when the right opportunity comes. So, it is more difficult for these kinds of people to cheat you after you have established a friendly contact and familiarity.

These ideas confused me at first, as Ambassadors were usually claiming that the whole point of the decentralized economy was the ability *not* to trust anybody. Embracing decentralized and trustless technology had always been presented at the Embassy as Satoshi's well-thought-out critique of risk-averse hegemonic views on such issues as individual financial autonomy, wealth inequalities, the reliance on debt in the fractional-reserve banking system, and the corporate structures that absolve financial elites of accountability when they abuse or misuse their corporate powers[7]. It is thus crucial to explain briefly, following Inês Faria, how trustlessness and trustfulness in fact coincide when viewed through the lens of communitarian collaborationism in the world of Bitcoin ideologists.

Trustlessness

Bitcoiners at the Embassy and supporters of what are now known as 'DeFi' economic models rely on blockchains for money transfers because these ledgers successfully automate actions that previously required rigorous human auditing and consent (Faustino, Faria and Marques 2022). A group of unrelated individuals can thus take part in decentralized financial projects whose governance is never deferred to any of these individuals. The pioneering implementation of trustlessness in Bitcoin has thus become a 'socio-technological' (Hayes 2019) force operating at the frontier of a new economic sphere. As I have already explained in Chapter 1, money forms that are produced by and exchanged on decentralized ledgers depend on algorithmic consensus, which in turn are seen as the mechanical equivalent of traditional forms of trust. Following Geoffrey Ingham (2004), Inês Faria (2022) summarizes this point well, arguing that money materializes social relations, and can thus engender what she calls 'communities of trust':

> In very generic terms, money can be defined by its functions as a medium of exchange, a means of payment, a store or standard of value, and a unit of account . . . Although monetary practices are very diverse, money always concerns an already established network of people that trust it, or, more accurately, that trust a kind of currency to serve as money . . . In other words, there is a wide network of people that trusts that it can be used to pay or be paid . . . As long as everyone accepts a currency, there are many things that can serve as money . . . and one single currency can also be managed according to various meaning-making, moral, and social rationales.

The genealogy of Bitcoin, its social pedigree or kinship, if you will, reflects in that sense the processual emergence of postmodern communities of trust, which progressively turned towards technological solutions at the expense of bureaucratic arrangements. This mirrored and extended Cypherpunk ideals, as they had been phrased decades beforehand, especially with regard to the use of digital technology outside the regulatory mandate of states and corporations. Some Ambassadors in Tel Aviv performed this connection materially; for example, by wearing black T-shirts imprinted with Hughes's iconic precept 'Cypherpunks Write Code'. By exhibiting a personal affiliation with Cypherpunk mythology, interlocutors tacitly consolidated a declarative boundary between their 'open-source community' to the 'centralized' institutions on which they were still dependent in their everyday lives. This explains why interlocutors in Tel Aviv reiterated the axiom that only a community of autonomous but committed 'peers' would be able to sustain the Bitcoin project in the future. Side by side with personal virtue, a collective version of Cypherpunk collaborationism was seen to arise from a plurality of irreversible 'P2P' transactions.

Cypherpunk idealism thus advanced the counterintuitive notion of a 'community' – the epitome of intimacy and familiarity – that was premised on so-called 'trustless' machinic processes. Vitalik Buterin – an early Bitcoin adopter turned crypto-superstar after cofounding Ethereum, the second-most-valuable cryptocurrency in terms of market capitalization and scale of use – turned the paradox of a 'trustless community' on its head when he argued that 'trustlessness' was simply a technological enabler for new kinds of *trustful* societal arrangements. In an article he posted online, Buterin (2015b) argued:

> Given any system that is maintained by humans, there exists a hypothetical combination of motivations and incentives that would lead those humans to successfully collude to screw you over, and so if you trust the system to work you are necessarily trusting the total set of humans not to have that particular combination of motivations and incentives. But that does not mean that trustlessness is not a useful direction to strive in. When a system is claiming to be 'trustless', what it is actually trying to do is ***expand the possible set of motivations*** that individuals are allowed to have while still maintaining a particular low probability of failure. When a system is claiming to be 'trustful', it is trying to ***reduce the probability of failure given a particular set of motivations.*** Thus, we can see the 'trustlessness' and 'trustfulness', at least as directions, are actually the exact same thing [emphases in original].

Buterin was not trying to whitewash the contradiction of an intimate sociality that is allegedly devoid of 'trust'. When I asked him about this potential contradiction during a short lecture he carried out in Tel Aviv in 2017, he told me that he described trustlessness and trustfulness as 'the exact same thing' merely to dispel the exoticism that had been assigned to blockchain technology. His utilitarian explanation, which focused on eliminating 'failure', suggests that trustless infrastructures would not jeopardize collaborative relationships. To work well at a grand scale, trustlessness *required* the horizontal cultivation of intimate familiarity between partners as much as it demanded a vertical sense of individual trust in the fungibility of the currency (see Vidan and Lehdonvirta 2019). On a clear night, after another drinking session at the Embassy, I confronted Dani Bloom with this question. Referencing David Golumbia (2016), I asked Bloom whether libertarian-leaning 'trustlessness' did not in fact contradict the communitarian tendency to build *trustful partnerships.* Bloom responded:

> I think it's more nuanced than that. Libertarians do not say that there can't be a community, only that nobody can *force you* to be in one. So, if you choose it, they are OK with it. Another thing is that, on the face of it, you might say that there is no trust, and you cannot trust anyone, but if we *do* want trust, we need to work on it. Every member in the community should make an effort to build trust, because on the face of it, if we are tabula rasa, there is no trust. Obviously online you don't trust people because you have no idea of knowing who they are, but [even online] it can be possible, once you take some steps to build trust. It is good

> to have trust – when you have trust you can build much bigger things than if you didn't have it. Without trust it is, you know, 'every person will grow his own corn and will live in a hut he built of mud'. But once there is trust you can build towers. Precisely because of the [libertarian] perception that there is no trust to begin with, that is why you need to build a community that will establish trust. That is why we need physical meetups and a common language and rituals; it creates a point of sharing, it generates the feeling that we really are working together.

Like Buterin, Bloom claimed that trust and trustlessness complemented each other and therefore were not posing a serious logical or emotional obstacle for the establishment of a decentralized community. For him, the conundrum was located elsewhere – the counterintuitive *moral* (as opposed to mechanical or technical) reliance on individual self-sufficiency as a source of communitarian and thus collective political authority. As Andrea Brighenti (2014: 58) claims, 'the unity of being is what makes society possible as a form of communication, of community; but such community can be achieved only at the price of violently opening up individual beings'. To work well, together or alone, the community had to reconcile the wholeness of the individual, the *integrity* of which stands as the core of the idea of P2P relationships, with the idea of communitarian consensus that Bitcoiners in Israel otherwise celebrated, and sometimes even fetishized.

It was possible to test these assertions on trust, trustlessness, intimacy and community in the hot autumn of 2017, when the price suddenly jumped from an all-time high (commonly abbreviated ATH) of about US$5,000 per bitcoin earlier in the year to nearly $20,000 in December (before correcting to around US$5,000 by early 2018). Bitcoin was suddenly all over the news due to this spike in value, in Israel and around the world, and new crowds began aggregating at the Embassy at an exponential rate. I documented this dynamic closely, and in the following pages I wish to demonstrate how it sharpens the distinctions Ambassadors themselves made between their ideologically motivated intentional community and the wider masses of potential adopters, who for the most part had not taken on board the values of decentralized sociality that for Shemesh, Bloom, Nissim and others were the central moral axis of the New Economy.

The Goldrush

In October 2017, Israeli media began reporting on Bitcoin almost daily, following its rapid increase in value. The coverage nonetheless provided little explanation of what cryptocurrency was or how the blockchain worked, focusing instead on whether it constituted a financial bubble or not. Until that point, the Embassy was a sleepy fringe community-hub visited mostly by those already 'in the know' and the occasional curious newcomer. By November that year, however, the Embassy would be crammed with hundreds of people daily, who would queue for about three hours on average to purchase bitcoin there. The first to come by were binary options gamblers, whose trading activities had been made illegal in Israel in October 2017.[8] Then came taxi drivers and trend-spotting bohemians. By December 2017, the established bourgeoisie had joined, including confused parents with internet-savvy teenagers and crafty tech entrepreneurs interested in the 'disruptive' potential of blockchain technology. 'We have been waiting for this for years now', Rami told me. 'I can't believe my eyes.'

The throngs of people who packed the entire floor and crowded around the pavement outside were queueing to buy bitcoin from what at the time was the only bitcoin ATM in the country. The machine was such an attraction because the process of identification and approval in the major cryptocurrency exchange platforms online was at the time still complicated, sometimes taking several weeks to complete. In 2017, some Israeli banks also unilaterally blocked transfers to cryptocurrency trading and exchange companies, opting for caution in a regulatory vacuum. Direct payment through the machine was therefore the simplest and most straightforward way to buy bitcoin. An immersive sense of thrill and urgency was heavy in the air, accompanied by an atmosphere of spontaneity, casual nonsense and overall chaos.

The chaos was to be reckoned with. To get a place in the queue, people were initially asked to sign their names on a piece of paper located on a table near the ATM and verify independently between them when it was their turn to approach the machine. While this practice is not unusual in the Israeli private sector – very few commercial spaces run orderly queues or monitor the lines – the sheer number of new arrivals, the constant flux of people and the extended wait times quickly made this whole system useless. Most were patient and friendly, but some did attempt to cut the queue. At least on one occasion arguments between people in the queue escalated to physical altercations, and many of those who used the machine managed to purchase substantial amounts of bitcoin without completing the necessary identification procedure. This could have meant trouble for Bits of Gold, which might have lost its trading licence if representatives from the Israeli tax authority audited the procedures.[9] Ambassadors could no longer take control of the situation, and the influx of people was only increasing as the price of bitcoin continued to soar.

Jeremy, one of Bits of Gold directors, appeared one day at the Embassy looking angry and determined to create order. He introduced several immediate changes. First, he hired paid administrators, whose sole role would be to sit next to the machine, photocopy ID cards and administer the queues. Second, he obliged *everyone* to hand over a copy of their IDs, even those purchasing less than NIS 2,000; which until then could be purchased anonymously. Third, he reduced the purchase limit from NIS 10,000 to NIS 5,000, thus allowing more people to use the machine, and extending the length of time before it had to be emptied. Fourth, he positioned at the entrance a ticket dispenser, obliging each new customer to take a number. And fifth, he hired an armed guard from a security company to monitor the line and the ticket dispenser 'just in case someone tries to catch a ride with us', as he put it.

While these steps stabilized the chaos, they did not reduce the workload for the Ambassadors. Veteran Ambassadors stretched their shifts in the hope of 'evangelizing' to at least some of the newcomers. The Ambassadors with whom I spoke during these intense weeks described it as not only physically but mentally draining. Until that point, they had enjoyed exclusive membership in a small community of aficionados among low human traffic to the Embassy; now they found themselves besieged by people who were not interested in Bitcoin ideology so much as a quick profit. More than once, for example, I saw people entering the Embassy to ask whether anybody 'sells the competing coin', meaning the aforementioned Ethereum. In some cases, newcomers would mispronounce relevant terms – saying 'atrium' instead of Ethereum, for instance – thus exposing superficial knowledge of the scene. Alternatively, some used flashy terms derived from the world of finance, seeking to create the impression that they were well versed in the cultural style of the stock exchange. They would often refer to Bitcoin as 'bit', a term that core ideological Bitcoiners considered derogatory, as I mentioned above. The Ambassadors began referring to all these newcomers mockingly as *nubim*, a term adjusted to the Hebrew plural conjugation from 'newbies' or 'nubes', UK boarding school slang referring to 'New Boys'.

Initially, most Ambassadors kept coming daily, doing their best to accommodate the influx. During the second week of the rush, Rachel took the initiative and printed out three sheets of paper that briefly explained what Bitcoin was all about. The improvised leaflet also included strong advice about how to manage digital accounts, where to save passwords and what *not to do* with Bitcoin (e.g. 'do not take a photo of your secret key', 'do not expect reimbursement in case of a mistaken transaction', etc.). Rachel attached this leaflets to the front window of the Embassy, and later also printed out further information on folded pamphlets to stack on a table at the entrance. This information proved helpful for some *nubim* who did not previously understand the ideological principles behind cryptocurrency decentralization and distribution, nor did they realize the technical challenges that came with the adoption of Bitcoin (see also Faria 2021; Schneider 2019). As useful as the newly available information had been, however, most of those waiting to their turn at the machine were not particularly intrigued. It soon became clear to Ambassadors that most of these newcomers were simply interested in quick profiteering. Disappointed by the general lack of interest in Bitcoin's good tidings at the level of societal reorganization most Ambassadors thereby stopped showing up.

Profiteering

As Embassy associates gradually disappeared into self-imposed exile, their place was filled with traders, speculators and profiteers. For example, a guy in his thirties called Yossi told me he had recently stopped working so he could concentrate on dealing bitcoin. Jointly with a partner he was touting bitcoin to and buying it from private people, as well as investing in other digital coins through specialized online cryptocurrency stock exchanges. Yossi could have been one of many professional investors who started speculating in bitcoin immediately after the Israeli regulator crashed the flourishing trade in binary options in October 2017. For such traders, Bitcoin was a pure financial opportunity, a way to achieve rapid wealth. I joined several WhatsApp and Telegram groups for trade and was amazed to see how traffic on these apps differed from the kinds of casual language regularly used by Embassy members with regard to Bitcoin. A common post, for example, would look something like: 'Selling Bit for 50k in Tel Aviv today, driving down from Jerusalem now.' Like Yossi, speculators would often buy and sell bitcoin quickly, while also investing in other currencies popular at the time, such as Ethereum, Bitcoin Cash, IOTA, Ripple, Cardano, Litecoin, Dash, Zcash, Monero and Verge.

Some profiteering was inevitably related to forms of money laundering. For example, for about ten consecutive days two people used to arrive in the vicinity of the Embassy and remain on the premises until it closed. The younger one, who was probably about thirty years old, had a buttoned shirt carefully tucked into his ironed trousers, and wore expensive Italian-leather shoes. His companion was probably about fifteen or twenty years older, a chubby guy likewise dressed elegantly and wearing expensive perfume. His knuckles were tattooed with letters. They drove a 2017 white crossover, which they sometimes double-parked right in front of the Embassy entrance, blocking the narrow street. In one of our conversations, the younger guy said he worked for 'an American firm based in New York'. He said that every month he had to provide fifty bitcoins to the firm, which then traded them online. The profit he and his partner made, he revealed, came through commissions for every bitcoin they transferred, as well as related transaction fees.[10] He said they buy exclusively from private individuals to avoid the 5 per cent commission to Bits of Gold. Indeed, I once was astonished to observe the younger man presenting a very thick pile of cash from an internal pocket of his jacket, counting NIS 25,000 in 100 and 200 notes, and handing them over to a seller. It is of course entirely possible that the pair avoided buying from the ATM not only due to the commission but also because they preferred to avoid identifying themselves via the KYC procedure.[11]

Such barter relations usually followed similar patterns. Take, for example, the following case: a man in his early twenties stopped his car outside the Embassy, walked hastily among the people crowding the pavement in front and declared, 'I am looking for buyers, I need the money now. I can sell you as much as you want. Who is in?' As if a scene from a Scorsese film, two young men who were still waiting for their turn to use the ATM quickly snaked towards him and asked what his 'rate' was (i.e. how much commission he takes for himself on top of the tradable bitcoin value). This sparked a process of negotiation also on the sum of money in NIS that the prospective buyers would be interested to invest in the first place. The seller refused the offer of one of these potential buyers, who wanted to invest NIS 7,000, insisting instead to sell a minimum of NIS 10,000. After a short haggle, he nonetheless agreed to sell bitcoin equivalent of NIS 15,000, divided between the two. He then asked them to join him in his car, which they did, and they drove off to conduct the actual exchange elsewhere.

Most such exchanges were subtler, however, taking place either on the pavement some metres away from the Embassy, or in nearby coffee shops. People negotiated transaction commissions, conducted the transfer and waited for about thirty minutes to receive at least two verifications in their digital wallets – as was the custom at the time – thereby making sure that the transaction on the blockchain has been completed and therefore was valid.

Purchasing bitcoin from the ATM felt less venal, probably because it was a transparent procedure, as people were required to provide their ID card and let Bits of Gold keep a photocopy on file. Those who did so – the overwhelming majority – could be sure they were acting in accordance with Israeli financial regulations while still satisfying their FOMO (i.e., 'fear of missing out' [see Vennonen 2024]). Noam, for instance, arrived in Tel Aviv by train from a Kibbutz in the north, where he worked as a bartender. He had to wait for hours before it was his turn to purchase bitcoin from the ATM, and at some stage we started talking. 'I am not an investor', he said. 'I just want to deposit 5,000 shekels to see what comes of it [over time]. I don't want to miss out in case this is really the next big thing.' Although calculated, this was still a measured appropriation of FOMO, which was not uncommon – I have in fact met people who saw Bitcoin as a bubble or even as a 'lie', as someone called it, but still purchased thousands of NIS-worth 'just in case'.

And there were also gold bugs with sparkles in their eyes. These were not money launderers, but normative people from all walks of life caught up in the FOMO. A fear of missing out, to be sure, or a feeling of distrust in the market due to successful FUDing campaigns – FUD being the acronym for 'fear, uncertainty and doubt' (cf. Vennonen 2024) – are both *genuine* affective states, rather than a mere abstract description of market dynamics or a semi-rational response to the imperative to make a profit. Even before they become rhetorical acts, such idioms are felt as authentic experiences of value fluctuation, which are embodied, and therefore turn the sociality around them into an emotive high-stakes game. I will further elaborate on this notion in Chapter 6. For now, I will provide two ethnographic examples that demonstrate how FOMO can lead to goldbugging.

First, Yotam, a forty-something, who one day came in with his fifteen-year-old son. Yotam told me he understood almost nothing about Bitcoin, but now with the recent media coverage had decided to finally take the advice of his son, who since 2014 had been trying to convince his parents to purchase bitcoin. 'In our house we never say no to the kids' whims', Yotam said. 'We thought of this initially just as a game, but when we understood how big the phenomenon is, we decided to listen to him and take him more seriously.' Not only did Yotam and his son purchase bitcoin, they had in mind a more ambitious plan. According to Yotam's son's calculations, they would be able to make a steady monthly income using a specialized mining rig that had recently been launched by an Israeli company. The problem was that the machine could only be paid for in bitcoin. They had joined the queue to buy NIS 10,000-worth of bitcoin, which they then intended to send to the company that produced the rig. I said that to the best of my knowledge making money from mining on individual machines would be exceedingly difficult, as this entire industry was controlled by mining farms that consumed monstrous quantities of electricity. Yotam shrugged. He said he simply believed his son's calculations were true.

In a second case, there was Oded, a marketing freelancer in his mid-thirties with a Trotsky-style beard and round glasses. I had met him at the Embassy before but that day he seemed changed. 'I have seen the light', he told me. Oded initially arrived at the Embassy to 'draw information from people' so he could establish a marketing strategy for a friend who was about to open a bitcoin exchange firm. That visit, however, convinced Oded that the Bitcoin craze was not merely a passing trend, an economic bubble or a risky investment. Rather, Oded said he had become convinced that its value would continue to rise. He began visiting the Embassy daily, buying about US$1,000-worth of bitcoin each time, either from private traders who hovered around or from the ATM, if he managed to get a ticket number. 'At the beginning my wife criticized me for wasting our money', he said, smiling.

'But then, when she heard someone at her workplace reproaching himself for not having bought bitcoin when it was valued at US$9,000, she realized I was right. So, she told me, "*Buy more!*" and that's what I'm doing.'

Oded was then drawn even deeper into the cryptocurrency trading buzz, selling some of his holding to people he happened to meet at the Embassy and using that money to buy more bitcoin. 'I covered my overdraft in the bank and then stopped using my credit card altogether', he affirmed. 'My handbag is full of cash now, tens of thousands of shekels in cash. Friends said I need to go to rehab because I have become a gambler. I just told them that we shall see in the future who was right.' We were sitting outside the Embassy on a bench next to Nissim when a middle-aged woman with elegant clothes and well-groomed hair arrived at the Embassy. She asked Nissim if bitcoin value fluctuation was not dangerous and Nissim began to answer, as always advising caution. But Oded interrupted him: 'Yes, of course, caution is important. And it may plunge tomorrow, but who cares? It is the best security you can buy these days! There is no reason to fear.' His eyes glowed.

Several days later I met Oded again. He said he had just bought some agricultural land near Hadera, a small town located about 60 km north of Tel Aviv. He presented this to me as a wise investment made possible by his newly acquired trading skills. As the story goes, Oded was explaining to a taxi driver on bitcoin when the driver's phone rang. It was a real estate agent trying to convince the driver to purchase a small plot of agricultural land, arguing it would soon be redrafted as an approved land for building development; so its market value was expected to rise exponentially. Oded joined the conversation over the speaker, asked to meet the agent and ended up buying that same plot the day after, using some of the money he had earned from his bitcoin trading. Later that week Oded was on television. He was being interviewed by one of the three national television networks that had arrived to shoot magazine items for their Friday-night news programmes, the peak of Israeli primetime TV consumption charts. 'Yes', he told the reporter decisively, 'I joined the Bitcoin cult!' Oded, however, disappeared soon thereafter, and I never saw him again.

For Rami, Nissim and other highly motivated Ambassadors, people like Oded represented everything that was wrong with the new adopters, who mostly seemed to have dollar signs reflected in their eyes. Ambassadors thus suddenly found themselves having to deal with people who were not the least bit interested in the ideology that was the declarative glue of their community. Instead, most of these newcomers, from professional money launderers to middle-class parents to gold bugs, wanted to make money, which Embassy associates saw as a 'centralized' habit that 'would not advance solutions' – as the local idiom went – to the many problems of the fractional-reserve banking industry. Rami explained this view in a conversation outside the Embassy during the hype:

> People who come here for quick profits get caught up in the illusion of becoming rich, but they don't last long. They get panicked when bitcoin begins to plunge – and it will plunge, because that's what bitcoin does – and then sell all their holdings at once. Then, usually they disappear. I am not sure why; they could be ashamed? They had no idea what they were getting themselves into and didn't understand they had to be resilient, not to mention convinced, because if you are not convinced that Bitcoin will be successful you really have nothing to look for here.

The goldrush has thus sharpened distinctions between the values that different adopters assigned to Bitcoin itself, as a mere financial asset on the one hand, and a tool of social reform on the other. Convinced ideologues were consequently disappointed with the general disregard towards the Bitcoin socio-philosophical-spiritual messages (see Land 2018) and physically exhausted from the daily jams at the entrance to the Embassy. Danni Bloom, however, saw things somewhat differently. In an interview with him about a year after the goldrush he said:

> It was impossible to explain about Bitcoin in the Embassy at the time because it was full of people who only wanted to buy bitcoin from the machine. Because it was so crowded and noisy, Ambassadors could not sit and explain about Bitcoin to people who were interested in knowing more, so those who were a part of the community, who felt that the Embassy was their home, who loved being there, no longer enjoyed coming in. That was a tough time, but it passed after a while for two reasons. First, [following the consequent fall in the Bitcoin value in 2018] there were less people who wanted to buy bitcoin, and second, more places were opened where people could purchase bitcoin. So, when things calmed down at the beginning of 2018, the Embassy could return to being what it was before – a community centre!

Bloom did not speak of ideological commitment or even 'conviction' as Rami did. He simply referred to the chaos at the Embassy as a decisive factor that made it impossible to explain the ins and outs of Bitcoin, as they were used to doing. He in fact spoke positively about the expansion of the market in 2018, which included several new venues in Tel Aviv established specifically to function as trade centres or shops for selling bitcoin. I visited several of these places. While some organized lectures in the same format established earlier by the Embassy, they did not pronounce commitment to 'community' at all; the three lectures I attended at these centres were either technical or economic in nature, and the people who attended them seemed more interested in cryptocurrencies at large as an emergent industry than as a potential tool of societal change. Bloom's pragmatism thereby recognized the *necessity* of such expansion, tacitly rejecting the puritanical attitudes of some of his colleagues.

Differing grassroots opinions concerning the goldrush reflected the ideological pluralism among Ambassadors. Yet they also suggested analytically that the boundary between the New and the Old Economies was not as sharply drawn as some ideologues preferred to present it. The masses that encroached on the Embassy violated in that sense its vulnerable, *ambiguous status*, as a space that I have begun to realize was located in between these ideal-type models of social organization. Rather than pulling the Embassy away from utopian decentralization, on the one hand, or accentuating these tendencies, on the other, it seems to me that the presence of 'centralized' capitalists at the Embassy during the goldrush effectively served to integrate both of these techno-social imaginaries (Swartz 2017, 2018) into a single frame of reference. I will further elaborate on the implications of this integration in Chapter 4. Remaining for now with the analysis of Embassy communitarian boundaries, I turn to demonstrate how different approaches to communitarian growth among Embassy associates might ameliorate some of the critiques directed towards the Bitcoin social movement with regards to the paradox of expansionism.

The Paradox of Mass Adoption

Critics with different agendas have in the past ten years identified different paradoxes, inconsistencies, biases and misrecognitions in the global scene of bitcoin trade (Dodd 2018; Faria 2019; Golumbia 2016; Nelms et al. 2018; Schneider 2019). Among them, Nigel Dodd (2018) has famously argued that Bitcoin communard ideology was paradoxical and unrealistic because it was based on the total disconnectedness of nodes (i.e. peers) from collective social processes. When Bitcoiners portrayed the blockchain merely as a neutral technical apparatus, Dodd claimed, they ignored the centralized forces and wealth hierarchies that sustained it, such as the dominance of mining corporations, the accumulation advantage that veteran participants gain over time, the leadership roles of a small group of experts and influencers, and the structured advantage heavy investors gain as they reproduce and expand their holding. Thinking of blockchain codes as value-free and neutral, Dodd argued, Bitcoiners ignore the fact that even mathematical consensus should be recognized as a social relationship. Individual freedoms that come with universal money systems make part of a *social process* (Simmel 2004), thereby contradicting the illusion that wealth objects in Bitcoin and cryptocurrency at large only serve individuated singularities. Dodd argues (2018: 37):

> My core thesis is that there is a paradox at the heart of the Bitcoin phenomenon. Bitcoin will succeed as money to the extent that it fails as an ideology. The currency relies on that which the ideology underpinning it seeks to deny, namely, the dependence of money upon social relations, and upon trust. Insofar as Bitcoin has been successful qua money, it is because of the community that has grown up around it. Ironically, however, this community is sustained by the commonly held belief that Bitcoin has replaced social relations – the trust on which all forms of money depend – with machine code. This belief is a fiction. Bitcoin has thrived despite, not because of, its reliance upon machines.

Dodd (2018: 51) identifies a paradox in the very definition of Bitcoin as money that relies on trustless technology – the blockchain. 'Bitcoin is currently being sustained by sociological features that are directly at odds with the political ideology of the theory of money that underpins it', Dodd explains. 'These include leadership, social organization, social structure, sociality, utopianism and trust.' Dodd understands the boundaries that define a 'community' of users as necessarily exclusive and limiting, while the idea of the blockchain's total openness, together with the notion of free-acting individuals, is inclusive. He stipulates that this contradiction cannot be mitigated – Bitcoiners must turn a blind eye when they express faith in trustlessness by way of ignoring the trust necessary to create a community (see Ingham 2020). This in turn institutes a collective misrecognition of the fact that the presence of money on the blockchain creates a strong tendency towards centralization, thereby re-creating an unequal monetary system like the one used globally until the US government decoupled the value of the dollar from the value of gold, known as the gold standard, in 1971.[12] For Dodd, this misrecognition whitewashed and thus strengthened centralized hierarchies both on and off the blockchain. As I began to demonstrate, however, Embassy associates actively dealt with these binaries in diverse ways, including the recognition that a designated 'community' of Bitcoin enthusiasts could one day become obsolete. The following excerpt from a conversation with Bloom explicates this:

> MATAN:
> What will happen to the community when all financial institutions are decentralized?
>
> BLOOM:
> First of all, in such a world we won't need a community, it will have achieved its targets . . . so people will find different communities. The vision is that in forty years there will be no Bitcoin community or Bitcoin association; it will be the only coin people use and that's it.

MATAN:
Can you really reduce Bitcoin to a form of payment alone?

BLOOM:
Yes, that's the main thing, but I think that strategically Bitcoin should be presented especially as money, because once people adopt it all the other things will come by default.[13]

MATAN:
This means that the play sessions, the hanging out, the parties, this will all be gone?

BLOOM:
We will still have programmers working on Bitcoin, there will be things, but it will have a different name. But at the level of a social movement, it is not going to exist, with a bit of help from God, in forty years. So, we can interpret this in this way – at some stage there will be people who would be using bitcoin but would not be defined as members of the 'Bitcoin community'. Today, because bitcoin is [still] quite niche, if you invest in bitcoin, you are already seen to be a part of a community. But in the future, this will be less and less; Bitcoin will be more pragmatic, much like the use of cars. If you drive a car, you are not a member of the car-loving community. There might be smaller communities of car lovers dedicated to specific things but using the car is just mundane.

Bloom then stopped, scratched his chin for a few seconds, and said:

> Well, maybe this contradicts what I just said. Maybe, there will be a community of Bitcoin supporters in the future, but this will no longer be a community *with a mission*. It will take a different turn, maybe [focusing] more on the ceremonies and the togetherness, less on the [goal of] adoption. So today the community is still dedicated to advancing [mass adoption]. The hardcore people are the fire or catalyst or engine that pushes the movement.

Since mass adoption would mean the destruction of collective intimacies, 'hardcore people' (i.e. true believers) were themselves entangled in what Bloom admitted was an internal contradiction. On one hand, as the community expands, they could lead it towards dissolution. On the other hand, as they reinforce the underlying ideas that sum up to a Bitcoin communard ideology, they would preserve their niche positionality vis-à-vis mainstream banking solutions. The intimate community of peers, whose members in Tel Aviv sought to demonstrate the generative power of collaborative P2P relationships, could no longer function as the beating heart of the project, and its survival amidst mass adoption would be a problem to reckon with (see Anderson 2016[1983]). Contemplating this same problem of scale, Roy took a step further to argue that the community of die-hard supporters will one day be sidelined by big corporations. In an interview he told me: 'The idea of community as a factor in the rising value of the coin is relevant up to about a US$5,000.' I asked why that was so, and he replied:

> Because from the moment that banks and VC funds dive in, they can invest huge amounts of money, more than the entire market cap [market capitalization volume] value that the community is [concurrently, in 2019] worth. It's like Williamsburg in New York or Florentine [neighbourhood] in Tel Aviv; at the beginning only bohemians and hippies went in, when the values were really low, but today properties in these neighbourhoods can get to $50k per square metre. The result is that the community, those people who actually live there, is squeezed out to look for more affordable neighbourhoods. Once the financial world begins to invest in bitcoin, the community loses its control, and so the power moves from the community to the corporation.

As opposed to Bloom, who saw mass adoption as outcome of collaboration – and unlike such ideologues as Rami or Nissim, whose near-mystical view of Bitcoin will feature in the following chapters – Roy simply assumed that the community would disappear altogether. For him, the moneyness of Bitcoin would eventually override its societal good tidings. In retrospect, however, the community survived. The entry of big money and centralized capital into the cryptocurrency market in recent years has been a major factor in the increase of trade volumes in Bitcoin, despite it fluctuating wildly, at times reaching such heights as US$70,000 and even US$100,000, or sinking to such lows as US$5,000. By the mid-2020s Bitcoin has become an almost mainstream investment channel – reaffirming one important aspect of Roy's predictions – but the 'community' remained a common idiom used by supporters in Tel Aviv and beyond, thereby providing a material foundation for collaborative networkers to experiment with decentralized solutions even in an era of corporate investments in DeFi.

Back in 2018, to be sure, most interlocutors did not conceive of their membership in the community in purely economic terms, and its boundaries were always considered at least partially porous precisely because there were so many distinct levels of association one could cultivate to belong to the New Economy. In fact, it was this flexibility with regard to alterity that attracted most of my interlocutors into the Bitcoin social space in the first place. Perceiving digital money primarily as a vehicle for social change, they created a community wherein economic trustlessness *enabled an ongoing ethical debate*, which, as I will explicate in the next chapter, inspired the cultivation of new individual skills and personal virtues fit for an emergent decentralized sociality at a large scale.

The question, then, is not whether Bitcoin could become an accepted money technology, or if as such it will destroy the intimacies that its supporters claim to cultivate and inhabit. Rather, the question is whether 'open source' values would influence society after the 'moneyness' of Bitcoin has already been established and its politics broadly accepted. From this perspective, there is no longer a paradox of scale in Bitcoin ownership, nor is there a clash between individualism and communitarianism, which many of the Ambassadors in fact saw as complementary. For most of them, to rephrase Bloom, the community ultimately demonstrated to outsiders that the vision was indeed realistic as long as people could coordinate real-world activities between them outside the intervention and supervision of formal hierarchic structures.

Conclusion

The goldrush was a major milestone in the popularization of Bitcoin in Israel. When its value began rising, and when a media hype was created around it, people who had never heard of Bitcoin were suddenly exposed to the scene. The profiteering bubble had nonetheless burst by January 2018, as Rami had predicted. Oblivious to the power of community collaboration that Bloom saw as a strategy to accommodate FOMO, many new adopters indeed sold out. For some people at the Embassy that was a moment of sobering up, which proved that a wide experiential gap existed between the change-oriented idealism of the small-scale community and the wider crowds towards which Embassy members' activism was initially directed. Yet, Ambassadors returned to their shifts and continued to work together towards mass adoption. When I asked Bloom about this in an interview, he smiled and said:

> In the end we want to do a revolution here, and for that you need a lot of work, and you need the fire that will push it through time. For someone outside of this world who would like to understand something about it, it certainly looks different if someone comes to speak with him about a commercial initiative or someone who comes with an ideology and [as a representative of] a community. This is akin to being 'a light for the nations' (*Ōr laGōyyīm*), although the gentiles can also be Jews in this case [grins] . . . we will do the best we can, so that people from the outside can see that we are a community that has values, and a technology that is something that people would not be able to see if there was no community.[14]

In Tel Aviv, references to the 'community' eventually encompassed four scales of reference. At the core, it included several dozens of committed Ambassadors who organized activities at the Embassy on a regular basis and took part in most of the events. In the second tier the community included a few hundred sympathizers working in the Israeli blockchain industry, related tech ventures and relevant research centres at academic institutions, who would occasionally come around but mostly participated in community affairs online. Broadening further, the community also included those who supported even remotely the dispersal of bitcoin as money form in society, such as the tens of thousands of followers on the Embassy Facebook and Twitter (now called X) accounts. Finally, the term 'community' was often used to encompass all other Bitcoiners around the world, effectively attaching the size of the community to the ever-expanding number of transactions on the blockchain. At this global register, activities were done via chats in designated forums or through social media outlets, while the notion of 'community' still strongly relied on the pragmatic exchange and accumulation of bitcoin; thus linking the existence of a collective identity with the material, rather than ideological or abstract aspects of Bitcoin sociality (see also Tsavelis. 2024).

For the most part, interlocutors did not rank these diverse levels of participation as I have done here; for them, the term 'community' simply signified their collective passion for Bitcoin, which inspired the establishment of shared avant-garde subcultural circles at both the local *and* the global registers. They spoke of direct interaction (i.e. P2P) at any scale as 'frictionless', thus resisting imaginaries of encompassing hierarchies by relocating the weight of mediation on the individual digital entities that take part in it. It was a resistance not only directed towards hierarchy and vertical linearity, but also an attempt to do away with the boundaries separating classes of people, groups and entities, locally and globally. A multiplicity of possible cross-scalar relationships were thus mediated by Bitcoin sociality. They came alive at the Embassy due to the belief that there, no dividing lines could subjugate any Bitcoiner to any articulation of higher-level authoritative will.[15] The term 'community' *included* all these multiple frictionless modes of relationships between individuals and groups.

The existence of a Bitcoin community at any scale, however, should not be taken for granted. First, from a technical perspective, the functioning of the blockchain depends on *distributed action en masse* to produce trustless consensus. This perspective designates the very idea of a communitarian, unified or coordinated operation of cohesive socioeconomic entities on and off the blockchain as an *attack* on the distributed network that algorithms must respectively block.[16] And second, ideological supporters emphasize their commitment to rational individualism in ways that at times contradict their own credence in the immersive power of the community. At stake here is the conviction that protection of individual interests can sustain whatever community structure people imagine might be relevant to their lives. But at least nominally, the idea that every Bitcoiner is exclusively responsible for his or her financial security goes against the structural encompassment that could be offered by groups; whether hierarchical or egalitarian. In the next chapter I will explore this apparent contradiction, wherein the holistic, collaborative community must rely on the atomic singularity of its distinct parts if it is to reliably produce value at both the moral and material registers.

NOTES

1. The organization still exists (see https://intelligence.org/). Accessed 31/12/2023.
2. Bloom was a regular contributor to Less Wrong forums, which are frequented mostly by technologists, mathematicians and philosophers interested in 'rationality' (see https://www.lesswrong.com/). Accessed 31/12/2023.
3. On Bitcoin mining see Chapter 1 or consult Antonopoulos and Harding (2024). In 2011, it was still possible to generate profit using homemade mining machines.
4. Initially using the second floor free of charge, in 2016 Bits of Gold took over rent responsibilities following Shemesh's decision to open an unrelated business in a nearby venue. They did so until the end of 2017, when the company suddenly made substantial profits due to the Bitcoin boom of that year. Forced to expand, the company consequently moved to a bigger space nearby. The mezzanine then became the office space for Inbar, the CEO of the IBA.
5. Bloom half-jokingly claimed in a public lecture that 'iron' was not a mere metaphor. Rather, during fusion at the atomic level, he said, 'everything converges to iron', concluding that precisely in the same way 'everything will converge to Bitcoin' when the New Economy becomes dominant.
6. A form of rapid chess for advanced players, which is played in pairs.
7. My colleague Dr. Janine Su had provided the following comment in a personal correspondence: 'This attitude appears to reflect a modernistic desire to distil interpersonal relationships to a "pure" form on the basis of affinity alone – the recognition and appreciation of the spark of humanity within one individual by another, in the sense classically unpacked by Weber (2002[1930]) with explicit reference to capitalism – and without the polluting emotional or social baggage of obligation, of which money is the emblematic complication.' This excellent interpretation merits its own empirical research.
8. Binary option trade is located somewhere between sheer gambling and legitimate bidding on future values of stocks. Since 2017, Israeli authorities consider the selling of binary options a financial fraud punishable by law.
9. Israeli money-laundering regulations on cryptographic assets were at the time lax, yet clear. Purchases lower than NIS 2,000 did not require identification at all, while purchases of up to NIS 50,000 by bank transfer only required one to provide a photocopy of an ID card. Only purchases of larger amounts required in-person identity verification and the signing of appropriate paperwork, which was then sent to the Israeli Money Laundering Prohibition Authority. Following the 2017 Bitcoin surge, the rules were changed, and now Israeli authorities oblige KYC (Know Your Client) procedures for every transaction, including taking onsite photocopies of ID cards to be filed and collecting bank account details.

10. This was likely false because bitcoin transaction fees are extracted directly to miners, not to traders.
11. Reasons to purchase bitcoin anonymously vary, however. These include fear of future regulatory crackdown and the collection of government tax on cryptocurrency profits. Consequently, not all face-to-face cash transactions necessarily involved straightforwardly illegal activities.
12. Called The Nixon Shock (Butler 2022: 84), relinquishing of the gold standard enabled the development of fractional-reserve banking, a system that requires commercial banks to hold in cash only about 10 per cent of the overall value that they circulate in the market. Consequently, economic growth became based on debt and deficit (Butler 2022; Graeber 2011).
13. Meaning new types of collaboration, decentralized organizational structures, etc.
14. *Ōr laGōyyīm* is a biblical term derived from the Book of Isiah (42:6). It is popularly understood among Israeli Jews as a reference to their alleged responsibility to shine a spiritual 'light' onto the world.
15. This same idea has in fact already appeared explicitly on the Ethereum project main webpage, which explains the advantages of programming a DAO for business purposes or otherwise (see Schneider 2019: 278–79).
16. I here allude to the so-called '51 per cent attack', wherein powerful stakeholders manage to own 51 per cent of the verifying nodes on the network. This allows them to divert transactions and syphon funds from honest users.

CHAPTER 3

INDIVIDUAL BANKS

Unborg Yourself

Among the many graffiti artworks and slogans covering the toilet walls at the Embassy, an inscription in bold black English capital letters stood out: UNBORG YOURSELF (see Figure 3.1). I never discovered who wrote it nor what exactly they intended to convey, but I believe the inscription referred to the Borg, an alien species from the sci-fi universe of *Star Trek*. In the series, the Borg are cybernetic 'drones' synchronized by a superconsciousness called 'the Collective'. Famously warning those they encountered that 'resistance is futile', the Borg inject 'nanoprobes' into other species' bodies as a means of assimilating their technological and biological characteristics into the hive mind.

The imperative to 'unborg' denotes a process of individual detachment from the collective, which is defined through the rejection of the hive mind. In the context of the Embassy, it implied purchasing and using Bitcoin as a self-liberatory practice. Other inscriptions on the toilet walls at the Embassy transmitted similar ideas, including 'Bitcoin is an international language of freedom that breaks down barriers and oppression'; and 'Bitcoin will destroy the Matrix'. These messages nonetheless also suggest that individual financial autonomy is at the root of a new kind of *collective* freedom. Yoav once explained this notion in an interview, arguing that the expected iconoclastic impact of Bitcoin has the effect of brining all those individuals who 'unborged' themselves into a mutualist relationship (Swartz 2018) in a community of equals. Rejecting the idea of violent revolution, he said:

> We don't want to overthrow anybody. We just [want to] create a world for ourselves, [in which] *we cooperate between us as a network of people who believe in a particular idea*. And those who wish to join us can do that. Those who don't want

to join can stay with [Israeli far-right populist politician] Miri Regev and the rest of the clowns.

Yoav tacitly outlined here 'a difference which makes a difference', as anthropologist Gregory Bateson (1958) might have said. The difference that is made here concerns two similar viewpoints, which are often mistaken to overlap: one that sanctifies radical individualism in and of itself, the other highlighting a *network* of individuals. Whereas both these views are focused on self-interest (or at the very least self-sufficiency and personal autonomy), the first emphasizes egoism while the second emphasizes cooperativism. The first view designates Bitcoin as a tool to achieving relative independence from 'centralized' social arrangements, and the second view holds Bitcoin as a tool to constructing a parallel utopian world (cf. Swartz 2018). The difference generated by this difference – to remain with Bateson's rhetoric device – manifests in a permanent tension that is attached to the status of individuals in Bitcoin sociality. On the one hand, since the blockchain makes trust obsolete, it encourages radical individual economic and political independence at a granular density. On the other hand, since individuals also sustain consensus on the blockchain through their roles as nodes, traders and miners, that same granular autonomy is always contingent on mass action. This tension suggests that a collective of fully autonomous yet interconnected individuals might never fully detach themselves from the reality of the Borg, leaving Bitcoiners with a need to constantly calibrate the level of their interconnectedness with other members of the network.

Figure 3.1. Graffiti on the Embassy toilet walls. Credit: Matan Shapiro.

This chapter focuses on how Embassy members collectively denied the hive-mind without completely sacrificing the synchronic interdependency on which their sense of individualism relied. I will begin this discussion with an analysis of the often-explicit imperative to 'HODL', an investment strategy that emerged in the Bitcoin subcultural genre when more and more adopters discovered they could support Bitcoin without necessarily engaging in trade or using Bitcoin as a profit-making device.

HODL

On 18 December 2013, amid a nerve-wracking drop in the bitcoin value against the US dollar, a pseudonymous Bitcoiner called GameKyuubi published a post on the 'Bitcoin Talk' forum, which he titled 'I AM HODLING' (errors and all-caps in original):

> I typed that tyitle twice because I knew it was wrong the first time. Still wring. w/e. GF's out at a lesbian bar, BTC [Bitcoin] crashing WHY AM I HOLDING? I'LL TELL YOU WHY. It's because I'm a bad trader and I KNOW I'M A BAD TRADER. Yeah you good traders can spot the highs and the lows pit pat piffy wing wong wang just like that and make a millino buvks sure no problem bro. Likewise the weak hands are like OH NO IT'S GOING D OWN I'M GONNA SELL he he he and then they're like OH GOD MY ASSHOLE when the SMART traders who KNOW WHAT THE FUCK THEY'RE DOING buy back in but you know what? I'm not part of that group.
>
> When the traders buy back in I'm already part of the market capital so GUESS WHO YOU'RE CHEATING day traders NOT ME~! Those taunt threads saying "OHH YOU SHOULD HAVE SOLD" YEAH NO SHIT. NO SHIT I SHOULD HAVE SOLD. I SHOULD HAVE SOLD MOMENTS BEFORE EVERY SELL AND BOUGHT MOMENTS BEFORE EVERY BUY BUT YOU KNOW WHAT NOT EVERYBODY IS AS COOL AS YOU.
>
> You only sell in a bear market [a market characterized by dropping values and a selling spree] if you are a good day trader or an illusioned noob [a newcomer, a novice in the crypto scene]. The people inbetween hold. In a zero-sum game such as this, traders can only take your money if you sell.
>
> So I've had some whiskey. Actually on the bottle its spelled whisky. w/e sue me (but only if it's payable in BTC).[1]

GameKyuubi was admittedly drunk, but those who replied immediately praised his title typo. One, for example, posted a meme adapting the movie poster for the 2006 historical-fantasy epic *300*. It depicted star Gerard Butler's character Leonidas holding his sword firmly as he let out a roar, his face scarred and bloody. Behind him were scenes of battling armies; in front was the caption 'HODLING!!!'. The meme has since achieved cult status among Bitcoiners, sending the message that any contemporary suffering due to HODLING will be worth the final victory. Jimmy Song, a Bitcoin evangelist from the United States who gave a lecture in Tel Aviv in 2018, projected this meme on the wall behind him (see Figure 3.2) as he delineated the difference he identified between short-term and long-term investment strategies; which he associated respectively with a view of Bitcoin as a 'medium of exchange' and as a 'store of value':

> Bitcoin is not that great as a medium of exchange because as a store of value it is just amazing . . . A lot of people don't want to spend their bitcoins because it's going up in value, so why would you want to spend that? Instead, you wanna spend money that is *less* valuable. The bad money is utilized, and the good money is kept back . . . this is my message to you – keep holding – because this is the killer use-case for bitcoin.[2]

Speaking just months after bitcoin had achieved its highest value to that point, Song did not have to work hard to convince his audience. When GameKyuubi wrote that post at the end of 2013, the fiat-equivalent value was around US$900 per unit, after having already risen exponentially that year from around US$30 per unit. This was a promising sign, but at that time even true believers could not imagine the price heights that Bitcoin would reach only four years later. At the beginning of 2017, the value stood at around

Figure 3.2. Jimmy Song on the stage during his lecture in Tel Aviv. Behind him is screened the famous meme promoting the imperative to 'HODL'. Credit: Matan Shapiro.

US$1,000 per unit but by the end of that year it surged exponentially to hit an incredible all-time high of US$19,000 per unit. Early adopters who had 'HODLED' thus became what the global media soon tagged as 'crypto millionaires' (Nelms et al. 2018: 24–26). The proof was in the pudding: the longer you HODLED – withstanding financial difficulties, bear markets, value crashes or whatever panic-inducing event – your assets would increase in value. Writing on Brazilian bitcoin investors, Bruno Cardoso (2024: 31) describes this in terms of 'stacking'. He argues that:

> Since all *fiat currencies* are often understood to be 'doomed' by default, with the BRL [Brazilian Real] being no exception; and since all other cryptocurrencies are about to sink to zero as well (because they are seen as nothing more than fancy and elaborated Ponzi schemes), there is a sense of rush and hurry, which is encapsulated in the somewhat famous slogan of 'stack *sats* and stay humble' (*sats* being Satoshis, the smallest tradable unit of Bitcoin, a 1/100000000 of a [b]itcoin), describing an ongoing process of gradual and disciplined *stacking* of bitcoins (emphasis and brackets in original).

An ideological principle as much as an investment strategy, HODLING in this context heuristically reflects the desire that Bitcoin will one day become an alternative to state-sponsored monetary system and fractional reserve banking. This serves two possible future conditions: (1) that Bitcoin will be regulated and thus become a widely accepted financial technology for payment, so those who 'stacked' will become a new financial elite by default; or (2) that its value will increase exponentially side by side with the centralized banking system – 'going to the moon', as a common Bitcoin adage goes – consequently providing an advantage for investors amid future financial uncertainty followed by the next 2008-style economic crash. Capitalizing on investments in the far future is thus seen as wiser than trading for short-term profit. Nathan, a gifted programmer actively contributing to the maintenance and development of the Bitcoin network, as well as a leading and much-appreciated figure at the Embassy, saw HODLING as a form of self-discipline:

> HODL is a *restriction you put on yourself*, it's not an external force that stands in your way to spending . . . but the meaning behind it is that you avoid commerce, you are not going to compete against sharks with lots of money that shake the market, you believe in the long-term value and just "hold", you don't get into this game.

Restriction as a form of self-control mirrors some of the practices used by financial 'edgeworkers' (Lyng 2005) such as stockbrokers, early-stage investors, speculators and other financial risk takers. As Charles Smith (2005: 192) demonstrated, successful entrepreneurs reduce risks by monitoring the market closely and acquiring knowledge about it. Aware of highly turbulent market forces, they engage with the market in a sensory fashion so that they can operate 'on the edge' with relative calm. To do that, they build a repertoire of skills, both in the sense of instinctive response and technical ability, which they use to identify what types of swings in the effervescent markets might benefit them. These skills, Smith (2005: 197) argues, 'are more than a means to an end'. He continues:

> Obviously, market traders . . . want to make money in whatever markets they participate in. For traders, however, making money only counts in the long run. This means making money by following trader rules. Put slightly differently, only profits made by the rules count. Money made in any other way is dangerous because it serves to undermine the trader's reliance and commitment to the rules, and it is only by relying on these rules that the trader can hope to survive in the boundary area – on the edge – in the long term.

When examined through the lens of edgework, then, HODL summarizes a bundle of skills that is activated to both enhance thrill and control risks. For example, when in February 2018 bitcoin plummeted from an all-time high of nearly US$20,000 to less than US$6,000, some analysts were speculating the inevitable crash of the entire project. Ariel, an interlocutor from Tel Aviv, called me at the height of this slump, saying he was going through 'a serious FUD' (fear, uncertainty and doubt; see Vennonen 2024 and Cardoso 2024), and was thinking of selling everything he owned. 'If bitcoin crashes it means losing a lot of money', he gasped. Contemplating this, however, and based on many years of HODLING, Ariel nonetheless decided to keep HODLING while reducing his risk factor. One method he used was to exchange bitcoin fragments (satoshis) with people willing to pay his utility bills in fiat, thus keeping most of his investment in his hands but also spending bitcoin on upkeep, which would in turn enable him to save money from his fiat-earned salary and buy more bitcoin when the value rises.

HODLING intelligently thereby does not mean abandoning completely the impulse to invest. Everyone at the Embassy spent fragments of their holdings on a regular basis, and so did Bitcoin evangelists and influencers who promoted HODLING online. Rami, for example, once told me that he perceived HODLING as an exercise in self-discipline and vigilance rather than as a form of static expectation that manifests in non-spending. For him, HODL required following the market closely and working out creative solutions to mitigate losses, especially when bitcoin drops. When I enquired further about this seeming inconsistency with regards to HODL, Ambassadors Yoav and Nathan explained that spending bitcoin on everyday services was indeed consistent with HODL positions as long as you avoided exchanging bitcoin for other cryptocurrencies. This approach, which Bitcoiners would classify under the heuristic category of 'maximalism', holds that by trading in other cryptocurrencies investors catapult themselves outside the community both pragmatically and ideologically. On the other hand, if you only spend on Bitcoin-related goods and services (e.g. encrypted 'cold wallets', especially produced to stock Bitcoin offline and off the blockchain) – or sell small amounts for fiat to pay bills – you will both gain value *and* contribute to the collaborative spirit that was valued by the community. HODLING thereby enables maximalists to support the community while still investing in their own future, as I now move to explain.

Maximalism

'Maximalism' is the idea that Bitcoin should function as a monopoly in the emergent decentralized crypto-economic market for it to be able to one day also replace the hegemony of fiat-based economic regimes (Buterin 2017; Shapiro 2022). At the end of the 2010s, maximalists in Israel and beyond saw Bitcoin as a direct competitor to centralized currencies and usually also argued that not even other cryptocurrencies could provide a reliable alternative (see Maurer, Nelms and Swartz 2013). Most Embassy associates self-identified as maximalists, which for them meant going beyond financialization to highlight shared cultural idioms and a set of 'beliefs' they claimed defined the singularity of Bitcoin vis-à-vis other financial assets, including cryptocurrencies, which as I explained in the Introduction, they derogatorily called 'shitcoins'. "One Bitcoin equals one Bitcoin", Rami used to say, often also gesturing with his two index fingers to indicate that the bitcoin value against the dollar, euro, pound, shekels and of course the bulk of available cryptocurrencies is simply irrelevant. The idea that Bitcoin can only be compared to itself – standing as a singular financial asset against all others – has with time become a common figure of speech at the Embassy, which for dedicated Ambassadors also expressed the very essence of maximalism (Shapiro 2022; cf. Cardoso 2024).

The events surrounding the establishment of Bitcoin Cash (or B-Cash) will exemplify this further. In 2017, Bitcoiners around the world debated a motion raised on the Bitcoin Talk forum to increase the processing capacity of each block on the blockchain. According to those who supported the move, such increase could enable heavier volumes of traffic and the payment of higher transaction fees across the network, mostly to the benefit of centralized exchange platforms and the mining industry. Pro-increase Bitcoiners also pushed for other changes that would make Bitcoin transactions more profitable for those companies and individuals whose financial investments dominated the blockchain. Some of them even openly challenged the idea that total decentralization predisposes liberty, which until that point had been a defining feature of Bitcoin. Their suggestions were nonetheless blocked by the majority of Bitcoin nodes on the Bitcoin Talk forum, and some of these revisionists consequently 'left' the movement to establish 'B-Cash' as an *alternative* cryptocurrency. They did it by 'forking' the blockchain – a process wherein the original programming codes are used to bifurcate a single blockchain into two identical systems. The new blockchain can then be modified and redesigned to comply with new rules, which are encoded automatically. B-Cash initially attracted heavy investment, although it never managed to dominate the cryptocurrency market. Both 'communities' came to view each other as a false version or inauthentic manifestation of the reality of decentralized finance. The mundanity of this conflict, its pettiness, overshadowed contested views about the nature of egalitarian practice in a decentralized community, radicalizing and extending the ideological disagreement between the two camps at a global scale.

Whereas most Embassy associates opposed this motion, a minority did support it, as well as wider circles of profit-oriented Bitcoin investors in Tel Aviv. Angry discussions on the issue in the 'Israeli Bitcoin' Facebook group thus included mutual accusations and genuine expressions of rage on both sides. At least on one occasion, rumour has it, the rivalry culminated in a fistfight between rival factions some streets away from the Embassy. This incident initially rocked the foundations of the community, causing serious discursive and emotional tensions between well-known figures in the Israeli Bitcoin scene. Tensions eventually died down when it became clear that the overwhelming majority of Embassy associates and community members both in Israel and abroad were not in fact flocking to the new coin, and that a Bitcoin Cash community would not threaten the hegemony of Bitcoin financially, ideologically or otherwise.

Lana Swartz (2018) insightfully construed an analytic distinction between these two techno-economic imaginaries of Bitcoin. 'Digital metalists', on one hand, consider Bitcoin primarily as a store of value (Maurer, Nelms and Swartz 2013; Zimmer 2017). This position 'embraces a theory of money in which the only truly sound money is one backed by a commodity like gold, which derives its intrinsic value from the market' (Swartz 2018: 630). 'Infrastructural mutualists', on the other hand, prioritize Bitcoin as an everyday unit of exchange. 'From this perspective,', Swartz (ibid.: 632) argues, 'Bitcoin is not primarily an alternative to state-backed money but an alternative to private payment intermediaries that seek to control and survey its passage. It affords a cooperativist vision of a money technology and therefore society.'[3]

As Swartz also recognizes, whether one leans more towards the first or the second group does not, however, matter much as this relates to the everyday maximalist ethics. That is so because both options primarily envision the Bitcoin ecosystem as a social space that requires strengthening and involvement at both individual and collective registers. Some of the maximalists at the Embassy in fact admitted that certain altcoins were useful for specific purposes; for example, some cryptocurrencies can enable fully anonymous transactions, a function that today is no longer possible on the Bitcoin network. Such approach remains maximalist due to the insistence that these altcoins should always derive their financial value from the dominance of Bitcoin (Cardoso 2024). In one of our many conversations Nissim once associated this idea with the term 'community', which, to my surprise he used uncharacteristically to refer to all cryptocurrency holders on the planet:

> A community is something that is alive. Why is Bitcoin unstable? Because inside the community there are people who are Bitcoin Cash [an alternative Bitcoin project initiated in 2017, see below], and others who are Ethereum, and others who are Cardano; they want it [the value] to rise; at the end of the day they all want Bitcoin but they do it in different ways. It [global cryptocurrency supporters] is a community in which everyone wants the value of Bitcoin. So, Bitcoin is like God, like Moses the Prophet, or you can call it whatever you want. Effectively, it focuses the energies of people on the target they wish to achieve.

Nissim thereby took a maximalist stance where other cryptocurrencies were permissible as long as they adhered to the primacy of Bitcoin. Only a completely decentralized cryptocurrency backed by a strong community of developers could according to this belief be efficient and resilient enough to challenge a corrupt 'old world' premised on centralized socioeconomic and political systems. That is precisely the reason that a HODL strategy can, in different constellations and situations, appeal to both these types of Bitcoin investors. Even Rami, who called government-issued notes 'colourful paper drawings' and identified most other cryptocurrencies as 'shitcoins', relativized his risk by investing about 20 per cent of his overall bitcoin holdings in these same 'shit' assets. When I asked him why he did that and how this was consistent with the strategy of HODLING that he otherwise promoted at any possibility, Rami said that for him such investments were just a game, a gamble on money he was willing to lose for the thrill of it. When he acquired profits from these investments in the wider cryptocurrency market, Rami exchanged it for NIS or USD and used the money to either pay for his everyday upkeep or, alternatively, to finance an occasional weekend of partying in Berlin. He would thus try to HODL his Bitcoin as much as possible, seeing in it a near-sacred source of funding for his future pension.

As Nissim also reacted when I summarized Swartz's argument: 'Those two perspectives on Bitcoin which you stated – mutualism and metalism – they are not contradictory but complementary.' He continued:

> What is HODLING? It means you have money. But it doesn't mean that because you have money you're going to buy a Rolls-Royce and drive around town, even if you can. This is because he [Bitcoin] doesn't tell you to show yourself and how much you've got ... [But] This money is not static, it's dynamic, as opposed to fiat, in which you can't make any profit at all in recent years ... Bitcoin says that instead of putting your money in the bank and getting one percent, or a quarter of a percent for a year or whatever, *here you become your own bank.*[4]

For Nissim, Rami, and many other Ambassadors, being 'your own bank' referred to being in exclusive control of one's funds, which they understood as a concrete act of liberating oneself from hierarchical power structures. In that sense, interlocutors treated both metalism and mutualism as forms of praxis by which people could train how to run 'their own bank'. They viewed HODLING as one of the main strategies by which one can develop the necessary skills. HODLING thereby discursively becomes the core exercise of the realization that in Bitcoin you *are and will always remain* 'your own bank', as opposed to more centralized cryptocurrencies and state-controlled inflationary money. To fully perceive the extent of these views, it is crucial to discuss Satoshi Nakamoto's own rejection of centralized money, which overwhelmingly focused on the notion of debt and the libertarian imperative to cancel it.

Debt and Freedom

In his now-famous study of economic indebtedness and the origins of capitalism, anthropologist David Graeber (2011) argues that before the advent of centralized political control instituted barter was enacted between groups that kept close economic and political relationships. Any debt created between groups was thus tied with honour, shame, and trust, which guaranteed repayment. He thus constructs debt between total strangers, with the idea of interest profiteering underlying its enactment, as contrary to much of human economic activity throughout history. Graeber consequently understands the shift from 'honour and shame' economic arrangements to contemporary debt-based markets as a proxy for the quantification of human relationships that would have otherwise forever remained entirely qualitative; as they were encoded in long-lasting patterns of gift and economic exchange, and often also embedded in kinship arrangements, moral imperatives, and religious or ritualized commitments (cf. Graeber 2001).

Based on this assertion, which goes against popular ideas about barter as the economic predecessor of money, Graeber analyses fractional-reserve banking as a disastrous anomaly. He argues (2011: 375–76) that President Nixon's decoupling of the dollar from the gold standard in 1971 (see Chapter 2) turned money from a concrete representation of economic ability into a floating signifier. Regulators, bankers and especially policy makers now controlled the money supply *as if* it were still a rare commodity, printing money 'from thin air'.

This game, Graeber further claims (2001, 2011), substituted the postwar social contract – which was based on striving towards economic security and wage growth – with a massive franchising of capitalism itself. In this new deal, people would now have equal opportunities to become 'rentiers'; that is, owners of the means of production, whatever these are, rather than mere producers for the capitalist elites. This emphasis on and effective decentralization of growth possibilities has in turn increased reliance on public as well as private debt, which caused governments to encourage people to borrow, thereby increasing the 'debt bubble':

> Any system that reduces the world to numbers can only be held in place by weapons . . . It can also only operate by continually converting love into debt . . . Just as markets, when allowed to drift entirely free from their violent origins, invariably begin to grow into something different, into networks of honor, trust, and mutual connectedness, so does the maintenance of systems of coercion constantly do the opposite: turn the products of human cooperation, creativity, devotion, love, and trust back into numbers once again. (Graeber 2011: 386–87)

Graeber's plea for sanity in the face of the growing debt monster – which was literally bailed out by numerous states after the 2008 crisis – encourages readers to rethink the assumption that national debts must be repaid at all. For Graeber, to be sure, the moralizing demand to repay national debts is grounded in an apocalyptic hysteria and colonial arrogance, which assumes that the end of the capitalist system itself is always imminent. To prevent catastrophe, we are told, we must handle credit responsibly, individually and collectively, in everyday life as well as a consideration in nation-states' long-term development plans. At the level of the individual, which is crucial for understanding HODLING in Bitcoin, 'responsible' economic rationalism is here premised on one's own reckoning of his or her place in a class hierarchy. Financial elites, on the other hand, often have the privilege of not fully complying with the rules that they had themselves determined. The entire capitalist financial establishment, as an apparatus and a political philosophy – which has been reaping the fruits of the credit system since the 1971 Nixon Shock – is thus exposed as unreliable (see Butler 2022: 84–86).

Unsurprisingly, this sounds very close to Nissim's argument above, and to Satoshi's (2008) own claims in the White Paper. Although they promote opposite political frameworks – Graeber accentuating the moral dimension of economic actions and Satoshi seeking to *neutralize* this same morality – both approaches in fact question the validity and credibility of the fractional-reserve banking system. While Graeber called for the subjugation of this system to wider social considerations beyond the logic of the market – prompting the destruction of the blind accounting systems used to verify that logic in the form of interest, deficit and debt collection – Satoshi sought to dispose of the banks altogether.

If Graeber is a provocative decelerationist, then, Satoshi definitely is an accelerationist. In both these accounts, however, and despite the stark opposition between these two solutions to the problem of debt, a vision of an alternative future is conceived as politically and economically attainable. In both cases this future depends on the relinquishing and denial of risk-focused narratives about responsible growth, trust in the banking industry, and the prevention of crisis at all costs. A future of prosperity is imagined even in case of financial meltdown, as it would also mean a new approach to indebtedness at a global scale. At the core of Graeber's and Satoshi's aspirations, so it seems, is the conviction that *extra-statist money could reorganize age-old corrupt hierarchies and power imbalances, turning them into egalitarian realities.*

These arguments thus complement one another. Both reject in different forms the system of power imbalances by which they claim that liberal capitalism maintains its vigour and hegemony. Both also attack the contemporary modus operandi of the dominant moral order, and offer instead pragmatic ways to replace it. Although Graeber and Satoshi would likely argue that the proposed solution of the other is inherently wrong, both indeed make a case for a conclusive and revolutionary socio-moral-economic transformation that in each framework is seen to promote human freedom. For Graeber, this task trickles down to the realignment of state and market, while for Satoshi it means a distribution of societal and economic authority into private hands. Although they represent antagonistic sociological and economic theories of human nature and social organization, both in fact call for pragmatic rather than philosophical responses to the problem of debt. In that sense, Bitcoin daily praxis would reject the same reductionist system David Graeber so vehemently criticized. As Nissim phrased it in one of his public talks:

> Many people say that the more you owe the richer you get. That's what people who accept the [values of the] general economy say. They say that we can't let the banks fall. They are the oxygen of the country; without them all of us will collapse. I think that the banks are the cyanide of the country; they poison the

> people. If they disappear it will only do good to the people. In 2008, when the economy collapsed in the United States, if they would have allowed the Lehmann Brothers to disappear, and not strengthen their bank [to bring it] to where it is today, we would have been in a much better world . . . the next fall will prove that money is not credit, that money, when it's not in your pocket, you don't have it, it's an illusion – take another mortgage, take another loan, but we shall be waiting in the corner . . . It's a system from which you can never escape because it drowns you ever deeper and you will never be able to pay your debts.

Extending from an origin story about how money was corrupted by the creation of a loan bubble, then, Nissim and many of his colleagues often argued that indebtedness itself was the typical manifestation of a centralized economic tyranny, which in turn limited freedom of choice and inhibited 'liberty' at a societal level. Bitcoin was the ultimate resolution, within this framework – 'a language of freedom', as one graffiti painted on the toilet wall at the Embassy proudly declared. Employing an even stronger analogy, another slogan on that same wall decisively pronounced: 'Bitcoin is not the bubble, it's the needle.'

Like David Graeber (2001, 2011), who identified a major geopolitical bubble in the perpetuation of unpayable debts, Bitcoiners in Israel thus fused ideas about debt and financial dependency into a theory of collective liberation, while still promoting their 'community' as a living model for true economic emancipation. Yet, as it has by now become clear, such emancipation both as an individual experience and a collective reality, required certain strategies conducive to the development of personality traits and even virtues, which Ambassadors generally saw as emanating from HODLING. I now move to discuss this notion in depth.

The Virtuous HODLER

Every person involved in Bitcoin sociality – traders, programmers, investors, influencers, miners or otherwise – is familiar with stories about people who compromised their HODL position and lost money as a result. One famous scenario is that of persons spending too much bitcoin in the early days on the Dark Net to buy drugs (cf. Maddox et al. 2016). Another common story is about people selling all their holdings when the value was priced under US$2,000, only to bitterly regret doing so when the value jumped just a year or two later. Yet another story refers to those who were HODLING but panicked when the next slump hit and sold, later regretting when it again boomed to even higher values. For example, Jimmy Song, the Bitcoin evangelist, described in his Tel Aviv lecture how he regretted buying a turkey in

2013 for about US$100-worth of bitcoin, which at the time of his talk in early 2018 was worth US$3,000. 'It was a very tasty turkey', he said, grinning, 'but was it worth $3,000!?' And there are plenty of reminders about people trying to make money by betting on trends, selling high and buying low, but who nevertheless erred or misread the market, ending up in a deficit.

Despite these well-known examples, however, Bitcoiners have always had to face the fact that by HODLING they were also stuck with assets they could not use. Embassy associates recognized that their economic autonomy thereby remained contingent on hazy potentialities and the necessity to receive their salaries in 'centralized' fiat money. Apart from its financial aspect, this problem also produced an intricate conundrum, as most veteran Bitcoiners at the Embassy initially purchased bitcoin to liberate themselves from intermediaries, state institutions, and corporations; yet, unable or unwilling to exchange it for whatever reason, they became *stranded* in intermediary territory until further notice. When I asked Nissim about this apparent conflict, he became angry. 'HODLING is not about getting stuck with money you can't spend; it's about being patient!' He went on to describe patient HODLING as a form of spiritual work:

> HODLING means that you freeze the material dimension in your thinking . . . it guides you to put the money aside [so that] it will do what it can do [i.e. grow in value] by itself, while you are dealing with the important things in life, which is finding solutions to your problems, advancing, [developing] your own capabilities and skills, and [investing] in your own actions that are sublime; those refined things you want to achieve as a human being, which do not necessarily include thinking about money. In the end, you must assume that this money is always available to you, you are the owner, so you tell this money what to do. When you tell him *[sic]* – 'listen, don't falter . . . when I come for you, will you be there?' He then tells you, 'YES!' And you ask, 'Will you be in the same situation [at the same value]?' So, he tells you, 'Maybe I'll be more and maybe I'll be less, *but I will be here because you put me here.*'

Almost like a monastic vow of chastity, Nissim describes patient HODLING as a cultivation of personal virtues that helps overcome destructive Dionysian whims. HODLING shields 'common' Bitcoiners in a market hugely influenced by the positions and interests of 'whales', 'bulls' and shrewd traders, whose actions, to continue the monastic metaphor, Nissim understands as forms of witchcraft and deceit. Associating a productive value to *avoidance* of trade turns the pursuit of money into a secondary consideration. Instead, HODLING helps people mitigate future economic uncertainty by incentivizing individual agency at a more abstract level. If you believe that Bitcoin will never collapse, HODLING reassures you that your money will be there and that you are the only person who would be able to access it. In turn, as Nissim claims, you can focus on your wellbeing, cultivate self-acceptance and live an alternative reality not dictated by credit or debt and free from obedience to powerful bureaucratic institutions.

In his analysis of Bitcoin maximalism in Brazil, Bruno Cardoso (2024) provides a point of comparison. Although his maximalist interlocutors spoke about 'accumulation' of bitcoin primarily as a financial strategy, Cardoso argues that they also associated it with a desire to strengthen the global Bitcoin movement. Alluding to Christian Borch's (2007) 'crowd syndrome' – that is, the affective urge to join in when we are suddenly swept away with the masses – Cardoso writes (2024: 31–32):

> The slow but steady accumulation of *sats* [satoshis] is depicted as a mandatory self-discipline for all dedicated Bitcoiners, who portray this financial practice as both an exercise of individual sovereignty . . . and a way of buying themselves 'a way out' when the BRL [Brazilian Real], and ultimately the dollar, finally turns into dust . . . This particular emphasis on accumulation instead of trading, fuelled by the FOMO on the hyperbitcoinization boom, highlights one of the main characteristics of the *maxi's* [maximalist] *syndrome*: if, possibly in the near future, all other goods and commodities are going to be denominated and traded for *[b]itcoins* and *sats*, there is no point in trading it now for everything else. The crowd-enforced positive feedback loops of accumulation, despite sudden price crashes or long bearish markets, are the main affect that drives *maxis* towards their promised Bitcoin-powered utopias [emphasis in original].[5]

I further elaborate on Bitcoin crowds in Chapter 6. For now, I only wish to note that as the Brazilian and Israeli cases suggest, HODLING cannot be understood in the narrow technical sense as mere 'waiting'. Rather, as Nissim argues, it is rooted in the *active* acquisition of self-confidence, skills and even virtuous personality traits (see Benkler and Nissenbaum 2006; Pianalto 2014), thus facilitating the strength and fortitude necessary to endure stress while incentivizing the process of personal development with the promise of future riches. It is a dynamic process, which requires discipline, attention and some sense of inner peace.

Beyond personal enrichment, HODLING is also connected with a collective value: if you stock bitcoin you will be contributing to its overall market domination. The higher this market capitalization gets, the more difficult it will be to 'beat' it. A circular movement characterizes HODLING, then, wherein accumulation favours volume, which enhances value, in turn incentivizing the purchase of more bitcoin, and so on. You would in fact be throwing your money away if you chose to sell it for *any* amount of fiat currency. Ripping the harvest of this prolonged process ultimately requires the cultivation of *patience as means to an end*. Philosopher Joseph Kupfer

(2007: 271–72) explains how this differs from *impatience,* which often prevents us from achieving our goals and thus quite literally costs us more in the long run:

> The obvious drawback to impatience is that we do not allow things to occur that need to take place in order to obtain the best results. The mediated object of desire is either not attained or attained in less than desirable fashion . . . If we are impatient about reeling in a hooked fish, we are liable to lose it. In the case of not waiting appropriately in teaching our child a subject like mathematics, the child becomes frustrated with us or develops a dislike for the subject matter . . . The cost of impatience is, ironically, not satisfying our desires, at least not in the way we wish. It is ironic because impatience is not being able or willing to wait to have our desires satisfied. Because we cannot wait to have our desires satisfied, then, we fail to have our desires *satisfied* [emphasis mine].

Kupfer (2007: 265) defines patience as 'the disposition to accept delays in satisfying our desires – delays that are warranted by circumstances or the desires themselves'. For him, being patient expresses the realization that the world does not always work in accordance with our expectations, and that the advantage we gain from exercising control over our desires is as significant as the fulfilment of these desires. Patience helps us find humility and resists the 'flawed human condition' (ibid.: 279) that makes us wait for too long on the one hand or not wait enough on the other hand. Being truly patient means balancing these vices out by learning how to keep advancing your objectives while remaining attentive to the needs and fallacies of others.

HODLING emerges in this light as an exercise in cash flow control *as much as* a process of obtaining virtuous personality traits that can help Bitcoiners to interact with people around them even in non-economic areas of their lives. Within this framework, as people begin to HODL they prove that they are also 'holding on' to the belief that Bitcoin will triumph both as a monetary system and as a sociotechnical political philosophy. This idea was even crystallized in a popular meme that humorously referred to HODLING as acronymous codification of the sentence 'Hold On for Dear Life', thus implicitly comparing Bitcoin to a life-saving object.

The two most important virtuous traits that Nissim and others at the Embassy associated with patient HODLING were accountability and responsibility, both of which translate in Hebrew as *akh-ra-yut.*[6] Take Anat's story, which elucidates well how this notion informed real-life choices in the early 2010s in Tel Aviv. At the time I met her, Anat was a fifty-something 'Yemenite of the old generation', as she presented herself, a statement that in this context meant she was from a poverty-stricken working-class family of Jews who had emigrated from Yemen. She owned a small restaurant in Kerem Hateimanim – which literally translates as 'the Yemenite Vine grove' – an impoverished (although by now gentrified) neighbourhood located near the colourful Ha-Carmel vegetable market in the heart of Tel Aviv. Anat first heard of Bitcoin from clients working at a nearby tech company, who asked if they could pay with bitcoin tokens. At first, Anat laughed and dismissed them. She, however, sought more information at the Embassy, which was located about ten-minutes' walk from her restaurant, and a while later began accepting payments in bitcoin. In an interview, Anat explained what led her to this decision:

> I had an ugly bankruptcy in the early 2000s, and the banks sucked my blood. They wanted to evict me from my apartment, a single mother with a small child, and claimed I owed them 350 thousand NIS. I took a lawyer and he managed to prove I only owed them 70 thousand. I made a payment arrangement with them and since then I swore never to rely on them again; I closed my bank account, opened an account in the Postal Office Bank instead,[7] and began working with cash and bitcoin. I had to exchange them all the time because I needed cash but I also managed to save. I took control over this problem [dependency on banks]. The banks are the worst thieves on earth, and I really don't want to have anything to do with them.

By taking control, Anat became the *owner of her own bank*. She also became one of the first business owners in Israel who accepted bitcoin payments. She consequently had to traverse between crypto and fiat but, as Anat says, she also applied an ethos of thriftiness along the lines of Nissim's poetic elaborations. Anat HODLED, but for her this ongoing careful accumulation of wealth lacked a spiritual or romantic edge. It was about survival, providing for her child and covering debts (cf. Szabo 2002). During the 2017 crypto boom, Anat capitalized on her HODL position by selling some of what she had accrued to nubes at the Embassy. The 'responsibility' part manifested in accepting the terms and conditions of a decentralized socio-economic arrangement, which Anat practised alongside her immersion in the 'centralized' economy, where she needed fiat money to make do and pay for regular upkeep. Anat eventually acquired her own economic freedom by being patient, taking control, and acting responsibly, a semantic connection that Nissim also made during a public talk he gave in 2019:

> Bitcoin first and foremost shows us the way; it gives us the possibility to decide who we are and where we want to go in life, and feel good in this freedom, feel good with our choices. Many people think that the term 'freedom' means no responsibility. But actually, freedom is *total responsibility over our lives*. If we are responsible, we are free. We can wake up and eat and work and hang out within this space of freedom . . . and with the freedom and responsibility we have today we can achieve very clear goals. The moon, the sky is the limit.

Nissim, Anat, Rami, Bloom, Nathan and other Ambassadors all claimed on separate occasions that the end of an era of HODLING is a known event at an unknown point in time, which will come when – not if – the banking system finally crashes. HODLING consolidated for them the difference between those who owned their bank and those who remained dependent on commercial banks. As a proxy for ownership, HODLING framed their accountability for their actions and their responsibility for the future of their money. At the same time, they were never alone. A network of individual peers who respected these principles across the world reassured HODLERS that the accumulation of Bitcoin was a public concern for many, thus cyclically strengthening such notions as personal accountability and mutualist collaboration.

A HODLING strategy thus supported both the ethics of collective decentralization and the ethics of individual trustlessness, which converged into a single action, and which proved to be efficient in the elimination of debts. To capture the full ethnographic significance of this convergence, I now return to the tension with which I began this chapter: the different forms of individualism that have defined the Bitcoin project since the very beginning.

Individual A vs Individual B

The model of individualism Embassy members promoted was far from the dog-eat-dog image that critics often associate with the world of cryptocurrency investment. It was not built on maximizing profits at the cost of breaking the rules (Smith 2005), but rather on situational cost-benefit calculations, all of which were premised on honest reciprocity between peers who interacted on equal terms as part of a network. That was the reason that Nissim contrasted the notion of 'being your own bank' with relentless trading, which he dismissed precisely because it represented the self-interested individualism that he saw as contrary to the Bitcoin spirit. Of course, Nissim and everyone else at the embassy HODLED to increase the value of their assets, and they never claimed that someone should compromise profitability to support the Bitcoin 'revolution'. Their idea of self-interest simply exceeded the tension between individuals and the community to seek instead a fusion of collective solidarity and personal autonomy.

In his lengthy discussion of the category of the 'individual', Louis Dumont (1972, 1977, 1986) distinguished between two main cosmo-ideological systems. Western-style individualism, he argues, constructs the individual as an immutable and elemental totality (Rio and Smedal 2008), a thoroughly bounded *self* that becomes an end in itself, thus transcending collectivist values (cf. MacFarlane 1993). This independent and unified self is imagined to be equal to all other selves, thus feeding the axiom that individualism and equality are two sides of the same coin and giving rise to Western 'methodological individualism'. Dumont (1977) associates this model historically with transitions in Christian theology that took place from the middle of the seventeenth to the middle of the eighteenth century. This process saw the detachment of individuals from a hierarchical cosmos imagined through levels or gradations of purity, sublimity and wholeness, wherein the only truly immutable entity was the divine trinity. Alongside this, Dumont reasons, individuals were increasingly defined by their relations to property and materiality instead of their relations to other people or divine forces. The path to achieving true individuality slowly emerged as the active pursuit of one's own self-fulfilment.

Dumont (1972) contrasts the duality of individualism and equality with 'holistic' perceptions, which he identifies as characteristic of premodern times in the West, and as a prevailing classification system in Hinduism that still affects the entire social structure in India. On such social and cosmological maps, people are not only embedded in sets of relations that determine their status in the material world, but these concrete relations are also defined by relations between abstract values such as 'purity' or 'holiness'; which are taken to be atemporal. In the holistic model, all aspects of sociality relate to all others, all fields of action are relative to others, whether they complement or negate one another through taboos. The individual is a category that makes integral part of this perfect wholeness, the *means* by which society regenerates itself as the epicentre of a wider cosmic order. The holistic person is dividual, rather than *in*-dividual, as he or she only acquires relational meaning with regard to the social relations that existed before, and that are inscribed in him or her both aesthetically and morally.

André Béteille (1986), Alan MacFarlane (1993) and others have criticized Dumont's strict structuralism and the logical inconsistencies that arise in his writings. Both these authors argue that individualism, holism, equality and hierarchy are all intertwined in more complex ways than merely being sets of oppositions, as Dumont claims. Like these two authors, I do not submit to the stark division Dumont establishes between the West and the rest, nor do I accept his dialectical treatment of binary oppositions, which annuls the very relationality of a 'relation', one of Dumont's main theoretical concepts. As Marilyn Strathern (1996) argued, classificatory systems extend or promulgate some types of social relations while simultaneously 'cutting' or limiting other types. Strathern's long-term exploration of personhood produced the anthropological truism that 'the (homogeneous) network of elements that make up the person – human and nonhuman – is also a (heterogeneous) network of social relationships. In turn, the person acts as both container and channel, blocking flow and bodying it forth' (Strathern 1996: 528, original brackets).

Dumont's ideas should nonetheless be recognized as a major contribution to cross cultural debates on the category of the individual. That is so because his argument emphasizes the crucial role of cosmological theories in highlighting the often-problematic relations between singularities and multiplicities in mundane practice (see Brighenti 2014; Mazzarella 2017). Building on this contribution as foundational, contemporary approaches hold that holism and individualism, as much as hierarchy and egalitarianism, are not in fact oppositions, but mutually inclusive social processes whose dynamic formations often produce a complex set of social obligations. These include, for example, commitments to maintain the myth of 'freedom' through the cultivation of encapsulated individualism while still respecting and operating within semiformal moral frameworks, which emphasize equality, dependency and contingency as organizing and even regulating principles (see Chapter 6; cf. Béteille 1986).

I consequently understand the celebration of rational-sovereign individualism among Bitcoiners in Tel Aviv and beyond as a *spectrum* that extends between two ideal-type models. The first, which I will call Individual A (because I below will associate it with Ayn Rand), holds that the 'individual' is in full control of most social domains or fields of action (MacFarlane 1993), often driven by a desire to mitigate risks and maximize one's own benefits. Any Bitcoin investor is, according to this idea, a player seeking to synchronize their gains and losses on the blockchain, in a sense surfing on (or swimming through) digital boom-and-bust waves that collectively influence the bitcoin financial value, with the overall objective of safely docking back on firm ground. Here, any intimate or otherwise community-oriented relational exchange with peers, near or far, is subjected to the singular motivation of making a profit by skilfully using crypto materiality, such as trade graphs, social media updates, trend-prediction propaganda, etc. Dislodged from social relations at large, Individual A is therefore imagined as self-sovereign to the core, denying any meaningful emotional contingency with the community.[8] Individual A fits into the ideal-type description of skilled traders that GameKyuubi condemned in his original post. Traders do at times HODL, as I emphasized above, but they tend to invest in many other cryptocurrencies or to sell copious quantities of bitcoin for profit in fiat when the market enables this, thus reducing a long-term strategy to a short-term investment tactic.

The second ideal type self-sovereign individual, whom I call Individual B (like Bitcoin), is framed, empowered and made distinct only *because of* their relational dependence on a 'network' of peers, locally as well as globally. In this model the network becomes the collective protector of a robust and 'free' economic zone online and offline. Unlike the short-term risk-averse, profit-oriented approach that characterizes Individual A, Individual B does not perceive market dynamics as deterministic forces that dictate every decision. To the contrary, the expectation of self-restraint, humility and resilience assigns a moral edge to every decision, with contribution to the 'community' being an important consideration. Individual B, therefore, is more likely to HODL for longer periods, which in turn can define his or her willingness to adopt Bitcoin-specific cosmological principles, such as the substitution of human trust with trustless machines, or the belief in an imminent economic crisis (see Chapter 4 and Chapter 5). Individual B tends to see the equivalent monetary value of their bitcoin holdings in dollars, euros or pounds *as means to an end*, that being to induce egalitarianism, decentralization and collaborative territories of work and play across society (see also Swartz 2018 on mutualism). I now turn to briefly exemplify how this distinction manifested discursively at the Embassy.

The Triumphant HODLER

A veteran Ambassador who had left Tel Aviv before I began my fieldwork, Shirly one day entered the Embassy looking solemn. One of her wallets had been hacked and she had lost several thousand dollars' worth of her hard-HODLED bitcoin. She arrived that day to seek help from experts, whom she believed could trace the source of the hack. 'Living in a world without a sovereign is a huge responsibility', she told me. 'In Bitcoin there is no customer service you can complain to; you really must rely on yourself. Accountability is entirely yours.' Facing the prospect of a self-centred universe, individuated to the point of having to self-protect from random harm (such as hacks, phishing and financial fraud), Shirly highlighted the intrinsic problem with the notion of financial self-liberation in Bitcoin – it negated itself by virtue of its enactment. When I asked Shirly if her views on self-reliance and 'accountability' were not simply whitewashing selfishness at the core of the Bitcoin project, she replied:

> Life obliges me to take care of myself. If my mind treats my own self as one with the universe I will just sit under a tree and let the lion devour me. Life compels me to have an individual identity, and this is not being selfish. When we use the term 'selfish' we are demeaning our essence because it generates a false opposition between us and society. Bitcoin is a basis for social organization at a completely different level of the mind . . . it is not the level of the individual but of the *network* of individuals who manage everything on the blockchain. It is actually an optimization [of the mind] because I am taking care of my immediate environment, and once the information exists in the network it returns to the system as feedback

> to generate an infrastructure for the existence of the whole of human society as a unified organism. That's why we are there [in the Bitcoin project].[9]

Shirly's ideas fused New Age concepts about humanity-scale mind-unity with communalist ideas about networking, self-realization, and autonomy. By taking your faith into your own hands, she claimed, you also take humanity's faith in your hands. At the root here was the view of society as an organic-cybernetic system whose mechanics enabled the circulation of care/goodness from the grassroots level 'upwards' to the collective. The collective was in that sense embodied in each subject, and each subject was subsumed in the collective. This fractality preserved distance but also abolished it when it came to communalist collaboration; having friends in the community enabled Shirly to temporarily let her guard down, and trust that they would not fail her even after sharing with them some of her passwords. At the scale of the masses, Shirly argued, the mutuality of individuals and society was coded into this cyclical movement. I was not surprised to hear Nissim reiterating these ideas in one of his public lectures some months after the conversation with Shirly. He explicitly turned notions of self-reliance into a form of collective resistance to the tyranny of centralized financial institutions:

> The [banks] flagellate us, and they lie to us, and they blame us; I call them *raptors*. And I know that we know the truth and that we must continue with our own integrity, and love unconditionally, because we are not dependent on the commissions, and the interests, and the salaries of the [bank] managers, because if we are controlling our own banks in a decentralized fashion, and all decisions are taken by consensus and not by a ruler, we can advance and achieve greater things than those we could achieve in a system that imposes on us all these things, which they consider to be correct and just . . . When each person fulfils his own will and desires, we automatically get a field of action that unites people who only deal with their own world. I think that precisely in this way this country was built seventy years ago. People came here to find safety and security and a community and a people, and [they] started working for that to happen. But the society was formed not because somebody coerced them. They *volunteered* to build the country.[10]

Nissim constructed the image of a community of fully enclosed individual-autonomous subjects, whose collaborative energy and good-willed mutualism was both the reflection and the instigator of the achievement of national independence. The community here excludes those total individualists who only care about themselves or refuse to volunteer for the general good. It is this kind of collective freedom that collaboration would make possible, in the case of Bitcoin, as this compares with the Zionist objective of establishing an independent Jewish state in the Land of Israel. This idea ultimately served for constructing the community as the overarching point of reference to any kind of economic or political revisionism in the contemporary world. It also reflected a hierarchical bias in the differentiation that Embassy members continuously constructed between Individual A and Individual B, which I now turn to analyse.

There Is Such a Thing as Society

As I have made clear, interlocutors at the Embassy acknowledged that financial incentives attribute value to every P2P exchange, and thus that the intrinsic monetization of any transaction on the blockchain turns the purported egalitarianism of all Bitcoiners into a game of snakes and ladders. GameKyuubi explained cogently that a zero-sum game like that of Bitcoin investment nominally sustains equality but pragmatically enables some peers to get richer than others. How people react to these processes is then dependent on their tendency towards self-autonomy (Individual A) or collective autonomy (Individual B). To complement Lana Swartz's (2018) notion of mutualism and metalism, I associate each end on this scale of individualism with existing cosmopolitical theories of capitalism, which go beyond economic considerations to constitute distinct moral-political interpretations of laissez-faire market dynamics.

The first is Ayn Rand's 'Objectivism', a political philosophy that presents the idea that rational self-interest is *objectively* superior to all other moral imperatives. In *Atlas Shrugged*, Rand's (1957) most notable Objectivist manifesto, the protagonist John Galt builds power at the margins of society by convincing major businesspersons to form an alternative community in an isolated valley. They seek to eradicate all forms of collectivism and relativism in society, and to establish instead a world in which people are exclusively valued according to their talents, abilities and achievements. Galt, an engineer shunned by managers and bureaucrats in a deteriorating and corrupt 'collectivist' society, eventually almost singlehandedly brings the collapse of the government after broadcasting the principles of Objectivism on the national radio and 'exposing' the moral decay of the regime.

Rand portrays Galt as the *prototypical* heroic individual whose absolute self-absorbed egotism guides him on a path towards excellence, during which he finds love and is merited for what he is 'really' worth. Rand purports that people must strive to fulfil their psychosocial ambitions as a precondition for happiness, and that the way to do this is to take care of one's own economic prosperity by any means necessary (although she disapproves of harming others in the process). For Rand, becoming the best possible version of oneself is the main driving force in life, the only viable moral compass that should guide behaviour, superseding any other consideration. Rand famously claimed that individual self-fulfilment should in fact *precede* romantic, communitarian or even familial commitments.[11]

I did meet Bitcoin supporters in Israel who embraced such notions of radical self-interestedness. For example, once I was on the phone with a former Embassy associate who had completely overturned his left-wing Socialist-leaning political convictions. He told me that he had 'sobered up' from his previous 'illusions' about the importance of communities for one's own prosperity and the feasibility of collective political struggle at large. He thus abandoned the Bitcoin Embassy and instead decided to become a crypto entrepreneur. He claimed bluntly that the world today is divided into two kinds of people – the smart ones, who know how to make money, and the stupid ones, who allow the smart ones to exploit them. He saw himself as one of the smart, clearly, thereby tautologically legitimizing the extraction of profit as evidence for the profiteer's alleged qualitative advantage over the odd simpleton and the incapable trader. I in fact once also met a trader who was passing through the Embassy to buy bitcoin from the ATM, who spoke at length on Ayn Rand and claimed that Bitcoin would enable the establishment of a real-word Galt's Gulch, the utopian society of free entrepreneurs unbound by any collective regulation. The ideal-type end of the spectrum embodied in Individual A manifests in these ideas as a form of political revolution that will turn collective responsibility in society on its head, promoting instead a romantic world premised on the successes or failures of individuals.

Despite this *Wolf of Wall Street*-esque attitude, however, most Embassy members explicitly or implicitly rejected the idea that self-fulfilment is a stronger motivation than other values. Ambassadors often claimed instead that individual financial autonomy can only be guaranteed by integration into a strong community. Once, for example, I overheard a conversation on power and anarchy at the Embassy, during which three of the Ambassadors claimed that the collapse of current power centres can only be achieved by the creation of a resilient Bitcoin community in Israel and beyond. Individual self-fulfilment, according to this view, was the result of new collaborative enterprises between equal partners. Recognizing that such enterprises were not merely financial, they went beyond Rand's Objectivism to represent cultural intimacy and peer-collaboration as major affective forces working in parallel with rational self-interest, which was justified at the Embassy with a Cypherpunk militancy.

Rather than associating these ideas with Rand's Objectivism, then, I began thinking of them as reiterating Margaret Thatcher's notion of individualism. Religious scholar Graeme Smith (2007) argued that Thatcher's political philosophy combined conservative arguments about freedom of choice and free enterprise with a Christian Nonconformist advocacy of charity, altruism and hard work, all of which were heuristically described by Thatcher herself as forms of virtue.[12] As opposed to Rand's fanatical rationalism, which claimed to be *amoral* because it subsumed considerations of value within individual rational economic choices alleged to have been objectively verified as truthful, Thatcher associated individualism with solidarity among the commons and interpersonal emotional awareness (ibid.: 235). Based on meticulous analysis of Thatcher's speeches and memoirs, Smith claims that Thatcher sought to incentivize private entrepreneurship in the UK primarily because she saw it as a *societal common good*. For Smith, the Thatcherite approach to private enterprise was soundly engraved in the idea that people have a natural moral responsibility towards their peers, family, friends and community:

> [In] the Iain McLeod Memorial Lecture of 1977 . . . Thatcher argues that the self-interest of the individual is inextricably bound up with the responsibility of that individual for others. She is seeking to refute the idea that socialists occupy the moral high ground through their emphasis on altruism, as opposed to the supposed Conservative stress on self-interest and selfishness: 'There is not and cannot possibly be any hard and fast antithesis between self-interest and care for others, for man is a social creature, born into family, clan, community, nation, brought up in mutual dependence. The founders of our religion made this a cornerstone of morality. The admonition "Love thy neighbour as thyself, and do as you would be done by" express this' (Thatcher 1977, in Harris 1997: 62). Thatcher offers reasons that are both naturalistic, by reference to human beings' physical nature, and emotional, to explain why self-interest must include care for others . . . The recognition of this shared humanity occurs first at the local level – that is, the family and neighbourhood – and then extends further outwards, with its limit seeming to be a shared national culture, as opposed to any idea of universal humanity. (Smith 2007: 244)

It is precisely this form of individualism which the ideal-type Individual B represents. To clarify this argument, I must briefly explain Thatcher's 'monetarist' economic policy during the 1980s, which was later adapted into Labour Party 'Third Way' policies under Tony Blair.[13] Based on Milton Friedman's theory of money, monetarism was seen in the 1980s as an efficient way to fight inflation, which had soared in the UK towards the end of the 1970s. To tame this trend, Thatcher and her ministers limited the money supply in the market through reduced governmental spending, while increasing the interest rate to encourage personal economic initiative. In parallel they deregulated key industries to encourage innovation and privatized national assets including transportation, communications and energy corporations. Monetarism succeeded in reducing inflation, but it did cause an unemployment crisis as well as the devastating dissolution of mining communities;

a result Thatcher saw as unavoidable on the way towards a more dynamic economy. Smith (2007: 243) argues:

> The reduction of inflation remained a core aspect of [Thatcher's] political rhetoric and what is interesting is that here we see it described theologically, as an 'evil' and a 'moral issue'. The explanation for the relationship between economic policy and ethical categories is found in her advocacy of nonconformist values. The rewards of thrift, hard work and enterprise are undermined by high inflation, and high inflation produces unemployment which was 'a waste of a country's most precious assets, the talents and energy of its people' (Thatcher 1977, in Harris 1997: 113). If nonconformity is not rewarded, then people seek other ways to achieve economic success which debilitates the national spirit and produces individual dependency on the state, a phenomenon which . . . Thatcher believed had exercised considerable influence on the British people.

It is true that Thatcher's policies were in part a destructive endeavour with calamitous implications for small communities in the UK. It is still unclear whether 'caring for others' could indeed be directed towards the collective with the same vigour as recruited to protect individual interests or the forming of new (arguably instrumental) in-group boundaries. This uncertainty is at the philosophical centre of free-market economics to this day, for better or worse. At the same time, Thatcher's monetarism also constructively ties together individual free choice with collective spiritual awakening (Smith 2007: 248), even if this conceptual link remains at the level of discourse alone. Thatcher's 1987 interview with journalist Douglas Keay from *Women's Own* magazine conveys this duality well, despite it initially being interpreted as a call for total societal fragmentation. It is worth quoting these infamous assertions at length:

> I think we have gone through a period when too many children and people have been given to understand 'I have a problem, it is the Government's job to cope with it!' or 'I have a problem, I will go and get a grant to cope with it!' . . . and so they are casting their problems on society and who is society? There is no such thing! There are individual men and women and there are families and no government can do anything except through people and people look to themselves first. It is our duty to look after ourselves and then also to help look after our neighbour and life is a reciprocal business and people have got the entitlements too much in mind without the obligations, because there is no such thing as an entitlement unless someone has first met an obligation . . . There is no such thing as society. There is living tapestry of men and women and people and the beauty of that tapestry and the quality of our lives will depend upon how much each of us is prepared to take responsibility for ourselves and each of us prepared to turn round and help by our own efforts those who are unfortunate. (Thatcher 1987)

This perspective is different from the ideas advanced in Randian Objectivism. If Ayn Rand's laissez-faire approach was focused on innovation and personal genius – which benefitted society only as far as it benefitted selfish individual entrepreneurs – Thatcher's political philosophy strongly disavows self-centred isolationism. Thatcher explicitly asserted elsewhere in her interview with Keay that 'freedom incurs responsibility', and in other interviews emphasized over and again that responsibility towards family and community is a lasting moral virtue that goes *against* excess and self-indulgence (Smith 2007: 244). In this logic, applying *free choice* should inform any mundane expression of individual desires, and free choice should thus become a constituent building block of a collective common good. This included the idea that human compassion was stronger than the impulse for total self-preservation, quite in contradiction to Rand's disdain towards altruistic behaviour of any kind. Thatcher's individualism included within it the relational moral indebtedness Rand aimed to dismantle, albeit replacing the collectivist imperative to '*Share*!' with the voluntarist question '*Should I Share?*'

Thatcher thus sought to redefine the social contract in the UK in the 1980s, going beyond Rand's ideas and merging instead Milton Friedman's free-market economic theories with an emphasis on collective accountability, virtuous behaviour and moral duty. Her monetarist policies were in that sense an attempt to incentivize 'free' decision-making an as indispensable aspect of people's engagement with those around them. Thatcher tacitly promoted a conceptual move from 'society' – imagined as a stable but inefficient bureaucratic monolith – to *sociality*, imagined as an organic, 'living tapestry' of men and women. This idea coincides with Nissim's perception of HODLING as something that goes beyond risk management to enable fine-tuning of one's own expectations from life, followed by a mutualistic ideology of wellbeing. The ideal-type Individual B conveys in that sense vivacity and rigour, features that in the context of the Embassy were used to describe accumulation (Cardoso 2024) of Bitcoin through patient HODLING as actively contributing to the emergent construction of a fairer society for everyone.

Conclusion

Although Thatcher was not mentioned at the Embassy during my fieldwork, her views resonate with the idea that personal development through HODLING was an act of direct support in and for the Bitcoin community. Unlike Rand's sanctimonious self-interest, which focused on individual heroism and rebellious iconoclasm, Embassy members spoke of responsibility and accountability, and to an extent also of patience, as virtues that all new adopters must acquire if they want to use their Bitcoin holdings productively. Most believed that a post-apocalyptic reality following the next global fiscal crisis would be premised on new sensibilities, new ways of seeing and feeling and acting in the world, which, while premised on the idiom of 'being your own bank', would encourage P2P collaboration at a scale never seen before. It is the coming into being of this personhood modality, as close as possible to the prototype of Individual B, that most of my maximalist friends at the Embassy anticipated and embraced.

These ideas, as I argued above, partially coincide with Dumont's initial distinction between two main cultural imaginaries that construct and inspire the relations between parts and wholes in a concrete social context. In a hierarchical imaginary, social categories such as 'class', 'caste', 'rank' or 'leadership' encompass other categories; that is, each level of reference contains a lower level of reference in its entirety within itself. An egalitarian imaginary, in contrast, produces many singular units, whose sum total makes up a whole, but wherein each unit also includes within itself the kernel of that which defines the whole as a whole. Building on Dumont's (1972) own definitions, Alan MacFarlane (1993: 2) further explains this issue as a question of morality that is parallel to ideas about the virtuous personality that Thatcher's egalitarianism aimed to promote:

> Dumont argues that, in contrast to the hierarchy and holism of all other civilizations, our recent Western civilization is based on individualism. What is meant by this? 'Our two cardinal ideals are called equality and liberty. They assume as their common principle . . . the idea of the human individual, humanity is made up of men, and each man is conceived as presenting, in spite of and over and above his particularity, the essence of humanity' (1972: 38). In other words, each individual, even when separated from the whole, is a complete moral being. This is the opposite of hierarchy, where the part only has meaning in relation to the whole.

Heuristic notions of individualism among interlocutors at the Embassy similarly held that any Bitcoin adopter was a fully contained moral entity, a totality that defines one's own vision of society here and now, as well as their aspirations for the future (see Tuddenham 2024). To achieve this totality, people had to redefine their dependency on institutions, while simultaneously also investing in the meaningful set of intimacies that membership in a community necessarily entailed. In this scheme, HODLING became a code for a process of personal change, in which an 'old world' ideology focused on cooperation between institutions and premised on a collectivist-centralized ethos of a strong state apparatus would be gradually replaced by a mycelium-inspired imaginary, focused at once on self-empowerment and voluntary contribution to a community or network of like-minded individuals. Virtues such as patience, responsibility and accountability, when practised at the personal level, would then also fix a broken system at the collective level. Nissim clarified this point in one of his public talks when he explained what distinguished the Embassy from other communities:

> I think that in this community people are dealing with the important things. There is no philosophy, or abstract values such as 'do meditation, do yoga, go to the Guru, go to the Rabbi, go to whoever'. This community deals with the essence . . . In other communities I was part of, many people lost their money because they believed in values that required them to give something to someone[14] . . . The beauty of this community is that [exercising] free will on the material issue, of the coin, of money, is individual and it is not dependent on anybody else . . . this gives us the possibility to live harmoniously in an individual way; each person comes and goes whenever they want, each person does whatever he wants, and that is why this community is the best of all communities I have seen so far.

As Nissim explicates, Individual B was not entirely 'holistic' and therefore not diametrically opposed to Individual A. As opposed to Dumont's model, which relies on a binary distinction, Individual B is seen here as an immutable rational being much like Individual A, a finite elemental component of the network, as Yoav claimed above. To put this in Dumont's terms, Individual B *could not be encompassed at any stage* by predetermined social relations, grades of moral hierarchy, established metaphysical truths or cosmologically constructed levels of purity (Dumont 1972); rather, they occupy a horizontal position on the network, metaphorically located alongside all others. Individual B is distinguished from Individual A by his or her differential contributions to financial decentralization, along the lines defined decades ago by Cypherpunk activists (Hayes 2019).

A HODL strategy could thus be seen as an exercise in self-control that also indicates commitment to wider communitarian values. HODL requires restriction, which anticipates the emergence of a new individual, an *Ubermensch* of a Nietzschean quality, who would transcend the moral framework of their time by 'being their own bank'. Free from the shackles of high-modernist moralities, living outside collective hierarchies, the individual bank owner would paradoxically no longer be worshipping Mammon. Here also would lie the potential for directing one's own creativity towards disruption and distortion, not by way of violent revolution but through careful observation premised on the accumulation of alternative economic resources; that would surely come in handy in the not-so-distant future.

Apart from debt evasion, hovering above these notions of virtuous individualism was the notion of egalitarian sociality. While sometimes overly fetishizing the praxis of P2P economic transactions, key research interlocutors praised the nominal equality of all 'individual banks' in Bitcoin. Some in fact claimed that the cultivation of this equality was the *only real innovation* Bitcoin could offer the world. Individual convictions or the rising value of bitcoin as a store of value were thus often considered secondary to demolishing traditional social hierarchies. The egalitarianism of virtuous individuals – of the kind that acknowledged communitarian and social goals rather than focusing on Randian-style self-interest – thus became a crucial heuristic force that maximalist Embassy associates embraced as the political pinnacle of their project.

In the next chapter I will examine how the liminality of the Embassy – a space in between Old and New economic and cosmological milieus – enabled the cultivation of these notions of individual virtues and personality traits. I will focus ethnographically on how the concept of 'Liberty' – or *Liberté*, in French, as most Ambassadors usually pronounced the term – was used in this context to further mitigate the tension between communard and individuated approaches to social and economic exchange.

NOTES

1. Original post retrieved 31 December 2023 from https://bitcointalk.org/index.php?topic=375643.0.
2. 'Killer use-case' is an adaptation of 'killer app', slang in tech circles for apps that profoundly transform the user experience of an online task or transaction (see Strahilevitz 2002).
3. Swartz here alludes to nineteenth-century notions of mutualism in the anarchist movement, popularized in the writing of Pierre-Joseph Proudhon and later applied empirically by such entrepreneurs as Robert Owen and Josiah Warren. Since anarchist theoretical principles were not a major topic of conversation at the Embassy, nor was the intellectual history of anarchism, I mention these here just as background information.
4. Nissim refers here to Bitcoin as an entity of sort, which can 'say' things or direct adopters to take certain actions. I deal with this semi-spiritual perception of Bitcoin in Chapter 5.
5. By hyperbitcoinization, Cardoso refers to the idea that Bitcoin will be spreading rapidly across the world and will ultimately replace fiat money as an organizing framework.
6. 'Accountability' in English refers to answerability or liability, a property of holding a position, whereas 'responsibility' refers to overseeing or making sure that certain actions are completed. This subtle distinction is absent in colloquial Hebrew, wherein the term *akh-ra-yut* (אחריות) includes both these senses at once.
7. The Postal Office Bank in Israel offers only the most basic banking services for a fraction of the costs of commercial banks. Postal Office Banks do not issue credit cards, and do not ratify overdraft agreements.
8. One of the most captivating visual signs of success in the early years, which later expanded from Bitcoin to other cryptocurrencies, was the image of a Lamborghini,

Tesla or Corvette, a definite status symbol that crypto millionaires often bought as a trophy, and that fans distributed online as memes.

9. Shirly used the Hebrew *to-da-âa*, which in English can mean 'awareness', 'consciousness' and 'mind', depending on the context. I chose to translate it as 'mind' because Shirly used the term to relate both to intellectual recognition of her own being, and in a quasi-mystical sense as a higher state of consciousness.
10. Nissim refers to the Zionist historiography of early 'pioneers', who encountered immense difficulties in pre-Israel Palestine but nevertheless worked together to build a shared national home for the Jewish People.
11. Without delving deeply into Rand's philosophy, I would like to briefly state my own critique of Objectivism. First, regarding the notion of reality as an object of perception, if we consider reality as a property of perception it cannot be studied and discovered separately from the perceiving mind, which is always interconnected with other minds. Rand imagines the world as completely detached from humans in reductive terms. She denies complexity – such as, for example, networks of perception and mutually communicating humans – as something that is both *in* reality and *makes it* at the same time. Her separations are binary and monothetic. Second, regarding the objective status of the theory itself, Rand argues that existence precedes reality but gives no evidence of that in her own theory, which is not derived from existence but is a reflection on the possibilities for existence. Hence, the theory is a fabrication of mind, which constitutes its own categories and coordinates, and then constructs on top of this additional coordinates and a whole set of structures that are imbued with objective status as real processes in reality. Since this theory is not a discovery or exploration of reality but rather an extension of the mind, it contradicts itself by showing it is possible to create reality from the mind, as opposed to using it to discover it. Consequently, the theory is not doing what it claims to do. This is a major weakness.
12. Nonconformist Christianity relates to reformist Protestant doctrines that refused to accept State authority over the Church, originating in seventeenth-century England and continuing to this day.
13. Tony Blair ran on a 'Third Way' platform in the 1997 General Election, offering to integrate monetarism with traditional Keynesian policies such as increased governmental spending on welfare. Simon Butler (2022) argues that monetarism is 'somewhere in the middle' between Keynesian and Austrian School economic theories.
14. In the 1980s, Nissim was a member of several intentional communities in Israel and the United States, including the Rajneeshpuram Community in Oregon, whose spiritual leader Rajneesh is popularly known as Osho.

CHAPTER 4

A SPACE IN BETWEEN

The Middle Ground

Until now, I have argued that Bitcoin handling in Tel Aviv should not be regarded a purely economic practice, but instead a project aiming to 'decentralize' and thus *reorganize* society more broadly. As a 'community', Bitcoiners in Tel Aviv protested the inherited logic of high modernism, which held that multiplicities and the individuals of which they were composed pertained to two levels of abstraction. In *Community and Civil Society*, Ferdinand Tönnies (2001[1887]) famously constructed a negative relationship between these two levels of abstraction, which he respectively called *Gemeinschaft* and *Gesellschaft*. The former represented a mode of reciprocity characterized by interpersonal immersion, while the latter represented superimposed societal arrangements. Both these modes of mediation, Tönnies argued, maintained a balance between unity and diversity, but *Gemeinschaft* did that by appealing to predisposed intimate connectivity, while *Gesellschaft* framed relations structurally through modes of repetition and differentiation. *Gemeinschaft* was thus imagined as organically created by – or naturally emergent from – inherited coresidential histories, whereas *Gesellschaft* was imagined as a mechanical framework that depends on individual docility at a mass scale (Weber 1921).

Embassy associates sought to challenge this very binary opposition through the establishment of a 'trustless' economic infrastructure. Empirically, this system was supposed to provide greater personal and collective freedoms. It was *personal* in the sense that Bitcoin fortified claims concerning one's own responsibility over one's life, while securing financial independence. And it was *collective* in the sense that, as a self-identifying group, the Israeli Bitcoin community was able to build itself around the libertarian values that Bitcoin embodied, especially the rejection of coercive methods in the institution of collective discipline. Freedom at a mass scale literally depended on the ability of any individual to self-encapsulate and preserve his or her financial autonomy. Individualization facilitated escape from both implicit and explicit societal contracts, but the possibility of escape was also contingent on the ongoing production of *consensus at a global scale on the blockchain.* This refracted the collective into the many individual elements of which it was composed, while simultaneously, and to an extent paradoxically, strengthening the overall boundaries as well as the authority of that collective.

Actively detaching economic power from the oversight of gatekeepers and regulatory bodies, Embassy associates empirically fused *Gemeinschaft* and *Gesellschaft* into a single – and declaratively revisionist – political-economic structure. They relied on Bitcoin to create what they believed was a trustful community of equal peers, whose collaboration emphasized voluntarism, mutual respect and intimate familiarity. But they also highlighted *trustless* economic reciprocity at a societal scale, effectively strengthening individual economic interests at the expense of collective mediation and overarching macroeconomic policies. In this way they generated a kind of holistic fragmentation – or fragmented holism, if you will – a cohesion curiously premised on refraction, which in turn is seen to consolidate the whole.

Given that most community members were living in Tel Aviv or nearby – which meant using NIS in everyday life, (mostly) working in 'centralized' jobs and being subjected to the sovereignty of the law – their activities in the Embassy situated them quite tangibly in between distinct economic and social orders. Not only was it impossible to live exclusively on bitcoin, even the few Ambassadors who worked for companies that agreed to pay them in bitcoin – most often these were companies building decentralized infrastructures in the emergent DeFi sector – had to exchange their crypto for fiat to be able to pay rent and buy groceries at the supermarket. Rather than practising decentralization and trustless sociality *stricto senso*, Embassy members thereby continuously transgressed across centralized and decentralized modes of economic cooperation, idioms of trustful and trustless sociality, and tropes of stability as much as of revolution. They even constantly moved between physical spaces that were identified with two systemic imaginaries. As this in-betweenness materialized at the Embassy (and a few other venues in Tel Aviv – e.g. Shemesh's new business, tech accelerator and incubator programmes, hackathons, etc.) – it generated a spatiotemporal experience of *synchronicity* between oppositions. Nissim, a known Romantic, saw it this way:

> For lack of choice, you must live in both these worlds [centralized and decentralized]. We are in a transition period. Of course, the idea is to live in the New

> World [of unmediated P2P transactions]; this is clear and bright. But everyday life dictates the rhythm of this transition. You intuitively identify the objectives you want to advance and act on them. It's a blind spot, but it is simultaneously also very dynamic. *You aim for a target, but you act as if it's not there.* The inner feeling itself creates the way [forward]. You just need to listen to it. It is true for today that we are in the middle [between these worlds] but when the idea [of Bitcoin] matures then freedom of action, imagination and everything else will be synchronized with the truth. And when the truth is active, my friend, growth is unstoppable, and its results are immense.

Poetic as usual, Nissim describes 'the blind' spot in the middle as abounding – in fact exploding – with potentiality. The New Economy is here imagined as having already existed in an embryonic state even *before* the apocalyptic event horizon of a devastating economic meltdown had happened, on which I will elaborate in the next chapter; an event most Ambassadors saw as necessary to replace the fractional reserve banking industry with a decentralized system. The Embassy could in that sense constitute a 'middle' space where community members would celebrate a vision of the New Economy while effectively still being subject to the 'centralized' social hierarchies of the dominant economic order. As I will now discuss, this fusion, including the distinct sense of freedom it represented, could only be achieved under the liminal conditions that defined activities at the Embassy.

The Liminoid

Nissim's notion of a 'middle' ground coincides with what Victor Turner had called 'a liminal space' (Turner 1969); that is, a defined environment wherein normative categories are temporarily suspended in order to enable some kind of social transition between personal or collective realities. A liminal space, for example, can be the epicentre of a pilgrimage site, where pilgrims temporarily become equal despite their divergent life histories and social background, united by their devotion to a saint, a prophet or a divine entity. The liminal character of the Embassy consisted in the attempt to build a New Economy there, meaning that it structurally allowed Ambassadors to continuously shift between mediated and 'frictionless' modes of P2P exchange. In fact, to remain with Turner – the grand priest of liminality as an analytic concept in modern anthropology (Kapferer 2024) – the Embassy can be identified as belonging to a special kind of liminality, which Turner (1974: 85–86; cf. Kapferer 2024: 14) called 'the liminoid':

> Liminal phenomena are centrally integrated into the total social process, forming with all its other aspects a complete whole . . . Liminoid phenomena develop

> apart from the central economic and political processes, along the margins, in the interfaces and interstices of central and servicing institutions, they are plural, fragmentary, and experimental in character . . . Liminoid phenomena tend to be more idiosyncratic or quirky [than liminal phenomena], to be generated by specific named individuals and in particular groups, 'schools', circles, and coteries . . . Liminoid phenomena . . . are [therefore] often parts of social critiques or even revolutionary manifestoes . . . [thus] exposing the injustices, inefficiencies, and immoralities of the mainstream economic and political structures . . . The liminoid is more like a commodity, indeed, often *is* a commodity, which one selects and pays for, than the liminal, which elicits loyalty and is bound up with one's membership or desired membership in some highly corporate group. One works at the liminal, one plays with the liminoid. [Emphasis in original]

For example, Turner (ibid.) argues that marketing and trading are more liminal areas of social life than production. This is also evident in the advertising industry and the whole attention economy, as a concept referring to the ritualization of industrial leisure. Consumerism, especially, is located somewhere in between ordinary work schedules – where social regulations or rules dictates and organizes your time, including obligations associated with private life, family, kinship, etc. – and the rituals of what Turner calls 'archaic' societies. Based on this debate, he contrasts liminal and liminoid phenomena, referring to the liminal as something that represents collective cycles of Big Otherness; that is, circles much wider than those of individual destinies. Commemorations enacted in liminal spaces are often seen as near-natural breaks in 'the flow of natural or sociocultural processes' (ibid.: 44). Liminoid phenomena, on the other hand, are not cyclical and unavoidable but linear and continuously changing (see Turner 1974). They are products of ingenious individuals – not collective arrangements – who model new social realities rather than mirror traditional values and collective ritual obligations. Revolutions, in other words, are made in liminoid spaces, which people carve within and through liminal social conditions (e.g. Hitler's liminoid rise to power in the midst of a liminal time of economic and political chaos).

The structural comparison with Bitcoin activism is self-evident. Satoshi had made use of the freedom they gained in the liminality of Cypherpunk forums to capture certain themes of social and psychological importance, which they then spread widely. Satoshi crafted a space for debating – and, according to the White Paper, also resolving pragmatically – such burning societal problems as widespread indebtedness, the corrupting links between political power and the flow of capital, and the utopian promise of machinic objectivity. These issues appealed to many, as the expansion of blockchain indicates, albeit not to everyone. The liminoid space Satoshi created nonetheless gained enough traction and momentum to inspire a global movement that from its inception claimed to have found the 'solution' to these intricacies through practices of decentralization and trustlessness. This method works at the level of the global movement as much as at the level of the community.

A liminoid middle ground contains here the empirical contradiction existing between a criticism of capitalism that local Bitcoiners expressed – most notably as this related to the utter disdain towards the banking system – and the fact that they also extended and perfected laissez-faire moral and economic principles regarding privacy, self-rule and the contribution of decentralized financial markets to the constitution of egalitarian social realities. Embassy associates inhabited a unique space between distinct ideologies, organizational principles, cultural imaginaries and cosmological theories. On one hand, they applied the inherited wisdom of twentieth-century collective organizational metaphors, which associated political change with institutions and 'communities'. On the other hand, they celebrated the twenty-first-century tropes of subjectivity, self-empowerment and distrust of institutions, all of which are premised on the transfer of power from authorities to citizens, the weakening of traditional truth claims and the emergent category of post-national 'global citizenship'. Stressing the latter option, interlocutors at the Embassy regularly argued that Bitcoin mass adoption would engender new forms of financial and cultural intimacies that could in turn make the former *obsolete*.

The Embassy thereby empirically *blended* tropes of 'centralization' and 'decentralization' into a single frame of reference. Consider, for example, the fact that bitcoin market capitalization itself was then and still is pervaded by 'centralized' hierarchies (Baldwin 2018; Schneider 2019; but see Butler 2022). At the time I conducted fieldwork, about 3 per cent of existing Bitcoin accounts controlled about 90 per cent of the coin supply, while several industrial mining corporations monopolized most of the generation and distribution of coins.[1] From a sociodemographic perspective, Embassy associates embodied another kind of centralized hierarchy; many of them, although certainly not all, were from middle- or upper-middle-class backgrounds, often with available family wealth or other securities that enabled them to invest in Bitcoin in the first place, and most had university degrees and normative work histories, all of which safeguarded their way out should the Bitcoin project one day fail.[2]

Ambassadors were aware of these contradictions. Regarding centralization on the blockchain they simply said that through time increased amounts of wealth would be distributed, and that in any case the money of small holders was always fully and absolutely under owners' control. They were not apologetic about their middle-class backgrounds – recognizing that they were able to get into Bitcoin early partly because of their sociodemographic positioning – but insisted that no prior education, technical knowledge, cosmopolitan tendencies or even ideological commitment was necessary to join the community. The fact that there was no formal gatekeeping – i.e. anybody around the world could buy bitcoin at any given moment, even a few shekels' worth – was used to justify the need to proselytize it to the masses. Embassy members *celebrated* the possibilities associated with dwelling in such liminal space because they experienced it as an inherently 'free' social, economic and spatiotemporal milieu. It is therefore now time to analyse the recurrent appeal of such idioms as liberty and/or freedom, which were often mobilized discursively at the Embassy to sustain its communitarian zeitgeist.

Liberté

In the recorded interview Yaron had done several years before I arrived at the Embassy, which I quoted in the Introduction, he described the adoption of Bitcoin as the only way people could liberate themselves from arbitrary scrutiny occasionally enacted by the Establishment. For him, the notion of popular liberty was mutually exclusive to the notion of centralized control, which he identified with the almighty 'sovereign'. He said:

> Bitcoin will destroy the Sovereign. There is no need for a Sovereign. Why do we need a Sovereign these days? Because it regulates the money, it keeps us safe, and so on . . . it hasn't got to do with anything [in the contemporary world]. Once there used to be carrier pigeons, Indian campfires, then there was the national post office, and today we have the internet. Everything changes. *The world wants Liberté – freedom (khofesh).* Freedom is to be able to decide if I drink Coke or coffee, or if I eat meat or I am vegetarian, [but] freedom also means that I decide whether I use a crazy Ponzi currency, a pyramid scheme [which is] like sand across the beach, and which is called 'the dollar', or [choosing instead] a currency that humanity has decided upon [its creation] . . . which is called Bitcoin. I will choose which currency I want to use to pay or invest, but more than that, Bitcoin is real estate, it's an amazing ore unlike any other, it is a language, it's much more than a currency.

Yaron presented Liberté as an *ethical contingency*. For him, the whole point of the Bitcoin project was to *liberate people*, not only from dependency on 'centralized' institutions such as banks, as Nissim would have it, but from oppression at large. Bitcoin mass adoption would turn individuals into autonomous socioeconomic units that could engage at will in P2P relations with all the other adopters. Simultaneously, it would consolidate 'communities', which could set their own economic rules because they would no longer be subject to the control, surveillance and scrutiny of the Sovereign. Distributing the economic power of mainstream stakeholders had thus become a task that required the empirical growth of autonomous citizens operating in economic and social spheres with little regulation from above.

Philosopher Isaiah Berlin (1958) memorably distinguished between positive and negative forms of liberty, the former experienced as the freedom *to* establish concrete motifs, goals and values, and the latter experienced as freedom *from* coercion. Negative freedom is deterministic in the sense that it establishes walls that could protect the autonomy of a subject, whether it be an individual, a group, a collective ethos (e.g. the nation), etc. Negative freedom territorializes subjects of action by distancing authoritative forces that could limit the ability to act. Positive freedom, on the other hand, is about idiosyncratic self-fulfilment in its broadest sense, which can be tolerant towards competing notions of liberty as much as it can amount to the uncritical negation of all other types of freedom. In both cases, Liberté is methodically related to issues of control and power; when stripped of its mystique and understood instead as a form of continuous negotiation of boundaries, the pursuit of freedom requires self-criticism and the ability to distinguish between positive and negative forms of liberation.

Although interlocutors at the Embassy did not usually make this differentiation, they did associate freedom with the ability to act in preferred ways, on one hand, and with the right to protect themselves from the 'Sovereign' on the other. The foundational aspect of both these forms of freedom was the ability to always 'verify' that blockchain automatic operations were working properly. Verification in this sense is a form of *power* derived from the distributed design of the network. Freedom could be guaranteed only under conditions wherein every peer could single-handedly verify at a 100 per cent certainty that others have somehow manipulate the blockchain. As Bloom presented this in an interview:

> You know, there are two [libertarian] schools in Bitcoin: one says, 'don't trust, verify!' and the other says, 'trust, but verify!' I really connect more with the second approach, because if you can't trust anything or anybody you won't be able to advance in life. But wherever you *can* verify [people's motivations, declarations and intentions], you *should* verify.

Both suspicion and verification were key symbols for libertarian activists already in the Cypherpunk years. Suspicion would expose traps (May 1992), and firsthand verification would prevent intended or accidental failures. Trusting any 'third party', especially State authorities, was thereby seen as deferring verification responsibilities to others, who could not be trusted in the first place. The obsoletion of third-party mediators in favour of a universal P2P structure – from its origins in Cypherpunk philosophy to the pragmatism of Bitcoin – in a sense compelled people to believe that someone would surely try to swindle them at some point (Swartz 2022; Shapiro 2025). It was necessary to 'verify', then, not only whether transactions on the blockchain had indeed been sent and received, but also that the trust put in people was being fairly reciprocated; or at the very least that it had not been exploited. In my conversations with Ambassadors who had obtained the relevant technical know-how, such as Bloom, they tended to describe verification as a proxy of self-reliance and personal autonomy, the epitome of practical liberation from 'centralized' dependency on third parties in the banking system.

Some Embassy members nonetheless understood liberty less as a pragmatic issue and more in the sense of the ability to develop oneself as a person. Nissim, for example, who did not have much technical expertise, experienced the ability of being one's own bank as primarily *spiritual.* As he saw it, Bitcoin adoption could teach people how to recognize their own limits, and, as this related to freedom, it would direct people in the path to achieving higher states of consciousness by forcing them to take responsibility over their actions and choices.

The liminoid character of the Embassy ultimately enabled celebrating both these aspects of personal liberation – pragmatic and spiritual – in ways that were not entirely iconoclastic, but neither were they self-righteous nor conciliatory. The middle ground connected the ethereality of exchange relations in cyberspace with a tangible materiality, while linking the local community with the global one, especially as the Embassy became a place that any Bitcoiner who happened to reach Tel Aviv – Israeli or not – *had to* visit. Liberation here emerges within concrete spatial boundaries. The Embassy was a stage from which Yaron, Nissim, Bloom and their fellow Ambassadors could disperse ideas about both these forms of personal liberation because its liminal positionality in the middle enabled them to freely cross between decentralized and centralized economic orders.

This movement also constituted a measure of timelessness, although not precisely stagnation, wherein people could reject the hierarchical 'past' of the Old Economy long before their aspirations for more egalitarian futures in a Bitcoin-friendly world could be realized. Dwelling in the middle ground thus also meant living to some extent in the present tense, a sort of prolonged or elastic present, which from a theoretical point of view is one of the most crucial elements of liminality (Turner 1969). True believers at the Embassy – Nissim being a good example – perceived this prolonged present as a waiting period leading towards a utopian future, as I will further discuss in Chapter 5. The types of freedom that Bitcoin promised were contingent in that sense on the instantiation of financial crisis, to which I now turn.

Crisis

Maximalist Ambassadors constantly argued that a major economic crisis was imminent. Such crisis, according to this narrative, would change society profoundly, especially if it were to take a colossal form reiterating the 2008 subprime crash, and bringing down the banking industry. Since their main objective was to establish a P2P-dominant economy, crisis was thus perceived positively as a watershed moment in history and a *necessary* step for change. Yoav and Avner, who self-identified as 'diehard' Bitcoin supporters, explained this issue vividly in a conversation we once had during a rainy evening over coffee and falafel:

YOAV:
I think that there is no chance that Bitcoin will succeed without the other side breaking.

AVNER:
If the financial system breaks down, people will have no other choice. They will have to either go back to sea shells or they will use Bitcoin.

YOAV:
More than that – without a crisis in the current financial system, Bitcoin cannot succeed. Adjusting Bitcoin to the current system will not work; it's like water and oil.

AVNER:
I do not think that there is a question of whether the banking system will collapse, it's only a question of *when* this will happen. You can ventilate [i.e. 'resuscitate'] the economy artificially only until a certain moment. When and where it will happen, if it will happen gradually or in one blow, or if [it happens] first in the US and later elsewhere, nobody knows.

YOAV:
I think we are still facing another stage of centralization [before the crash]. Whenever existing ruling institutions encounter obstacles, the solution is to centralize. [In] all of the recent big crises, resolution depended on centralized institutions. For example, the solution [for inflation] in the Great Depression was the [establishment of the] Federal Reserve. During the Depression, the centralizing act was to say, 'Bring me all the gold.' The next act, in 1971 [by the Nixon administration], was to cancel the gold standard. This is even more centralistic, because it keeps the control over the money in [the government's] hands. And in 2008, the act of centralization was to merge several banks together so they would be too big to fail. In every crisis we have seen everything boiling down to larger and larger acts of centralization. So, for sure there will be another crisis followed by a centralistic growth, which is a form of artificial resuscitation, and only then the fall will come.

MATAN:
You are talking about a global catastrophe. People will lose everything.

YOAV:
Yes. In 2008 we were on the verge of such a global catastrophe.

AVNER:
But let me ask you [plural] a simple question – what will happen when people stop believing in the shekel?

MATAN:
Yes, good question, I guess they will buy dollars . . .

YOAV:
Well, that is what happened in Israel in 1984 with the inflation.

AVNER:
Yes, and it keeps happening; just recently it happened in Venezuela. Their currency lost its value, and at some stage it will happen everywhere in the world. The governmental coins will get out of control – something will happen, I don't even know what, and then people won't have a choice anymore, they'll have to either use currencies of other states or move to digital coins.

MATAN:
And how will the value of Bitcoin be determined in such a world?

YOAV:
I think it's very simple. Let's think of an enclosed world, an island, for example. If you put there 100 ounces of gold, and inside the island there is a set amount of goods and a set number of services, so one is divided by the other. This is the pricing. You add more goods, the more value you have. The value grows relative to the growth of commodities and products . . . But of course, all of this will come after a crisis strikes; the powerful will not give up their power so easily.

Yoav and Avner relished the idea of an impending crisis, or at the very least they did not think that people should prevent such crisis if it came. They were not, however, naïve with respect to its destructive effects. They were used to feeling some measure of distress when facing boom-and-bust cycles and thus acknowledged that a major crisis could involve anxiety. I already described Avner's FUD (fear, uncertainty and doubt) in Chapter 3 as a reaction to the volatility of bitcoin, whose periodic value crashes or a hostile regulatory environment have threatened numerous times to break any maximalist's determination to HODL. Avner was not an exception. At the end of 2017, for example, when bitcoin was at an all-time high of nearly US$20,000 and many people were feeling elated, Yaron came into the Embassy with a gloomy face and claimed that 2018 would be 'a very long Bitcoin winter'. He was right. Bitcoin fell sharply in the subsequent months, returning to its pre-goldrush values of around US$5–6,000 per unit, invoking fears even among true believers. From the perspective of maximalists and HODLERS such fears were an ongoing reality: If Bitcoin loses its value before the collapse of the banks, none of the freedoms it was supposed to guarantee will ever be attainable.

Interlocutors in Tel Aviv were thus aware of the difficulties they would have to endure until the crisis materializes, and they recognized the potentially devastating results of such crisis for the global economy. Yet, perceiving crisis as the only feasible remedy to the ills of contemporary capitalism – especially the uneven concentration of wealth and the abuse of power that Embassy members associated with the Sovereign – it has been constructed as a necessary, albeit agonizing step, on the unpaved road to ethical self-transformation (but see Kapferer 2010). Ambassadors often stated that they held Bitcoin to secure their 'pension' – understood vaguely as a post-crisis paradise – thus betting on an apocalyptic version of the future as a financial exit plan (see also Swartz 2018 and Swartz 2021).

Importantly, these views are directly opposed to a rational-pragmatist perception of crisis, which is supported by risk science modalities aimed at maximizing safety (Shapiro and Skartveit 2025; cf. Beck and Kewell 2014). This latter approach holds that societies must collectively invest resources in systems that could *foresee and hinder* technological breakdowns, moral panic or natural disasters. Defying this logic, most Ambassadors saw crisis as *essential* to any form of deliverance or reward that Bitcoin could deliver, both in terms of acquiring individual liberty *and* building a collaborative community. I will further elaborate this point in the next chapter when analysing millenarian attitudes at the Embassy. For now, suffice mentioning that this theory of crisis was so commonsensical that it was hardly ever challenged during my fieldwork. Alas, this changed unexpectedly when Satoshi Nakamoto suddenly stepped into the Embassy.

Meeting Satoshi

In 2019, a group of entrepreneurs organized a major cryptocurrency conference in Tel Aviv with the participation of some of the most prominent thinkers, technologists, investors, academics and entrepreneurs in the global cryptocurrency scene. One of those who participated was a veteran computer scientist whom I will call Brian. Known due to his affiliation with the Cypherpunk movement in the 1990s, Brian was a Bitcoin early adopter, who, some claimed, could have been involved in writing and reviewing Satoshi's original White Paper. Many Bitcoiners across the world in fact believe that Brian *was* Satoshi Nakamoto, given his scientific reputation as a programmer and years of recorded techno-libertarian political activism. Dani Bloom, who was one of the speakers at the conference, therefore invited Brian to the Embassy for an open chat with Embassy staff, and they both arrived there in the early evening.

Since it was an impromptu event, only about twenty Ambassadors took part in the conversation. We all sat in a circle, Brian looking embarrassed by the attention. After a short exchange of witty but meaningless jokes, Shlomit finally broke the ice, asking, 'So, are you friends with Satoshi?' We all laughed and Shlomit then asked Brian why he had decided to research cryptocurrency protocols. Brian nodded. He said that his lasting support for Bitcoin was the result of his engagement with Ayn Rand's *Atlas Shrugged*, which he described as 'a manual teaching how you can protect yourself from the government'. He then singled out Tim May's techno-libertarian politics as a source of inspiration. Shlomit followed up with a question on the ties between Bitcoin and the hegemonic fiat economy. Brian answered:

> I am a fan of local exchange outside the big centralized exchanges, so if you are taking the *lightning network*[3] that you are doing, and start doing business among yourselves and establish supply chains, start paying each other just in the local community, off-chain or on-chain, it doesn't matter, whichever layer works best for you, if you make a whole cycle, you never have to go through exchanges. It's less convenient that way . . .

'Why is that so?' someone interrupted, and Brian replied:

> Well, it's more convenient to just deposit your money in the bank and . . . you don't have to worry about these specific cycles. But that makes you dependent on a central entity. So, in order not to be dependent on a centralized entity like exchanges and banks you are going to have to create these cycles [that protect] monetary calculation.

Bloom explained that the Ambassadors were trying to do precisely that by sending each other fragments of bitcoin through the lightning network; for example, to repay a person who ordered food for everyone. Bloom nonetheless admitted that such exchange was far from encompassing 'the whole supply chain in the economy'. 'We just need the collapse of the Old Economy', Inbar threw into the air. Bloom replied, 'This is not necessary, but it could help'. Although Brian was reserved and calculated, the conversation flowed well from that moment on. Brian shared his opinions about such issues as smart contracts, the resilience of the Bitcoin network and the necessity to establish an internet infrastructure independent from governmental control. It was all very intimate and thrilling, especially as everyone had in the back of their heads a slight hope – an intuitive certainty, in fact – that Brian was indeed Satoshi.

Things, however, went slightly off track when Brian began expressing opinions that Embassy members – especially those who embraced Bitcoin maximalism – found hard to process. Asked whether he was surprised to see Bitcoin develop the way it had, Brian responded that it was for him 'something very abstract', and that he did not have an 'emotional response' to the process of value acquisition in Bitcoin. To smooth the shock that Brian could see on people's faces, he added, 'But seeing it happening among the people that sit in this room is already something very emotional for me.' Someone then asked Brian if he was not afraid that the entire project would be hijacked by 'a CEO type'; that is, would it increasingly tilt towards corporatization, as with the mining companies and cryptocurrency exchange outlets. Brian maintained a poker face, thought for a second or two, and said:

> That's a possibility. That is certainly a threat. But that just decreases the value [of Bitcoin], because the main values are the censorship resistance and global seamlessness, and general trust minimization, otherwise just use the banks. I am not *that* anti-bank as some people in this community are; you know, they are useful, they work reasonably well for what they do, [although] they are getting worse [because] they are getting more censorship and stuff. But you know, there is no magic to crypto; [its utility] comes from trust minimization and censorship [resistance], whereas a lot of people just think of it in magical terms, as, 'Oh well, it's crypto, it's got to be good; even if we destroy [its decentralized characteristics] and it's actually centrally controlled [by the banks], we'll still call it crypto.' And they are still working on it now. The banks are going to work better than that; you can't beat the banks.

Brian seemed to have deliberately phrased these ideas vaguely. On one hand, he attributed the hegemonic appropriation of the blockchain to 'magical thinking', suggesting irrationality or mysticism, but on the other hand he claimed that the banks acted *rationally and efficiently*. Brian thus acknowledged the inevitability of some measure of corporatization in the cryptocurrency industry, which simply reflected the infinite power of established centralized institutions that could not be 'beaten'. This answer was surprising because it presented a pessimistic (or realistic?) view with regard to one of the most important aspects of the Bitcoin ideological imaginary: that all 'shitcoins' would crash with the fractional-reserve system and the banks, erasing debts and thus making Bitcoin a hegemonic currency. After a moment of embarrassment, the conversation moved to other issues, as Bloom asked some of the Ambassadors to tell Brian how they got into Bitcoin. Nissim traced his maximalist view of it as a world-making device; Brian remained composed, merely nodding here and there, his face sealed. He did not react further. Someone then asked him about the hyper-use of the term 'community' in the world of Bitcoin:

> I think it's an often-abused term. I think of 'community' as people that communicate with each other in a kind of peer-to-peer fashion, so if you are watching TV and somebody is talking one-way that's not a community, that's just you observing someone telling you something. So, community is people who talk to each other but that's not a very socially skilled thing, that's a very small thing, so to say that there is a 'Bitcoin Community' is a real abuse. [In fact], there's a ton of Bitcoin communities – you guys have a really good Bitcoin community. There's lots of other Bitcoin communities, and hopefully on core issues we see eye to eye but we're not actually all talking to each other, so . . .

Bloom disagreed, bringing up as an example the productive communication taking place between Bitcoiners online. 'Technology does make it [community] possible', he argued. 'I mean, we have the Facebook community page in Israel, and there are several thousand people there who haven't necessarily met each other, but some did, and they are all talking to each other.' Brian was amused. He looked straight at Bloom and said, 'Well, there are [still] a lot of silent people who are largely [only] listening . . .'. Some of those present nevertheless attempted to demonstrate the kind of communitarian localism Bloom was trying to convey, speaking, for example, about the slang words invented within the community (such as 'tahini', 'iron' and 'Harry-Pottering'; see Chapter 2).

Brian smiled courteously, but likely remained unconvinced. A few seconds of silence were a sign that the conversation was ending. 'Before we close this', Ronen whispered, 'one more thing. In the community we believe that Bitcoin has a similarity to the honey badger, and we usually open and end each of our meetings with the Honey Badger Dance . . .' Bloom picked up from there:

> Have you heard of this analogy, Brian? It is based on the idea that the honey badger is a fierce animal that can take whatever you throw at it . . . and Bitcoin is very similar, because you know, Bitcoin had so many ups and downs . . . but it just keeps moving on and on and on. This is a global thing, not just us. And here in the Israeli community one thing we like to do is to dance to the 'Honey Badger Song' at the end of formal meetings, so I suggest we all do it now and later you can stay around for more informal conversations with people.

With that, we stood up still in a circle and performed the quirky up-and-down movements of the 'Honey Badger Song'; waving our hands at the side of the body with knees bent, forcefully slapping the air. Brian performed it like everyone else. Nobody said a word as we shook our bodies in front of each other. Only incredulous laughter would occasionally cut through the silence. The 'dance' lasted for about a minute, ending with a wild standing ovation.

Inbar then handed Brian a T-shirt with a logo of the honey badger, which he was delighted to accept. 'It's an important party, you know', Bloom told Brian, referring to the Ten-Year Party for which the T-shirts had been printed (see next chapter), 'because it's been ten years since you released the Genesis Block. . .' Brian grinned, neither confirming nor denying.

The 'formal' meeting thus ended with a *Fight Club*-esque moment of revolutionary companionship. Brian remained at the Embassy for a while. He played chess with Bloom and others, drank a beer or two and occasionally engaged in private conversations with Embassy members. Whether he was Satoshi or not, it looked like he was having fun.

Bitcoin Realism

A sense of discomfort still lingered at the Embassy a while later. It had resulted from the gap between Ambassadors' expectation that their views would gain Brian's explicit support, and the reality that this expectation went unfulfilled. Instead, Brian developed a nuanced critique of these positions, especially their collectivist aspects. Rather than supporting the establishment of a new society Brian demystified Bitcoin's utopian capacity, arguing that nothing in the world would change even if Bitcoin grew further. He seemed to agree with the Ambassadors that the banking industry and the government are forces to be wary of, but he also claimed that banks do their job well and might suit some people. He indicated that a totalizing destruction occurs seldom, and consequently rejected the possibility of substituting the Old Economy with the New. Instead, he argued that the tension between centralized and decentralized institutions in most societies would probably remain as it exists today, wherein 'decentralists' must continually find new ways to dodge centralized control and avert censorship in an eternal cat-and-mouse game.

Brian thereby tacitly rejected the romantic notions some Embassy members presented to him. Instead, he defended only the values he saw as essential for the perpetuation of an incipient Bitcoin revolution: (1) 'censorship resistance'; (2) 'global seamlessness'; and (3) 'trust minimization'. Brian thus promoted a rebellion without end, one that required *determination.* Proponents of iconoclastic revolts, as Martin Holbraad (2014) argued convincingly, often sustain the 'revolution' in a fervent ontological state that is continuously reaffirmed, no matter if the objectives have been met or become irrelevant due to the realpolitik of everyday life. Dealing with the Cuban Revolution, Holbraad (ibid.) deconstructs the contradiction between people's dissatisfaction with the realities that their revolution has wrought and their passionate belief in the basic values of that same revolution. In a memorable passage, Holbraad (ibid.: 383) thus argues that 'the object of everyday discontent is by definition something other than what the revolution takes itself to be, so criticism and dejection, however incessant and growing, leaves the revolution proper [i.e. the revolution that demands the people's loyalty] strictly speaking untouched.'

Not only did Brian endorse this kind of ongoing struggle, but he also rejected the collective existence of an ideologically motivated 'global community', which until that point most Embassy associates had accepted uncritically. While encouraging his audience to develop grassroots economic networks, he also claimed that they would not be able to demolish macroeconomic policies. He even argued that nation states would remain a crucial societal regulatory factor – especially on issues 'like borders, security and military power', as well as the provision of critical infrastructure. Although he did not say so explicitly, Brian thereby negated the expectation for apocalyptic crisis and purification, after which only the faithful would thrive. That was so, first, because he did not seem to care much about cosmo-historical or other eschatological narratives – on which I elaborate in the next chapter – and second, because he believed that the 'system' was too strong to crack anyway. These views did not completely disavow the idea of an 'alternative' system, of course, but they realistically recognized the inability – or extreme difficulty – to reinstate an all-encompassing technological utopia.

Instead, Brian focused on the pursuit of one's own interests through economic independence. His suggestion consisted of the unwitting *acceptance* of big government and 'centralized' control apparatuses, alongside invigorating economic relationships in generic communities. He did not see a meltdown in the sense imagined by those who supported the substitution theory; that is, the idea that the Old Economy would gradually give way to the New Economy, culminating in implosion and followed by mass adoption of cryptographic money. Some of the Ambassadors shifted uneasily in their chairs as Brian claimed that even in the New Economy banks might still appeal to those who do not worry about centralization and censorship. No longer a temporary transition period between the tropes of 'Old' and 'New' Economies, Brian described an eternal struggle with authorities, banks and even the sprawling DeFi crypto market. It was an approach that framed Bitcoin as a proxy for resistance to censorship of any kind, a life dedicated to negation – which was in fact a permanent and ongoing revolution in the Marxist sense, only attributed to individual struggle and personal economic encapsulation rather than 'community' as a political or economic factor. This kind of ongoing resistance would never end, Brian tacitly hinted, because it could never fulfil its final objectives.

Embassy associates found this position difficult to accept because it forced them to revise their views on the attainability of collective forms of freedom. Most of the Ambassadors admitted that preserving their freedom of action also required self-discipline and training (Turner 1974; see also Laidlaw 2013). But when Brian described the grit of anarchist resistance he also put on the table the recognition that, as general concepts, freedom and liberty would not simply prevail; rather the contrary, it had to be reinforced and situated in concrete power relations, which also had to be carved out and defended *all the time*.

This critique contained a barely concealed contempt for the kind of collectivist Liberté that Bitcoiners at the Embassy held dear, as it subtly dismissed the very possibility of reaching consensus. It also concretely disowned the idea that crisis is an essential step for the triumph of Bitcoin, including the aspiration for a totalizing revolution that will replace the fractional reserve banking system once and for all. Instead, Brian offered to mobilize suspicion (and self-verification) as a way of life. This brutally realistic meeting thus exposed the fragility of decentralization as a political mechanism, while indirectly undermining the sense of communitarian solidarity among Embassy associates.

This also reflected on Embassy members' ideas of individual autonomy. Double-checking of algorithms, even double-checking as *a metaphor for independence,* was after all dependant on one's own technical knowhow, as it tacitly assumed that only firsthand knowledge could be fully trusted when such issues as privacy and money were at stake. In that sense, Brian's ideas not only revealed that a collective form of decentralized freedom might be a myth, but it also suggested that individualism in Bitcoin required a radical break from the mentality of 1970s communards. While communards sought collective sustainability, a requirement to 'verify' assumed that Liberté could only be achieved in relative isolation.

Brian's ideas suggested that interlocutors in Tel Aviv were eventually suspended *between* self-styled polarities, which they sometimes constructed at the mythical level rather than as a reflection of empirical realities. Brian's non-romanticism was an important reminder of some of the consequences of this suspension. It made clear that beyond liberation, voluntarism and decentralization, being in the liminal 'middle' also accentuated the rigidity, resilience and power of the 'centralized' system that Ambassadors wanted to revolutionize. Recognizing that revolution was unlikely, however, would obviate the very passion and moral commitment required for such actions as HODLING. That was the reason, I believe, that people felt embarrassed facing Brian's ideas about a gritty, endless resistance, which effectively precluded the potentiality of a totalizing (or 'final') crisis and a consequent 'liberation' at a massive scale.

Conclusion

In this chapter I claimed that the Bitcoin Embassy in Tel Aviv should not be seen as an ex-territorial space, where state power could be temporarily withheld. Rather the contrary, the Embassy was a space in which centralized and decentralized economic models successfully and consistently blended into each other, thereby forming a single, liminal geographical epicentre. While attempting to liberate themselves *from* the state and its centralized institutions, then, Ambassadors unexpectedly found *liberty to transgress* between the hegemonic political-economic order and its ideal-type decentralized mirror-image. They could do that individually online through trade, of course. But at the time of my fieldwork the Embassy was one of only few places in Israel where they could transgress across these models as an organized collective. This ongoing motion put the community somewhere in the middle between these two schemes.

Such sense of transgression was heightened during the goldrush, as I discussed in Chapter 2, partly because it physically extended community networks at the Embassy into the streets around, while bringing in huge crowds from the outside. In that sense, and for lack of effective legislation on cryptocurrencies in Israel at the time, the Embassy quite literally unified the Old and the New economy under one roof. That period demonstrated that as much as the Embassy could function as a community centre for die-hard believers, it was also a provisory portal through which the masses could join the global Bitcoin movement.[4]

A liminoid space for action, the Embassy paradoxically enabled people to practise decentralized sociality right in the very 'middle' of the Israeli 'centralized' financial system. The fact that the Embassy was located just across the street from the Tel Aviv Stock Exchange distilled this wider sense of middle-grounding; I could not imagine a better way to explicate the subversive potentialities of the liminoid in this context. The middle ground was not only a liminal space for those who dwelled in it ideologically or morally but also a place where brokers from the other side of the street could experiment with the promises and challenges of the New Economy.

The liminality of the Embassy thus reflected the larger-scale context in which it was located; that is, the debt-based fractional-reserve banking system, which encompassed it legally and financially. In 2008–2009, when Bitcoin became operational, the banking industry was amid an earthquake (Faria 2022). Bitcoin emergence in that moment, even if entirely coincidental, situated it within a grand historical superstructure, constituting semantically the idea that it was an intrinsic part of late capitalist economic realities. Bitcoin emerged from within the system it sought to replace, to put this straight, and it gained widespread visibility precisely because this happened in a moment of total meltdown (Faustino, Faria and Marques 2022).

The liminoid character of the Embassy is in that sense at least partly also rooted in the mythical image of Satoshi Nakamoto themself, who identified a fissure in the capitalist system and made something out of it; thereby creating, deliberately or not, a transitional space conducive of subversive economic discourse. Whether Brian was Satoshi or not, the fact that he dedicated time to converse with Ambassadors roughly ten years after the creation of the Genesis Block only accentuated the liminoid quality of the space and its resilience through time, as it still provided the perfect setting for invoking aspirations for a socioeconomic revolution.

The issue with the liminoid, however, is that it must be continuously sustained *as liminal*. It cannot become institutionalized (i.e. defined strictly in terms of work or leisure, or any other binary) because it would then lose its unique characteristics and consequently become banalized. The distinct sensorial forces of the liminal and the liminoid, as is the case with the revolutionary space of the Embassy manifesting the global Bitcoin revolution, are thus intertwined, temporarily, swirling like a hurricane, cutting across and through social domains, or fusing other domains previously perceived as disconnected. The flux of bitcoin value keeps generating its own liminality with different rhythms and intensities, all of which are earmarked by ritual pulsations, on which I elaborate in Chapter 5. It is this form of middle-ground liminality, or indeed a multiplicity of demarcated middle-ground openings (experienced as breaks or delays or holdbacks to the common logic of things), which produced a convincing theory of 'decentralization' and 'distribution' that could be felt as revolutionary (or at the very least as groundbreaking).

'Bitcoin is magic', Nissim told me once. 'It is the rabbit hole from *Alice in Wonderland*. It is the tunnel that leads you away from darkness into the light, from the Old to the New. You just need to imagine an alternative reality.' The 'tunnel', the 'blindspot' and the 'middle', all of which were Nissim's favoured descriptors for the in-betweenness of Bitcoin sociality at large and the interactions at the Embassy more specifically, suggested an intrinsic, ontological connectivity, between old- and new-world imaginaries. Bitcoin sociality, which in the context of Israeli society took place in and around the space of the Embassy in Tel Aviv, enabled passage from one socio-moral order to the other (Handelman 2021). A liminoid middle ground thus pragmatically included paying the rent for the Embassy in fiat *as well as* using a bitcoin wallet to reimburse Ambassadors for expenses they had on different Embassy activities. These included public events that emphasized relational affective dependency among participants, whose prescribed unity depended on their moral rejection of 'third parties'.

Simultaneously subversive and reversive, defying political-economic hierarchies but still dreading the authority of State regulators, Embassy members could experiment with decentralized sociality only because the 'centralized' system tolerated a space in which they could do that. Idiosyncratic and 'quirky', as Victor Turner (1974) described it, the experience of a liminoid middle ground accommodated the juxtaposition of oppositional tropes, imaginaries, idioms and values. The prototypical economic realities that this engagement exposed were dynamic in and of themselves, and thus they transformed attitudes and ideals in accordance with such real-world events as the overvaluation and undervaluation of Bitcoin market capitalization, macroeconomic decisions and the growth of the blockchain industry. Embassy members maintained in that way a sense of communitarian solidary that was based on being able to survive in the middle, embracing a *mode of relationality* that was unique to them and which encompassed their common interest. Sociologist Craig Calhoun identified the constitution of such 'modes' as the essence of any community: 'Community life can be understood as the life people live in dense, multiplex, relatively autonomous networks of social relationship. Community life, thus, is not a place or simply a small-scale population aggregate, *but a mode of relating*, variable in extent' (quoted in Delanty (2018[2003]: 179–80, emphasis mine).

Precisely because they embraced a concrete mode of relating, then, Embassy members could celebrate and promote iconoclastic ideas. Especially after they encountered Brian, regular interactions between community members were more consciously identified with the 'middle ground', whose liminality deterred rather than advanced the arrival of a full-scale revolution. Suspicion and verification would instead become equally important and mutually inclusive with the implementation of Liberté as a form of personal agency that also enabled people to learn about themselves, as spiritually oriented interlocutors such as Nissim saw that. All this was based on the belief that bitcoin was a reliable financial asset that would survive in the far future.

In the next chapter I will explore another critical trait of liminal spaces – their ability to contain and even encourage the creation of myths through ritualized commemoration. I will examine Embassy members' millenarian preoccupation with human destiny and social justice, showing that the semantic boundaries Ambassadors set up between them and the so-called centralized society – as well as the total societal reformation they imagined – should be understood as a coherent cosmology, a spatiotemporal theory of the upcoming decentralized universe they aspired to build.

NOTES

1. This distorts the notion of decentralization envisioned in Satoshi's White Paper, wherein every node/peer could take part in the collective task of transaction verification, mine new bitcoins and circulate them in the network.
2. This said, it is important to recognize that among the group of devoted members were also people from a working-class background, such as Nissim, who worked in the construction industry most of his adult life, and Menashe, who worked as a butcher.
3. The lightning network was developed as an additional layer superimposed on the blockchain, enabling the sending of fragments of bitcoin between peers without having to go through a blockchain node. This minimized transaction fees while also reducing the load on the main network (which could be jammed and slow down in a bull market).
4. As I mentioned in Chapter 2, at the time it was still difficult to purchase bitcoin in Israel for several reasons, so the cash machine at the Embassy had become a literal gateway to bitcoin trading for thousands of new adopters.

CHAPTER 5

DECENTRALIZING THE UNIVERSE

The Ten-Year Party

On 3 January 2019, Israeli Bitcoin supporters gathered at haÔman 17, one of the oldest, most respected and largest nightclubs in Tel Aviv. They were there to commemorate ten years since the mining of the Genesis Block. Bitcoiners across the world frame this 'genesis' as the big bang of an emergent socioeconomically decentralized age that would one day replace the fractional-reserve banking system, eliminating its reliance on inflation and growing debts. As the event was subsidized almost entirely by the IBA, all 1,300 entry tickets were sold in advance. Apart from Embassy personnel, the audience included many IBA members (membership at the time was in the hundreds) and followers of the Israeli Bitcoin Facebook group. The party began with a fireworks display outside the club. Minutes later, inside, Dani Bloom strode onto the stage, raising his hands. He spoke firmly into a microphone that was clipped to his jacket:

> Bitcoiners, listen to me! It is true, what many of you have heard. The 2017 bubble has burst, and as I speak, the bitcoin exchange rate [against the US dollar] keeps falling. Believe me when I say that difficult days are still ahead of us. But if we wish to be prepared, we must first shed our fear. I stand here in front of you, truly fearless. Why? Is it because I believe in something you don't? No! I stand here fearless because I remember! I remember that I am here not because of the path I see before me, but because of the path I have left behind. I remember that for ten years now we have been fighting the bankers . . . for ten years they have been sending clerks to destroy us. And after a decade of wars, I remember that which matters most: We! Are! Still! Here! Tonight, let us send a message to this troll army. Tonight, let us shake this nightclub. Tonight, let us shake these walls of blocks, chains and bits. Let us be heard from the Embassy to the moon! Tonight, let's force them to remember: This is Bitcoin! And we are not afraid!

Bloom's speech recalled a scene from the blockbuster film *The Matrix Reloaded* (2003). Addressing a rapturous crowd in a cavernous, subterranean 'Zion', resistance leader Morpheus affirms his faith in the human spirit, which will defy the machines that had been persecuting the community for the past century. Bloom used this imagery to allude to the regularly drawn contrast among Bitcoin supporters between the open nature of the payment system, and the exclusivist and centralized characteristics they associated with all-powerful banks and national governments. Like Morpheus, Bloom wanted to make a point that would inspire his audience: he alluded that their fearlessness was epic, their power was in their unity, their fight was eternal, and victory was at hand. It seemed he did well, as the audience cheered wildly, excited not only by Bloom's message but also by the atmosphere of exuberance that filled the place. Food stalls offering freshly prepared vegetarian dishes operated throughout the evening, all drinks were on the house and a pair of professional dancers dressed in shining alien-like costumes occasionally passed through the crowd, adding a dark-yet-carnivalesque edge to the party. The electronic club music that rattled the walls enabled a total suspension of reality.

Towards midnight, as the party continued to rage, Nissim collapsed. One of the event's main organizers, he had been in the club since the early hours of the morning, had eaten very little and had already drunk a few beers. Those of us who were nearby rushed over to help, and after Nissim recovered, we all walked out for some fresh air. He vomited, then said he felt much better and wanted to go back into the party, but his daughter Iris, who was also there, insisted he go home. He reluctantly agreed. We chatted a little as we waited for Iris to get the car. Nissim was melancholic. 'I am like Moses overlooking the Promised Land', he said, looking away into the dark night. 'I made sure that everything was in its place and now I am too sick to enjoy it!' He then professed that as shares in Apple were crashing – they had fallen by 10 per cent the day before – the whole fractional-reserve 'loan bubble' would once again burst, paving the way for Bitcoin to emerge stronger than ever before.

It is tempting to interpret such statements as mystical or even religious. In recent years, diverse commentators from academia, finance and the media have indeed begun using terms such as 'financial religion' (Humayun and Belk 2017) or 'religious cult' (Golumbia 2018) to describe the 'quasi-religious zeal' (Dodd 2018: 49) they claimed characterized the Bitcoin movement (Nelms et al. 2018). Commentators argue that supporters themselves speak of their 'belief' in Bitcoin; they engage in ritualized activities (Caradonna 2020; Faustino, Faria and Marques 2022); they relate to Satoshi Nakamoto as a prophet or as a timeless reformer (Humayun and Belk 2018); and they are said to have developed an eschatological perception of blockchain technology, which they characterize as a pathbreaking invention, while often ignoring some of its problems, misgivings and conundrums (Dodd 2018; Faria 2019 and 2021).

Then again, celebrating Bitcoin is different from worshipping it. The fact that Nissim and other Bitcoin maximalists in Israel and beyond find a spiritual dimension in their activities does not mean they perceive Bitcoin as an entity that influences world affairs independently from the people who use it (Cardoso 2024; Shapiro 2022). Rather, this realm of spiritual practice is a murky emotive ground existing between collective and subjective registers, which is dependent on firsthand experiences of transformation. 'Belief' is an outcome of such experiences (see also Luhrmann 2012). To further explicate this assertion, I now turn to discuss religiosity in the Embassy and explain why a faith-oriented understanding of 'religion' fails to encompass the spiritual dimensions of Bitcoin sociality.

Religiosity Revisited

Following Nigel Dodd (2018) and David Golumbia (2018), Faustino, Faria and Marques (2022) argue that the 2008 subprime crash produced an existential sense of 'uncertainty' (see Faria 2021). Consequently, decentralized financial technologies such as Bitcoin were infused with a romantic passion and a sense of enchantment. The magic of blockchain was thus promoted by 'persuasive narratives . . . secular rituals and events, which bring together members of a perceived community, reinforce their cohesion and networking, and produce comfort during moments that are often guided by charismatic preachers and specialists' (Faustino, Faria and Marques 2022: 76). The authors do not ignore the pragmatic utility of the blockchain or its appeal to 'individualists', but at the same time they argue that narrative structures used by blockchain evangelists to mobilize supporters were anchored in a 'quasi-religious' (ibid.: 68–70) mystique.

Bitcoiners in Tel Aviv indeed spoke often about their 'faith' or 'belief' in the power of Bitcoin (*Emunah*, in Hebrew). Rather than focusing on mysticism, however, these beliefs were directed towards two main goals. First, in terms of value, they expected that bitcoin would one day 'fly to the moon', with estimates given between '100,000 dollars' per bitcoin and 'a million'. The second goal was the establishment of a decentralized society anchored in collaborative grassroots economies, which would rely on bitcoin both as money and as a philosophy of living. While some interlocutors did sometimes attach a mystical aura to the realization of these goals, others explicated their 'belief' using mundane or utterly pragmatic terms. In both cases, Embassy associates believed that algorithmic trustlessness was *morally* superior to reliance on fiat money. Yoav and Avner, whom I quoted in Chapter 4, explained that aspect in our conversation. Both grew up in ultra-orthodox families but left the religion and were leading secular lives, and both spoke of 'freedom' (*hofesh*) as the core of their 'belief' in Bitcoin, but both emphasized that this was a very different kind of belief than that which is common in structurally religious settings:

> YOAV:
> Freedom is my ability to do anything that I want as long as I don't hurt anybody else. It's about choice, free choice, the ability to choose and not to be forced to do something I don't want to do or [something] I do not believe in . . . For me freedom is the supreme value. I have no problem with being a Zionist in my culture, and I see nationalism [in Israel] as folklore, but when there is a conflict between values, *freedom will always win over*.
>
> AVNER:
> This means also that there is no doctrine. A rulebook always begins with the 'ten commandments', then it turns into a bible, then the Mishnah, and then the Gemarah [i.e. Jewish Halachic law] . . . It always develops and it ends up limiting your freedom of choice.
>
> YOAV:
> I think that there is a connection between the fact that we undermined authority [of religion], leaving a framework that was slightly restricting, and the fact that we were able to adopt very quickly the idea [of Bitcoin as a proxy of freedom]. I can see how people who are more conservative . . . it's hard for them to digest this idea.
>
> AVNER:
> In religion you believe in something external, in God or the Messiah, and so on, but in Bitcoin *you basically believe in belief itself*; if you want to survive you must believe that there are other people who believe in what *you* believe, so they count on you, and you count on them.
>
> YOAV:
> If someone leaves the orthodox lifestyle because his ideology changed; for example, he stopped believing in God, he will probably remain secular. But if he left it because he wanted to engage in hedonism, he is likely to return to the religion when he faces a difficult moment. I have several [ex-orthodox] friends who became secular because they wanted to hit on girls but ended up repenting and going back to an orthodox lifestyle when they had a crisis . . . It works precisely in the same way with Bitcoin. If you are there just to make a quick profit, you won't last long. You only keep holding if you truly believe it will set you free. Faith helps you endure; this is the real value of the coin. Because what secures [the value of] a coin is trust. And therefore, the true believers – the HODLERS – are the people who give value to the coin.

Antagonism between secularism and religion, like a disparity between belief and doubt or between abstraction and materiality, are relational classificatory distinctions often made by observers rather than by practitioners, whether they adhere to pantheistic, monotheistic or 'secular' lifestyles, rituals and belief systems. It is interesting in that sense that Yoav and Avner avoided this binarism, constructing instead the differentiation between 'belief in something external' and 'belief in belief itself'. When analysing this conversation, I thus thought of Talal Asad's (2020) deconstructionist project, which instead of defining 'religion' seeks to identify the concrete advantage of that category as an explanatory framework for certain lifestyles or sets of practices. Asad writes (2020: 427–28):

> The concept of 'religion' can't be reduced to a universal essence of beliefs and practices because (a) that pair is common to all human life, and (b) as part of different forms of life the grammar of this concept functions differently, expressing and guiding different ways of inhabiting the world. Our craving for abstract definition that [Wittgenstein] deplores is evidenced in the way people insist on using 'religion' as a universal, abstract term – a tendency reinforced, incidentally, both by the policies of secular modern governments and by the relatively recent establishment of university departments of religious studies. The question is not, in other words, whether or not one can ever have a better, or more inclusive, definition of religion (or of the secular, for that matter); the crucial question is how, by whom, and for what purpose a definition is required, and what the implications of that concept are for particular forms of life.

Phrased differently, the desire to classify any faith-based practice as 'religious' is problematic because a pure universal model of 'religion' to which we can compare such practices does not exist in the first place. Any routine that people uphold to 'inhabit the world' spiritually is at least partially religious, while the lifestyles reflected in these routines are not necessarily theistic, and the space of belief in them changes even within the social context into which it is inscribed. Seen in this light, it becomes analytically problematic to trace the origin of ideas, symbols, moral convictions and experiences as explicitly religious. For that reason, I presume, Faustino, Faria and Marques (2022) used the term 'quasi-religious' to describe Bitcoin spirituality. It is thus possible to think of spiritual practices simply as passionate endeavours to live one way rather than another, subject to the establishment of designated social institutions that enable that lifestyle. Bitcoin spiritualism should be understood in that sense as a *social framework* that contrasts some sets of values and convictions with others; a philosophy of living whose distinct materiality boils down to the conviction that the future of economic practice is dependent on both individual and collective resilience vis-à-vis state and corporate apparatuses.

Yoav and Avner claimed that belief in free choice represented the empirical practice of trust, which they juxtaposed to religious dogma (cf. Faria 2022). This declaration of faith is very pragmatic in the sense that if nobody 'believed' that Bitcoin would be valuable, the entire project would not gain traction. A Bitcoin 'true believer' can therefore reject the rules of 'religious' doctrines, while still believing in or trusting the Bitcoin global community and its values. Epistemological convictions underlying Bitcoin sociality here become equivalent to other high-modernist relational theories of exchange, such as the many existing variants of neo-Marxist *and* neoliberal frameworks, whose distinct claims on human nature and societal organization demand large-scale social reconstruction (see also Asad 2018). Ambassadors did not, however, need to establish a clergy and a rulebook for such a reconstruction; as I explained in the previous chapter and as I elaborate below, they simply waited patiently for crisis to materialize.

The acquisition of personal freedom and collective autonomy – that is, the achievement of Liberté from contemporary societal hierarchies – here nonetheless goes beyond economism to reflect a *millenarian sentiment*, which revolves around a presumed inevitable destruction of the hegemonic economic system, along with its core values. By 'millenarian sentiment' I mean simply that most Ambassadors believed in imminent cataclysmic crisis as a prequel to a *golden age*, in which banks and other powerful economic gatekeepers would no longer be able to limit the development of grassroots economies. As opposed to theological millenarianism – which seeks the implementation of celestial order on earth (Cohn 2004) – Bitcoin millenarianism nonetheless promotes a human-induced revolution, after which new forms of earthly collaboration and free choice will flourish. Most Ambassadors thereby did not expect Satoshi Nakamoto to be incarnated as messiah. They did aspire, however, towards a secular reorganization of society and the beginning of a new political-economic millennium.

Bitcoin Millenarianism

The concept of total societal reorganization as a necessary step to redeeming injustice is consonant with the definition of 'millenarianism', a term that originally referred to the belief held by early Christian groups (based on the 'Book of Revelation') that 'after his Second Coming Christ would establish a messianic kingdom on earth and would reign over it for a thousand years before the Last Judgement' (Cohn 2004: 13). At the philosophical core of this revivalist idea is the notion that suffering can be eliminated, and that good will triumph over evil. This idea is not limited to expression within Christianity, however, as Cohn (ibid.: 16) argues:

> There are countless possible ways of imagining the Millennium and the route to it. Millenarian sects and movements have varied in attitude from the most violent

> aggressiveness to the mildest pacifism and from the most ethereal spirituality to the most earthbound materialism. And they have also varied greatly in social composition and social function.

To support this claim, Cohn surveys an extensive list of millenarian belief systems that positioned crisis at the centre of their approach to society, human destiny, divinity and power. A positive view of crisis is essential for such traditions because, much like Bitcoiners today, adherents understood it as unavoidable. In Charismatic Pentecostal circles, for example, revelation of the divine kingdom via apocalypse is part of God's premeditated plan for humanity. Consequently, one prepares for the *aftermath* of the apocalyptic crisis rather than spending energy on futile attempts to prevent it (see Shapiro and Skartveit 2025). Importantly, Cohn (2004) argues, this positive view of crisis has not disappeared with the rise of rationalism and scientific positivism. Early modern and Enlightenment ideas of history as social progress were themselves deeply rooted in the millenarian conviction that the nature of human life can be radically altered, and that a perfect civilization can be designed and realized, sometimes by actively invoking social, economic, political, biological or other forms of crisis. Communities devoted to exceeding the moral and material horizons of their predecessors could thus begin constructing their own worlds, by their own means, to achieve salvation. In his thorough historical analysis of millenarianism in the West, Cohn (ibid.: 15) supplies five reference points to typify a millenarian association of crisis and salvation:

> Millenarian sects or movements always picture salvation as: (a) collective, in the sense that it is to be enjoyed by the faithful as a collectivity *[sic]*; (b) terrestrial, in the sense that it is to be realized on this earth and not in some other-worldly heaven; (c) imminent, in the sense that it is to come both soon and suddenly; (d) total, in the sense that it is [enacted] utterly to transform life on earth, so that the new dispensation will be no mere improvement on the present but perfection itself; and (e) miraculous, in the sense that it is to be accomplished by, or with the help of, supernatural agencies.

All five points fully apply to the case of the Embassy and its people – even miracles. For example, when Embassy associates celebrated the Jewish holiday of Hanukkah in 2017, they humorously compared the unbelievable rise in the value of bitcoin in that year to the 'Hanukkah miracle' (see below). I have also met observant Jews in Tel Aviv who saw the Jewish God as the main inspiration behind Satoshi's impulse to create Bitcoin, thus associating it with a mystical spirituality or at least an otherworldly origin. As with the actualization of salvation in traditional (Christian and other) apocalyptic myths, Bitcoin ideology is rooted in an idea of breakout and redemptive substitution, the replacement of an 'old world' – as the sign on the wall of the Embassy declared – with a clean new start. Amir, a veteran Ambassador, expressed these ideas clearly in an article he published online in 2012:

> The new money [i.e. Bitcoin] must preserve some of the characteristics of the old [i.e. fiat] – easy to transfer, hard to forge, divisible, etc., but it must be different with respect to one thing – nobody will be able to produce it arbitrarily and charge interest on it. If we had such money, *we would be able to build a global community whose members trade with one another outside the existing system – a parallel economy*. Wherever it is possible, one pays and charges using the new currency. The community uses this currency as usual [i.e. as in the fiat economy] but it goes back to its natural place as a technical tool that enables trade through the representation of value. Community members do not only benefit from their role as ideological messengers, but they also thrive economically by doing so. They do not have to bear the taxes of interest and inflation, they do not pay commissions to banks and credit card companies, and they do not fund the financial market. *Every action done within this community is one that has not been enacted in the old economy, so when the community grows, the old economy shrinks together with its damaging elements*. The self-destructive mechanism that is built into the old economy will make the transformation quicker; we see these signs already today and they will proliferate. When the final collapse comes, we would have already prepared the alternative [system], which will gladly absorb the refugees [emphasis mine].

When I spoke with Amir in 2018, he said that the very fact that he could make such predictions five years before the global bull market of 2017 was itself proof that 'belief' can create a community and an economy, which then reassures people that their intuitions were correct, and so on in a circular fashion, until the new economy replaces the old one. This theory of substitution is not the only scenario Bitcoiners envision, but it is an idea that most true-believers I met at the Embassy embraced. The expansion of Bitcoin will, according to this theory, come at the expense of the hegemonic fiat-based economy, compressing the State-produced currency supply across the world while remaining immune to the volatility and meltdowns that adherents believed would probably shock established financial markets.

Amir had every reason to assume this theory would work. In 2012, when he authored his article, the value of bitcoin against the US dollar was somewhere between \$5 and \$13. By 2018 it had already passed the \$20,000 mark (although, as noted, it dropped back to \$5–6,000 some months later). As an early adopter, Amir could see how the Bitcoin economy was growing in volume and significance, albeit not yet 'compressing' the hegemonic economy. This only served to strengthen his belief that decentralized 'sound money' was the key to achieving free choice, which would enhance personal autonomy and therefore facilitate political liberation.

Several versions of this storyline circulated at the Embassy, emphasizing the following points: (1) the current economy is based on consumer purchasing power; (2) consumer income nonetheless stagnates while productivity dips, thereby creating larger gaps between available commodities and the purchase power of the population; (3) profits created within this expanding gap increasingly go to wealthy elites, big corporations and financial institutions; (4) elites do not spend enough to meet the demands of the rising productivity; (5) to fill the gap and avoid shortages, states and commercial banks print money, using the interest rate as an inflation control mechanism; (6) interest rates, however, cannot fully depress high levels of inflation, which reduce the value of money for those unable to make large profits on their investments, assets or salaries; (7) banks make the situation even worse due to their built-in conflict of interest with the customers, wherein the bank seeks to maximize its profit and the customer to minimize their losses; (8) consequently, people increasingly must borrow money to make a living, and fall deeper into never-ending debt; (9) in the long run, it will become impossible to pay off the accumulated weight of debts in the richest nations, and the entire world economy will crash; (10) after the crash, a New World awaits. This story also at times includes references to State protectionism of big banks (as with the bailouts of 2008), 'rigged' regulations that allow corporations to act irresponsibly and tales of corruption in influential circles. In all versions, the result is an inevitable crash that will affect billions.

True believers who held fast to such predictions conceptualized the timeframe of the crash in two main ways. First, in the material-mundane sense, time was technically encoded into the blockchain to produce rarity as the conditioning of monetary value. The fact that there is a limited number of bitcoins, and that the mining of new bitcoins will come to a halt sometime in the early 2140s, guarantees that the price will always be derived from its absolute finitude. Deliberately designed as a deflationary currency, whose quantity in each block on the blockchain reduces by 50 per cent every four years, Bitcoin is thus supposed to maintain its value *over* time, potentially even increasing it (despite frequent fluctuations). Second, time was eschatologically attributed to the progression of current hegemonic neoliberal political-economic policies, which were seen as deterministic in the sense that they were 'destined' to instantiate a devastating economic recession of global proportions followed by a social revolution of sort. One prolific Facebook contributor and Bitcoin Embassy member, for example, posted a picture of a Gilets Jaunes protester whose vest was inscribed with 'Buy bitcoin'. He titled his post '*Viva la revolution*'. Chaos and violence here seem to communicate the fight to obliterate old truths and thus maybe 'reshuffle the cards' – as Yaron phrased this in the 2014 interview that I quoted in the Introduction – thus redistributing economic and political powers to the masses. In that same interview, Yaron imbued this stance with a millenarian passion by literally incorporating the term 'millennium':

> With Bitcoin everyone can buy bitcoin[1] at any given moment at a per-market price subject to the same conditions; me and Obama ... There isn't more [money] to the banks and less to us ... Bitcoin does not redistribute the chips on the table but it does straighten the table up. It will not eradicate poverty and injustice in the world, but it will bring the fall of the abhorrent [financial] barriers and the profit of a select few – banks, Big Brother, weapons industries, the Sovereign – a mad apparatus that *rapes* humanity [with] borders and wars and [the politics of] divide-and-conquer ... Bitcoin renders useless the entire sinful, insane, road bump that is called 'the Sovereign', including its huge apparatuses that produces criminality ... Why did the Soviet Union collapse? Why did Detroit go bankrupt? The Sovereign WILL fall. It has to fall ... Everything that happens today [in the established economy] is insane, and it is held together by a deliberately inflationary economic policy, which creates money like sand across the beach, in the service of the select few, of the banks and gigantic industries. And Bitcoin will liberate [us] from all of this. Bitcoin is truly Moses, the Prophet of the Third Millennium!

Millenarian ideas that developed at the Embassy were not commonly focused on the revelation of a Bitcoin deity that would end human suffering. Instead, they anticipated critical temporalities that would fuse 'the great deflation' with an end to the hegemonic Sovereign. The positive view of crisis among maximalists, along with the holistic features of Bitcoin activism in all its pragmatic manifestations, thus distinguishes the Bitcoin ideological framework from other cryptocurrency communities. Israeli Bitcoin maximalists generally perceived other cryptocurrencies as hollow imitations of the 'real thing' since most were centrally controlled. The notion of colossal or millenarian breakdown was thereby central to the understanding of the flow of time as a dynamic that would lead to breakdown, if not total collapse, not only of world banking industries but also of every other competitor to Bitcoin. Ambassadors did not expect to annihilate the hegemonic economic order actively, in other words, but to simply wait for a 'cosmic' event that would perforate the fractional reserve banking system until it bleeds to death. This millenarian framework, as I will now discuss, was anchored in a series of rituals that Embassy members regularly celebrated; not as a serious 'religious' endeavour but humorously, as a parody that allowed them to consolidate Bitcoin sociality as simultaneously ceremonial and secular.

Rituals

Embassy members regularly engaged in different celebrations, which, aside from Genesis Block Day, included other important days on the Bitcoin cultural calendar. For example, the 'block-halving party' commemorated every four years, when the amount of bitcoin produced by each sealed block is cut in half (Faustino, Faria and Marques 2022). Another common celebration is the annual Pizza Day on 22 May, which marks the first known use of bitcoin to purchase a commodity. Laszlo Hanyecz, an early adopter who at the time was twenty-eight and living in Florida, wrote a post on the Bitcoin forum on 18 May 2010 declaring that he would pay 10,000 bitcoins for anyone willing to send him two large pizzas. Jeremy Sturdivant, then nineteen and living in California, accepted the challenge. He used his credit card to send Hanyecz two pizzas from a Papa John's branch, while Hanyecz sent 10,000 bitcoins directly into Sturdivant's personal bitcoin wallet. Several authors have described these bitcoin-specific celebrations in other contexts (see Faustino, Faria and Marques 2022), wherein Bitcoiners commemorate Bitcoin both as a financial tool and a philosophy of decentralized sociality. At the Embassy, these events took a similar form, providing a space for community members to play chess, drink beer, listen to music and hang out.

I use the terms 'ritual' and 'ceremonies' firstly because Danni Bloom regularly used them, either in Hebrew (*tekes*/*tkasim*) or English, when speaking about the different commemorations he and his colleagues often organized at the Embassy. In addition, based on Don Handelman's (1998) understanding of the elementary forms of ritualized events, this designation is also accurate analytically. Combining Victor Turner's (1969) analysis of initiation rituals and Johan Huizinga's (2000[1939]) pioneering study of 'play', Handelman argues that 'rituals' can be divided into two main categories. The first relates to rituals designed to serve as a *mirror* held up to society. This type of ritual encourages contemplation of and strengthening faith in commonly accepted values. The second category refers to rituals designed to *model* society. This type of activity shapes new social realities.

In both these cases, Handelman incorporates Huizinga's (ibid.) definitions of 'play' to delineate the traits of a *ritualscape,* which must (a) be clearly demarcated in time and place; (b) be circular or repetitive, both in the sense of concrete dates and in the sense of highlighting the same symbols or values; (c) be rich with symbolic action and artefacts; (d) be formal, rather than casual; and (e) convey a meta-message on the activity that has been taking place during the ritual – that is, it must produce a statement about the ritual itself as valuable. Based on these ideas, I will provide a structural analysis that demonstrates why the rituals enacted at the Embassy were both uniquely 'Israeli' and globally 'Bitcoin', emphasizing simultaneously the values of the local community and the underlying millenarianism that characterized the wider ideology.

The Ten-Year Party is a good example of the 'global' side of things. The event was published online as the 'birthday commemoration' of Bitcoin, thereby framing it deliberately as a formal celebration with a motif of growth, success, happiness, optimism, etc. This framing also constructed a sense of linear progression, which was coupled with the circularity of its annual commemoration on a designated date. Demarcated in time and place, then, the event included typical Israeli 'birthday party' stunts, including putting a block of concrete wrapped in an iron chain on a plastic chair – a visual representation of the Genesis Block – and lifting the chair in the air eleven times (see Figure 5.1).[2] Bitcoin symbology enhanced the seriousness of the event: a large screen projected bitcoin-themed graphics prepared especially for the occasion and the whole club was decorated with banners, balloons and huge images of the moon hanging from the ceiling. Whereas the moon symbolized Bitcoin's stratospheric flight, the banners and the balloons proclaimed related global terminology such as 'the Genesis Block' and 'Satoshi', as well as local community slang such as 'iron' (as stated above, *barzel*, refers to Bitcoin's impenetrability).

Distinguished from regular nightclubs through this aesthetic, the party reached its peak deep into the night when Bloom and others performed the Honey Badger Dance on stage. Bitcoiners incorporated the image of the fierce and fearless badger in 2017 as a kind of mascot, as Bitcoin had withstood

Figure 5.1. Cement block symbolizing the first block ever mined on the Bitcoin blockchain by Satoshi Nakamoto in 2009 being lifted on a chair during the Ten-Year Party in Tel Aviv. Credit: Matan Shapiro.

continual attacks from regulators. While partygoers engaged in the deliberately quirky dance, an animated clip of jumping honey badgers was also projected on the screen behind the stage. The dancers, some wearing Guy Fawkes masks, jumped frenetically from one side of the stage to the other, and the audience responded with cheers, turning the dance floor into an ecstatic mass of writhing bodies. Finally, Bloom specifically articulated a meta-message, suggesting that Bitcoin was here to stay, the community was growing and they were 'not afraid'. Enhanced by Bitcoin symbology and performances, the party thus ritualized Bitcoin as a mode of personal action and a collective lifestyle, rather than emphasizing its financial value. The party did not only *reflect* the prosperity associated with 'genesis', but it also *modelled* the spirit of resilience that should inspire future Bitcoin activism. Speaking over coffee, I once asked Bloom what he hoped to achieve during these ritualized celebrations. He replied:

> The ceremonies are something that consolidates and unites, and [they] build trust. When we do these rituals, it helps to feel that we are together in this boat, and in many cases I see this also as something that I do, not only for the people but also for Bitcoin itself as an abstract concept. In a way it is even a form of gratitude, because for me, Bitcoin deserves it; it did so much for us, so *this is about recognizing goodness*. And this also helps to show people from the outside that we really believe in something. Some of these rituals remind some people of a cult or a pyramid scheme, but if we filter them out, we can simply show that there is a difference between Bitcoin as a business and Bitcoin as a community. People who want to make money with bitcoin are not going to put it on a chair and celebrate its birthday party . . . whether it is the Ten-Year Party or other ceremonies we do, it is meant to show outsiders that we really believe in this [vision].

Bloom looks at rituals in a classic Durkheimian sense, wherein the ritual both absorbs and directs the energy of the community. But he also mentions Bitcoin as an abstract concept, a pachamama of sorts that should be recognized for its indifferent but continuous delivery of goodness to those who respect it. He argues that enactment of rituals is not meant as worship of Bitcoin or Satoshi, but rather to demonstrate that a community of Bitcoiners can thrive, and that its members believe in the technology. The dream of living a decentralized sociality here furnishes a desire to inhabit a concrete socio-communal space, wherein people can collaborate freely. Their mutual trust mirrors the trustlessness of algorithmic governance, and both of these key universalist elements in Bitcoin thus paradoxically come together to model and reconstruct the emergent local Bitcoin community in Israel as a locus of personal and collective salvation.

The Embassy also commemorated distinctively Jewish-Israeli holidays such as Purim, Hanukkah, Pesach and Independence Day, which were all adapted to the context of Bitcoin sociality in often hilarious ways. In the context of all these celebrations, belonging to the 'community' did not depend on people's activism. In fact, the fusion of Jewish-Israeli holidays with Bitcoin themes and values fomented local Bitcoin folklore, tying together millenarian attitudes with the concreteness of the Embassy as an *Israeli* social club. Despite the elements of comedy and improvisation that often characterized these celebrations, they were as 'ritualized' as their formal Bitcoin-specific counterparts, in structure as well as content. As I will now show, these events enabled Embassy associates to adapt the spiritualist aspect that accompanied (and cemented ideologically) the global scene into the specificity of their own cultural milieu.

Bitcoin and the Maccabees

The Hanukkah party organized by Embassy associates in December 2017 took place just a few weeks after Bitcoin soared to US$20,000 per unit, an all-time high that had corroborated predictions and prophecies dispersed by Bitcoin evangelists since the beginning of the 2010s. The mood of the audience was particularly jubilant due to this exponential rise in value, and the space of Yoni Shemesh's store – which hosted the event because it was bigger than the Embassy – was full. The Bitcoin goldrush in October that year had also been covered extensively by the Israeli media, and three national TV channels had sent crews to film the celebration. Their reports were broadcast in the weekend news on Friday night, producing what are still among the highest-rated segments for each of these channels. It was a celebratory event, and the sense of excitement was palpable.

Bloom led the event with a humorous spiel, riffing on the Jewish myth of the Hanukkah miracle, which celebrates the recapture of the Jewish Temple in Jerusalem by the Maccabees in 164 BCE, as well as its consequent 'purification' from Hellenistic idolatry. The problem that required divine intervention was that the liberators lacked oil in sufficient quantities to light the sacred menorah – a multibranch candelabra – which was essential to institute the spirit of God in the desecrated temple. The priests searched everywhere, eventually locating a small tin with oil enough only for one day. They were spiritually and mentally defeated, but God blessed them with a miracle, and the menorah inexplicably remained lit for eight consecutive days. The victory was complete and divine grace returned to the temple.

Bloom's version was different, and very funny. Beginning with a comparison of Bitcoin to the dreidel – a spinning top associated with Hanukkah festivities – Bloom argued that Bitcoin was a self-generating 'spiritual' force that 'will last forever', as opposed to 'the bubble of fiat currencies', which he described as an earthly force doomed to come to a halt at some stage. He then retold the Hanukkah myth. Two thousand years ago, he explained, the Jews practised the 'commands' of the Bitcoin Protocols until a new Sovereign decided to forbid the 'reading of the White Paper' (allegorically the Torah) and the mining of blocks. The Sovereign also ordered that everyone must 'trade altcoins' instead of Bitcoin, a reference to the 'sinful' Hellenistic Jewish customs of the period, which differed from the saintly rabbinical decrees that had inspired the Maccabees to fight. This provoked laughter, as most of the people present saw altcoins as 'scams', which implied that trading in these coins was equivalent to worshipping foreign gods. Bloom kept a straight face, however, and continued the tale. When the Maccabees managed to recapture the temple, he said, they looked for a source of energy they could use to light the menorah. They looked everywhere, eventually encountering 'Bitcoin oil' in 'a small cold wallet'. There was only enough 'oil' for one day of use, but it miraculously began to 'mine' new 'oil', and ultimately produced enough energy for a full eight-day period of light. The crowd laughed again, as this part of the story cleverly compared the original Hanukkah miracle to the recent rise of the bitcoin value against the dollar and the incredible all-time high that in a matter of a few short weeks had turned many of the people present into multimillionaires.

Since Hanukkah folklore is generally well known even to secular Israelis, no orthodox background was required to understand the humour. It did, however, require familiarity with the subcultural style of Bitcoin maximalism practised at the Embassy, which Bloom planted across the entire spiel. For example, Bloom mentioned fighting the Hellenists with 'iron' (used to describe Bitcoin, as I explained in Chapter 2), thus cleverly alluding to fighting the banks with Bitcoin. Bloom also provoked laughter when he referenced 'tahini' as equivalent to 'impure oils', thus mocking trade in altcoins while indirectly comparing it to the forbidden sacrificial offering at the time of the Maccabees. These rhetoric devices metaphorically repositioned Ancient Jerusalem at the Bitcoin Embassy in Tel Aviv of the present day. The audience, which included mainly Embassy members and their close friends and colleagues, clapped wildly as Bloom completed his show. He then moved to perform the traditional Hanukkah ceremony. He lit the candles, sang the blessing and broke into Hanukkah songs, familiar to both orthodox and secular Jewish Israelis, joined by the community members who assembled there. That was not yet the end of the night, though. When Bloom left the stage, Menashe, a well-liked Ambassador and a practising Orthodox Jew, took the microphone and added the following short speech:

> When Satoshi was considering [how to] bequeath his doctrine, he examined which spiritual frameworks were generated throughout the generations and

> which were acclimatized most efficiently. So, he looked at Judaism and said, 'No doubt, Judaism is the best religion!' After all, it is written [in Jewish mystical scriptures] that if you want to do much in the world you need to become infected with God's ways. *Satoshi too was infected.* At the beginning, he brought us the White Book [i.e. Paper], which is just like the written Torah: whatever is written cannot be changed. This later inspired the oral tradition, which is set by the rabbis of the generations.

The idea of the White Paper's immutability references the sacred status of the Jewish Torah, the opening five books of the Old Testament. Menashe used this to imply that the Bitcoin protocol should not be altered due to its total truthfulness, noting that earlier that year a dispute between Bitcoiners around the world resulted in a split and the consequent creation of a new cryptocurrency, unimaginatively called Bitcoin Cash (or B-cash). Most self-identified maximalists in Israel and beyond opposed the split because it was a thinly veiled move to increase the profits of big investors and mining corporations (see Chapter 3). But this also had a spiritual edge, of course, as Menashe went beyond humorous allegories to attribute Satoshi with the power of divine inspiration, and maybe also to reconceptualize Bitcoin in that way as a distinctively *Jewish* invention.

Claiming that Satoshi was 'infected' with the realization that Judaism was a religion true to God's ways does more than transform Satoshi into a prophet or a rabbi; it unifies the status of the Torah as a sacred text with the status of the White Paper as the Bitcoin Instruction Manual. This infuses millenarian arguments about crisis and salvation with a wider story of cosmic creation, which is also inscribed in Bloom's story, albeit ironically. I further elaborate on this aspect below. For now, I will suffice arguing that both Bloom's mischievous interpretation of the Hanukkah miracle and Menashe's designation of the White Paper as a holy text presented Bitcoin sociality as a form of *spiritual awakening*. It is important to note in this regard that, depending on who commemorates them, Jewish holidays are widely celebrated in Israel either 'by the book' – that is, as instructed by Halachic Jewish law – or 'lightly', as a secular tradition that focuses on the symbolic aspects of each holiday rather than on doctrinal demands. Menashe's short speech wonderfully adjusted both of these ceremonial protocols to fit the Bitcoin philosophy, thus turning the event into something that at once associated and distinguished the Israeli Bitcoin community from the global Bitcoin movement.

Celebrating Bitcoin at Hanukkah legitimized the entire movement, in that sense, as the truthful carrier of a universal socioeconomic theory capable of 'freeing' anyone worldwide, while at the same time planting its *local* roots, charging Bitcoin praxis with a specifically Jewish-Israeli feel. The millenarian version of the Bitcoin belief system could now be taken seriously because people could relate to its techno-utopian vision through local idioms. What might at first appear as a joke or play on words in fact harnessed the good tidings of Bitcoin to the sensibilities of Embassy sociality and familiar local knowledge. That was so even though Judaism was never the focus of any of the Embassy celebrations. Performances, speeches and humorous acts always conveyed support in the Bitcoin project of societal reorganization rather than encouraging a particular approach to Judaism. At a Hanukkah party held in December 2018, for example, exactly a year after the event I described above, moods were different. At the time, Bitcoin was going through another periodic crash, and people were worried. The 2018 party was not euphoric, although it was not particularly glum either. During the party, Rami declared on the microphone: 'Bitcoin will prevail! Do not worry! You're all HODLing until further notice, otherwise you'll have problems with me and Nissim!'

Faith was still being tested, Rami seemed to argue with this statement, and it should be expressed pragmatically by keeping bitcoin for a rainy day rather than using it or selling it, despite the sharp decline in its value. He thus also tacitly reminded his listeners that they should keep waiting patiently for something to happen, such as economic catastrophe, after which the bitcoin value would soar to the moon or even turn some HODLERS into the new elite of a post-crisis dystopian reality. There was something concretely local even in Rami's alleged implementation of a wider Bitcoin-focused economic framework in Tel Aviv. Going beyond HODLING, and indeed beyond individualism, Rami tacitly mobilized the *community*, its intimacy and its familiarity, to protect values that were deemed objective, at least regarding the status of Bitcoin.

Rami and others' public performances in fact often included a blend of neo-spiritualist universalism, Jewish myths, typically middle-class Tel Aviv humorous idioms and a concretely Israeli aesthetic. This suggests that practising an open-source community at the Embassy was not a perfect embodiment of ideas imported from across the sea and superimposed onto Israeli folklore. Its specificity was the result of the cultural intimacy between Ambassadors, who understood well the satirical nuances of political references raised in ritualized events such as the Hanukkah party. Encounters at the Embassy, the meeting of ideas, values, ethical convictions and emotions, whose origins and contextual significance were diverse, encouraged associates to activate their political imagination and invent something new. And this, as I discuss below, produced an original cosmogonic theory of late-capitalist financialization.

Neoliberal Cosmogony

Anthropologists have classically used the term 'cosmology' to indicate the perceived order of things in vernacular understandings (Abramson and Holbraad 2014). Cosmology was thereby used to frame attitudes and practices that were taken for granted at the level of everyday life in specific cultural contexts, as these reflected localized conceptions of nature, society, history and human fate (Cohn 2001, 2004). Such attitudes include, for example, the assumed relations between parts of the cosmos and the whole (e.g. medieval Christian maps of the Holy Land represented Jerusalem as significantly bigger than other parts of the land); the 'correct' positions of centres and their presumed peripheries (for example, the replacement of Earth with the Sun as the centre of the universe in Western-secular cosmology); and the dynamics of moral transformation in the human world (e.g. an eternal struggle between good and evil is mutually exclusive to the idea that a crisis will lead to salvation at the end of time). Native (or grassroots) theories on the place of humans and divinities in cosmos were often presented in early-to-mid 20th Century Anthropological literature as 'holistic' in the sense that they were seen to commit those who shared them in a deep moral sense that was refracted through all areas of social activity. Anthropologists thereby presented cosmologies as quasi-static, and as a property of small-scale non-Western social wholes though to have largely disappeared from Western society after industrialization and the triumph of scientific tropes of progress.

In their critique of traditional anthropological approaches to cosmology, Allen Abramson and Martin Holbraad (2014) argue that those who accept the premises of cosmological theories experience them as ontic rather than as 'holistic'. By this they mean that cosmological knowledge is not only a representational storyline on gods or infinity or eternity in an entropic universe, but rather a generic re-creation and proliferation of *particular* gods, *particular* infinities and *particular* eternities through the generations. This critique holds that cosmological ideas are rooted in cultural practices everywhere, including in scientific theories, economic modalities, and secular lifestyles. People do not turn to cosmological explanations because, for example, they encountered a moral breakdown, financial uncertainty or another crisis; rather, cosmic logos is always-already infused in permissible local descriptions of most social and physical phenomena. This ontic, ground-level approach holds that a cosmology is intrinsic to any sociality, in antiquity as well as in modernity.

According to this view, cosmology also manifests in economic terms. As media scholar Finn Brunton (2019: 11) has shown recently, all money technologies can be seen as 'cosmograms'; that is, 'things, stuff, which order the cosmos and our place in it, embedding a system of relationships, roles, and actions within their operation'. These cosmograms, of course, are also relational, or at the very least comparable across contexts. Marxist theory, for example – which follows Hegel's dialectical analysis – is cosmological in the sense that it envisions a transhistorical conflict between slaves and their owners, conceived differently in each epoch. Likewise, Keynesian economic theory is cosmological because it is grounded in the idea of ontological security, guaranteed by the 'vaulting' double effect of the state 'from above' and the nation 'from below' (Abramson and Holbraad 2014: 12). Based on these examples, Abramson and Holbraad (2014) argue convincingly that neoliberal cosmology is often called 'postmodern' precisely because its guiding cosmic logos represents a break from dominant imaginaries and historical narratives that Keynesian and Marxist paradigms have stretched to the limits. Neoliberalism, accordingly, is premised on imaginaries of fragmentation and acceleration, which are perceived as positive values, and they thus inspire the mundane weakening of sociocultural and empirical boundaries, including those of the nation, the state and the community. As Abramson and Holbraad (2014: 12) describe that:

> In many texts, anthropological ones amongst them, neo-liberalism dolefully means the commodification of everything, the consequent reduction of all human value to price, and the hyper-individualization of agency. True enough. However ... if we theorise beyond the social categories of this 'conscious mode', also register a more profound ... spatiotemporal consequence of this politicoeconomic re-arrangement. Indeed, the crucial cosmological outcome of economic de-regulation and tacit de-nationalisation spelled out politically as 'freedom' has frequently been for populations to feel not only severed from traditional communities and receding homeland, but also inchoately 'thrown into the world' without limits: in effect, to be cast into a space that is no longer vaulted by the state above and by the nation below. the result is that, with the much-vaunted death of society, the social becomes part of an ill-definable felt infinity which can be portrayed in many registers, all of them allowing for the possibility – and in some cases the inescapability – of significant continuities with the immensities and nano-spherical minuteness of cosmic process 'out there' and within.

As I began to show, precisely such process of invention can be seen to characterise most Embassy associates' approach to neoliberal economics. Interlocutors vocally argued that mass adoption was contingent on the acceptability of P2P and decentralization as organizing principles in the emergence of new collaborative communal networks. Being able to imagine a new world, Yoav and Avner told me during our lengthy conversation, was more important than any rational cost-benefit financial consideration. As became clear at the Ten-Year Party, the Israeli community at large saw Bitcoin's survival against insurmountable odds as *proof* that this theory was correct. Dismissing the value of bitcoin against fiat currencies as unimportant, interlocutors identified instead a process of slow emergence, a spiritual and pragmatic broadening of consciousness, a trickle that they believed would become a flood – an opening, to use another metaphor, that would gradually habilitate Bitcoin as a sound financial tool across the world. This process empirically informed the development of a generic cosmogonic theory in Tel Aviv.

Bitcoin Syncretism

My interest in local manifestations of neoliberal cosmology (as an encompassing term for both ideology and belief) began after a conversation with Ben-Tzion and Yosef-Hayim, both Orthodox Jews whom I met during the goldrush at the Embassy. Ben-Tzion claimed that Bitcoin was a viable financial tool according to Halachic Jewish Law, which forbids gambling but demands that every person divides their capital into three: one-third in liquid cash, one-third in real estate, and one-third in commerce. Ben-Tzion, accordingly, saw unfettered trade in multiple cryptocurrencies as potentially problematic – as it gets dangerously close to gambling – while mining and trading in Bitcoin was kosher given its simultaneous status as both currency and asset. Yosef-Hayim exclaimed that 'Bitcoin is a third thing, a mixture of gold and real estate, and that is the reason it is not forbidden'. For them, there was not even a requirement to weave Bitcoin values and spiritual lessons with Jewish ones. It was enough to designate Bitcoin as a financial product that does not contradict Jewish Law, thus also classifying it cosmologically.

An act that Ben-Tzion and Yosef-Hayim could otherwise have interpreted as blasphemous syncretism, then, was justified both from the Jewish-Israeli perspective and the universalist techno-utopian perspective. This suggests that at least in principle, there is no contradiction between the nominal permission to use Bitcoin 'within' the context of Jewish Law and taking part in the development of a secular millenarian cosmology. Israeli Bitcoiners at large have thus consciously been transforming the values they associated with Bitcoin into concrete cosmological references that they could relate to, as much as Orthodox Jews were doing so for different reasons. While Bitcoin-specific ceremonies at the Embassy usually took a carnivalesque form, commemorations of formal Jewish or Israeli (national) holidays thus had a deeper sense of enclosure, intimacy and familiarity. The syncretic fusion of Bitcoin themes with cosmological assertions about divine entities or purity, zeal and devotion, have thereby created a special dynamic that added a sense of singularity to the Israeli Bitcoin community as a distinct group.

These ideas should not be read as particularly deviant, neither heuristically nor analytically. After all, scholars studying the relations between grassroots economies and macroeconomic processes (Kalb 2017; Goddard

2016) now assume that economic decision-making include many 'non-economic' considerations, along with their symbolic and spiritual aspects. For example, care for meaningful others, fulfilment of personal desires, and belief systems – all make their impact on nearly every economic decision, as well as on norms and rules guiding the exchange of money, favours and debts (cf. Zelizer 2005). Susana Narotzky (2012: 630) locates such decisions across scales of relational engagements with the world around us, arguing that 'in pursuing their livelihood, people have to negotiate the scales of macro-economic models, meso institutional regulation and micro forms of responsibility that govern their actions (including filial, community, religious or state responsibilities)'. This approach, which some call 'neo-substantivist' (Narotzky and Besnier 2014: S6), rejects the formalist rational-choice model as incapable of capturing the richness of human economic behaviour.

The Hanukkah party was cosmogonic in this neo-substantivist sense because it creatively projected an aspired economic order in our time through the retrospective imaginative localization of Bitcoin in the time of the Maccabees. This associated Bitcoin sociality within a universalist framework that emphasized such ideals as freedom and financial autonomy, while also attaching Bitcoin sociality to a popular Jewish-Israeli framework. Expressing both of these logics simultaneously, the party constituted an emergent theory of decentralization that did not reject traditional spiritual references, religious dictates and local folklore in the name of a grand metanarrative. Rather, if it *did* reject anything it was the real-world hierarchies of a capitalist system gone wrong, and the injustice at the heart of a debt-based system, all of which are ideals found in some Jewish traditions, customs and myths. Bloom might have generated a techno-theoretical 'mishmash' (Barbrook and Cameron 1996) as he integrated Jewish folklore and Bitcoin millenarian attitudes, but this mishmash could thrive empirically precisely because it successfully *meshed* (rather than mashed) P2P sociality, decentralization and trustlessness with Jewish-Israeli customs, jokes, symbols and values. During a casual conversation at the Embassy, Nissim used a set of images that likewise built on local cultural practices to pronounce the universalist essence of Bitcoin as a tool for personal and collective salvation:

> Bitcoin gives you the tools to take care of yourself. You produce these tools by yourself, for yourself, to do better [in life] and upgrade your internal being as a human. But only a person who understands he has an essence and that he is walking along a path can do this . . . Not everyone can learn the Torah, so likewise not everyone can deal with Bitcoin. If you are putting on a *kippah* (yarmulke) just so that people see you have a *kippah*, you are not *really* religious. You are only using the religion to get something else. In Bitcoin, if you want to make money and show off, you are also just using it. There are values behind Bitcoin, there is

> an added value, but not everyone understands this. Someone who talks with me about bitcoin in terms of 'going up, going down', and how much it's worth, will eventually get bored and move on.

Nissim's spiritualist ideas 'work' semantically *only* because he compares Bitcoin to the Torah and thus locates Bitcoin techno-utopianism in the context of folk Israeli idioms. This also explains why the collectivist aspects of Bitcoin sociality could be developed organically in Tel Aviv despite the strong individualist dimension that many of Bitcoin's global supporters have attached to their involvement in the movement. A cosmology of financialization, profit and prosperity dynamically emerges here from below, in other words, rather than being a reflection of struggles and local histories from far away social contexts. As Bitcoiners in Israel engaged in public events and ritualized celebrations, they generated cosmic-oriented aphorisms that strengthened their millenarian commitment to building a grassroots economy of the kind envisioned by Amir in 2012; which thus also inspired the cultivation of personality traits and investment strategies that in Chapter 3 I included under the category of Individual B.

Socioeconomic cosmogony in Tel Aviv still nonetheless builds on universalist rather than strictly isolationist models. The foundation myth of the Genesis Block traces the origins and limitations of power in society, thus serving as a basic index for the aspired rearrangements of objects, forces and relations in *all* human societies. The belief in techno-utopian futures, shared by all Bitcoiners around the globe, juxtaposes millenarian ideas of crisis and salvation against a set of concrete human vulnerabilities and faults that are usually described negatively as the source of injustice in everyday life, in Israel as elsewhere (see Shapiro and Skartveit 2025). The upcoming crisis is predictable, according to this cosmic understanding, because it had happened several times before, impacting global markets to different degrees. The crisis is therefore mathematically verifiable, interlocutors argued, its redemptive potential justified based on scientific rationality in its most positivistic sense. Embassy associates' imaginaries of crisis-laden futures should therefore be taken at face value – they created symbolic iconologies that organized action *rationally* as they relied on universalist scientific motifs. These in turn served to verify the truthfulness of localised assumptions in a cyclical fashion (cf. Schrempp 2016).

Conclusion

I understand cosmic logos as a representation – much like a map – whose totality makes for a spatiotemporal theory of the social and natural world. The idioms that constitute its factual pillars, such as key symbols or the designation of boundaries between conceptual and actual spaces, as well as a cosmogonic foundation myth (for example, the Genesis Block), inspire an array of life-making principles. In the case of Bitcoin supporters at large these include a sense of temporal distinction (e.g. the New vs. Old Economy); preferred models of spatial distribution (e.g. decentralization vs. centralization); central mythical figures – both living and dead, anonymous or recognized (e.g. Satoshi); a dynamic or a movement that defines how entities interact, assemble or separate (e.g. P2P, community); boundaries or border zones that distinguish friends from foes (e.g. 'shitcoins'); and grades of key values (for example, 'freedom').

These spatiotemporal features suggest that the underlying libertarian rigour that Satoshi encoded in the White Paper could not be reduced to capitalist profiteering in the narrow sense, nor could it be understood exclusively in techno-financial terms. As a phenomenological experience, which was always at least partly 'local' and partly 'global' – an intimacy that emerged at the Embassy – the relative success of the community in Tel Aviv should be understood as inseparable from the concrete social conditions in which the local Bitcoin scene had developed and the cosmogonic theories it generated. Inductively, then, any experimentation with Bitcoin-centred sociality could be said to include revised notions of time, space and deliverance, which could encourage the generic formulation of new rituals, beliefs, linguistic idioms and myths that would then progressively define the expected emergence of a radically 'decentralized' world order (Faustino 2019; see Faustino, Faria and Marques 2022).

An emergent cosmology of Bitcoin is interesting because it represents a contemporary radical shift and a new way of thinking about economic processes, cultural styles and social organization. Given the fusion of local myths and global redemptive theories, which also reframe individual boundaries in collective terms – and vice versa – this cosmological framework might even represent an axial moment in modernity itself, wherein large-scale transformations of 'logos' take place simultaneously in many places (see, for example, Cohn 2004). In Bitcoin, this axial moment is imbricated in the scalable imagination of the world, which is reduced to two plains of reference: it is as large as the sum of the overall parts of the transactions in the market ('a market cap') or it is as small as the particular transaction conducted between two peers. What is 'axial' here is the requirement to dynamically switch between these perspectives *all the time* in order to gain any real power (mainly in economic and moral senses).

In the next chapter I will suggest that this act of 'switching' has the effect of forming online crowds, an emergent mass of unrelated individuals who are occasionally thrown into intense interaction based on their cyberspace roaming activities. It is my thesis that crowding has become an immense social force (Hayden 2021), and that the crowding phenomenon on the Bitcoin blockchain is one of its most significant current manifestations.

NOTES

1. As I mentioned in the Introduction, I use Bitcoin with a ‘capital B’ to describe the system or movement, and bitcoin with a lowercase ‘b’ to describe its money qualities.
2. In Israeli birthday parties for children, the child on the chair is lifted according to the number of years passed, plus one for the year to come.

CHAPTER 6

BITCOIN CROWDS

Crypto in the Plural

Whether you think of Bitcoin as money, equity, asset or symbol, it must be understood in the plural. The quantities of units involved – of digital bits, of electricity voltage, of chips and processors, and 'coin communities' that branched out of Bitcoin or were created as parallel digital assets in the emerging crypto-economy – derive their meaning from their collective density. In fact, the total number of Bitcoin addresses cannot empirically decline as every account remains forever on the blockchain even if it is inactive.

Pluralism also means dynamism; the more people are involved, the more transactions are enacted between nodes and peers, and the fluctuation of value further accelerates. Exchange of satoshis across the blockchain exemplifies this connection between pluralism and dynamics. As mentioned, every bitcoin is composed of 100,000,000 bits, each called a satoshi; these fragments are used to pay for goods and services as well as the small transaction fees each individual user transfers automatically when they buy or sell something on the blockchain (see Cardoso 2024: 31). Bitcoiners consequently disperse millions of units of value across the system, while also changing their own relative position to one another in their shifting roles as buyers or sellers. A functioning cryptocurrency economy is thus premised on: (1) masses of people who trade masses of units; and (2) the smooth, continuous, constant and reliable flow of value.

Pluralism and dynamism can therefore be seen to condition the value-fluctuation of bitcoin vis-à-vis fiat currencies. Since 2013, when bitcoin first acquired significant monetary value, it has crashed numerous times, occasionally losing 50 per cent or more of its value within days, only to 'fly to the moon', as the famous allegory goes, several months later. Bitcoiners treat such fluctuations as part of what Bitcoin 'is' and how it behaves financially as an object of the market. While mainstream economists and the media at large have been consistent in presenting wild value fluctuations as irrational and risky – claiming on that basis that bitcoin was a particularly volatile investment route – Embassy associates interpreted these fluctuations as indicators of synchronic mass action, which in turn influenced individual investment choices (cf. Pickles 2024). When bitcoin dropped, for example, maximalists at the Embassy would normally buy more of it, at times joking that they must not miss 'the sale'. Although they did not always sell or buy as soon as the market morphed, committed Bitcoiners I met always referred to market trends as a dominant factor in their own private economy, if only as navigational beacons in a the rapidly changing, uncertain and unpredictable waters of blockchain investment cycles.

In this chapter I build on these assertions to show how the Bitcoin blockchain turns a plurality of co-temporal and trans-spatial automatic calculations into self-perpetuating crowds. Pluralism and dynamism, I argue, are the foundational technical characteristics required to synchronize a multiplicity of transactions taking place in parallel to one another in a network of interconnected nodes. The dynamic of trade on the blockchain, then, forms a distinct ontology, in which *quantifiable units* (such as individual people and pieces of bitcoin) acquire *qualitative* meaning (as a human reality or a set of moral values to live by) *only through the relational aggregation* of all the transactions that are being done in real time across the entire network. As long as there is electricity in the world, this process should in principle pulsate *ad infinitum,* thereby incessantly producing new crowds of Bitcoin investors on an ongoing basis.[1] Beginning with the notions of suggestion and contagion, in this chapter I will show that more than a mere ledger, the blockchain should actually be understood as a perfect digital crowding machine.

Suggestion, Imitation, and Contagion

Sociologist Gabriel Tarde (1903) coined the term *suggestive imitation* to explain the phenomenological and psychological power of mass action (Borch 2012: 56; see Barry and Thrift 2007). Tarde argued that the spread of ideas and customs in society, both old and new, was grounded in processes of mimesis and 'contagion'. By this he meant that new norms, taboos, values and political pressures, among other social things, could only gain traction at a societal scale through replication and representation, enacted over and over again, until they were finally standardized or canonized. Tarde argued (ibid.) that contagion accelerates during mass gatherings, wherein previously unconnected individuals come together as a *crowd.*

Bruno Latour et al. (2012) exemplified how contagion works by analysing the 'olé' wave that was fashionable in the early 1990s in football stadiums around the world.[2] The synchrony of fans rising stand after stand to participate in a 'wave' is not organized by stadium authorities or any other 'sovereign', to use the common Bitcoin analogism. Here, there is simply an intense kinetic energy that moves inside and through people, which draws them into action. It thus synchronizes mass movement between them as they watch the wave coming, 'infected' by the thrill of participation, and prepare to join in. The 'wave' overcomes every distinction used to outline sociological boundaries between the people that put it into motion – including, for example, contrasting loyalties to different football teams – and its movement is self-generating in the sense that it lacks coercion; the wave impels people to stand up and raise their hands in the air merely by approaching them. By participating, spectators then feel a collective density, a kind of unity or a momentary equilibrium that includes everyone, which is contagious in the sense that it engulfs the entire stadium to instigate a jubilant or joyous mood.

Understood as a psychological mechanism that rules crowd behaviour, then, suggestive utterances can spread like fire, gripping people and mobilizing them en mass into mimetic action, sometimes even if they had no premeditated intention to take part in any form of collective rallying. It can begin with an utterance, a cry, an action or a gesture, which 'contagiously' travel across the ranks – let us say of marching workers – much in the same way that a bugle call can cause soldiers to leap to attention. Whatever the contagious key is about, depending on the context of the gathering, it would then instigate movement in a mass of people, which consequently begins to act as a coordinated crowd to spark a riot, for example – even though they are not controlled by agitators or leaders (Brighenti 2014: 47; Mazzarella 2010: 716–17).

In this scheme, a form of energy is understood to be rushing through crowds like a lighting ball, blurring personal boundaries, bringing people together, 'semi-hypnotizing' them, as Tarde would have it, into believing that their entire selfhood is dissolved into the collective, while curiously also sharpening their idiosyncratic sense of self as members *of* a wider multiplicity (see Borch 2009: 282). This makes it easier for people to pick up and rearticulate words, gestures or behaviours, which either emerge from the crowd itself or are inspired by leaders. As people imitate each other and their leaders in a mass demonstration – or being 'infected' by mood – they become one, and their actions are expropriated from the regular checks and balances of everyday conduct. Personal expression and mass consensus thereby become synonymous, or at the very least reciprocal for a determinant period; thus, temporarily resolving the tension existing between investors' own agency as individuals and the contagious drive to meld into the crowd. Writing on social media, Raymond Lee (2016: 86) expresses well how this takes place in digital environments:

> Digital technology provides the hard- and software for making possible extensive online connections. These connections activate and disseminate thoughts, feelings, and actions without requiring physical co-presence. Only by connective rationality are these thoughts, feelings, and actions systematically channelled and organized. It implies that the connected participant is individually engaged in interpreting messages, assessing affect and making decisions on future actions. At the same time, the participant is also a node with linkages to other nodes. This assumption allows the preservation of individuality as well as its insertion into a collective modality. It creates the basis for online crowds to represent the individual and group simultaneously.

Lee's assertions are relevant to the analysis of Bitcoin crowds because trade on the blockchain is *heavily influenced by this duplicity of individual and collective modes of expression.* FOMO, especially, is the classic articulation of emotional contagion among crypto investors within and beyond Bitcoin, which combines the aura of skilful financial edgework (i.e. rational individualism) with the physically embodied, unmitigated excitement inscribed in collective risk taking (as sellers or buyers that are subject to market dynamics). To elucidate this issue further I now turn to discuss Elias Canetti's conceptions of modern street crowds, which can still be applied almost in their entirety to postmodern digital crowds.

Discharge

Elias Canetti (1984[1960]) famously argued that the crystallization of any crowd can only take place when something at stake *might be lost.* Crowding is not merely symbolic play or a leisure activity, in other words, but a kind of social impulse surging bottom-up in certain situations in order to make a claim on whatever inalienable issue that the crowd manifest at the time of its formation. To understand this assertion, think of the energy we often feel viscerally when we take part in a mass gathering, which sometimes includes an element of 'losing ourselves' in the crowd to the point of forgetting that we are in fact separated from it. This very phenomenon can be framed positively as a type of collective effervescence (Durkheim 1995[1912]; see Brighenti 2010) rather than be seen as the violent unleashing of a mob mentality (Le Bon 1895). When a collective sentiment of potential loss transmutes itself through the crowd, people lose 'the fear of being touched by the unknown', as Canetti (ibid.: 15) puts it. A flattening of social reality takes place through emotional immersion with those who are around us, accompanied by a visceral sense of physical density or crowdedness.

Canetti (ibid.) used the term 'discharge' to describe the materialization of this phenomenon in a mass gathering. For Canetti, discharge is an unpredictable affective phenomenality that appears suddenly when people in the crowd are no longer deterred from being touched by others. Put another way, discharge causes people to feel closer to those around them, obviating existing norms that regulate the implicit imperative to hold appropriate distance between strangers. Discharge literally enables people to 'free themselves from their burdens of distance' (ibid.: 18); that is, to be comfortable when their bodies are pressed against others.

More broadly, discharge cancels dependency on the hierarchies that previously separated these people individually and collectively. The group of previously differentiated individuals then enmesh to become an *undifferentiated* social unity, a supra-human entity, which lacks top-down vertical governance. 'It is for the sake of this blessed moment', writes Canetti (ibid.), 'when no-one is greater or better than another, that people become a crowd'. He thus claims that *crowds are an egalitarian universe*; a space and time in which people feel equal and leaderless, a framework of action free from moral defilement that overcomes people's instinctive tendency to sustain their personal boundaries. As Christian Borch (2009: 285) expresses well:

> It is only by uniting closely with others that the individual acquires the rare opportunity to emancipate himself or herself from the burdens that have accumulated in him or her and hence to understand himself or herself in new ways ... [This] even amounts to a democratic transformation: the crowd incident destabilizes existing power structures, creates a momentary equality and freedom, and in that sense empowers the individual in a common act. As a part of this, power and politics are no longer imposed on the individual from outside but emerge from within in a joint enterprise of total equality.

The hundreds of people that packed the Embassy space every day during the goldrush in the autumn of 2017, exemplified how the affective force of discharge can mobilize crowds. As I claimed in Chapter 2, intensified synchronicity of trading at the global level increased virtual density to such an extent that the dynamics of the marketplace discharged an affective sentiment that crossed into actual spaces. In the case of Israel, this generated a genuine sense of FOMO across Israeli society at large, attracting numerous newcomers into the scene. As the crowd congregated inside or in front of the Embassy, people mingled regardless of the reasons for which they decided to invest in bitcoin. They thus crystallized into an amorphous yet distinct crowd whose members were loosely connected but whose collective power and energy were felt on the ground until the expected drop finally arrived towards the end of 2017.[3]

Whether they meant it or not, Satoshi's original design of the blockchain empirically enabled the spread of FOMO to the critical point of discharge, which resulted in the formation of crowds online and later also offline. People might have read the newspapers, or decided to listen to their children, or realized that a new method of money laundering with a high profit potential had just opened; and a few people even 'saw the light' (see Chapter 2). But in all these cases it was not a mere linear, rational, transmission of data – neither technical nor economic knowledge – that incited them into action. Rather, it was a deeper sense of anticipation crystallized as a collective phenomenon, an excitement associated with a moment in history in which the value of bitcoin washed through the dreams and fantasies of people far beyond the limited subcultures to which it had been previously confined.[4] It was this collective thrill that made the act of buying bitcoin meaningful in the first place, even an emotional experience to some (see for comparison Navaro-Yashin (2007) on the affective quality of documents). Enacted through the masses, as I will now discuss, the force of such affects impacted the blockchain also *topologically*.

The Topology of Blockchain Landscapes

So far, I have demonstrated that fluctuations of value on the blockchain spread affects that in turn instigate crowding. Crowding in this case generates a structure; rather than forming amorphous masses, it has the pragmatic impact of assembling buyers and sellers into clearly defined groups (Vennonen 2024). A tension between buyers and sellers in a way defines the entire experience of Bitcoin crowding, as traders follow the synchronic action of both these groups in real time to determine the best investment strategy. At the Embassy a forty-inch screen was always tuned to a popular internet site that visualised groups of sellers and buyers as intersecting graphs, which were glowing in red and green (or sometimes blue; e.g. www.coinmarketcap.com). Embassy associates would often turn to these graphs, which were available 24/7, to analyse the flow of capital in real time, understand the changing conditions of the market, debate whether they should buy or sell, and try to predict future trends.

The process of reading and analysing such data involves affective contagion (Lee 2016; Wiedemann 2014), side by side with a sense of clotting (Baker 2011). The double impact of discharge – a visceral sensation rushing through the body and a change of spatial perception – ultimately materializes *values* in terms of both (1) worth (as sums of money in a digital wallet increase or decrease); and (2) moral judgement (of maximalist expansionist realization, on one hand, and the gold-seeker dream of quick enrichment, on the other). Mathematical value is here *qualitatively* equivalent to certain political and philosophical convictions, which in the world of Bitcoin are signs for autonomy, independence, and freedom. The algorithmic distribution of satoshis across the blockchain, in other words, creates a space, a landscape, which is measured *topologically* in relational volumes of commerce.

Relationships between peers on the blockchain are therefore not merely quantitative. Rather, the weight of most investments is linked to deeper considerations, such as economic uncertainty (Faria 2022), lifestyle choices, and political goals (Swartz 2017). Consequently, seemingly 'pure' economic decisions – such as fund hedging, HODLING, shorting, etc. (cf. Pickles 2024) – are simultaneously experienced as both ethical and affective (King and Koutmos 2021). FUD attacks, for example, are especially frightening not just because of their potential financial implications but also because they expose ideological dilemmas.[5] As Nissim explained in the Introduction, FUDs are known to have broken the determination of quite a few die-hard believers, who have sold all their holdings at times of weakness.

Not only that trade volumes can be experienced spatially, but the space itself is also relational given the comparative ability to influence the space-volume occupied by other traders in the market at any given moment. For example, bull market qualitatively differs from a bear market, and both depend on the decisions of heavy 'whales' whose space on the blockchain is relatively large. The entire bitcoin market capitalization can in fact be measured topologically relative to the overall market capitalization of the entire cryptocurrency market; the monetary volume of other cryptocurrencies traded parallel to bitcoin; and fluctuations in fiat currency volumes. Spatial logic manifests even semantically in the jargon used to describe trade: values can be 'adjusted' or 'corrected', data structures 'verified' or 'validated' and then 'contained' or 'sealed'; wealth volumes can 'inflate' or 'deflate'; manipulations cause 'bubbles', which might pop; trade positions can be 'occupied'; and the market functions in 'loops' or 'cycles'. These topological representations of spatial shapeshifting – which are all based on approximate volumes of trade and their rapid changes vis-à-vis the dynamics of the market at a global scale – determine the relative, albeit constantly transforming, positioning of peers on the blockchain.

To clarify this, take for example Bitcoin Rain (http://bitcoinrain.io/), another site that represents transactions in real time. Rather than providing numbers or graphs, this site visualizes every exchange taking place concurrently online in the form of a bubble, whose size depends on the size of the transaction relative to US dollars. Bigger bubbles (or 'raindrops') thereby represent higher-volume transactions, and vice versa. The relations between these bubbles are measured mainly in size and volume, not in numbers. Sending money out and seeing your bubble among so many others during a moment of high-volume trading – while measuring the sizes of other bubbles on the screen – is quite literally a live representation of spatial density online.[6]

Such sites enable the imagining of value fluctuations as something that has spatial characteristics, including size, depth and address (of a Bitcoin wallet). A relational topology of values-as-volumes can thus be seen to control crowding phenomena on the blockchain. Crowding does not however involve here the shortening of physical distances between people, as Canetti (ibid.) had argued for the case of street crowds. Rather, crowding is expressed here in terms of changing *intensities* of trade volumes, which then translate into measures of digital distance. Andrea Brighenti (2014: 47) beautifully defines this broader topological sense of distance-beyond-metrics through the concept of intensity, leading me to the next section:

> Canetti (1960) . . . singled out the inception of the crowd as a moment he called 'the discharge'. It is the moment when distances and social differences imposed from the outside are suddenly abolished and people begin *accepting being touched by unknown others*. The discharge is the crowd-event, the crowd as event. One could object that such a discharge is mostly a speculative moment, impossible to be empirically observed . . . But the analytical insight here is clear: distances, in the widest possible sense of the word, correlate not simply with density, but with intensity. Even when distances are not thoroughly abolished, distance management is of utmost importance in most social experiences and contexts. The management of distances relates to the creation or, on the contrary, prevention, of social intensities [emphasis in original].

Distance Management

Although not all interlocutors in Tel Aviv regularly followed websites that represented values topologically, an awareness of the spatial dimension of the blockchain had to exist by default. Evidently, people rarely revealed how much bitcoin they owned, although it was taken for granted that early adopters probably had plenty of it. Precisely because numbers were excluded, and since the relative size of people's holdings was a major topic of conversation (along with the value against the dollar), common linguistic utterances gave way to topological connotations (see also Lash 2012).

As I mentioned above, 'heavy Bitcoin whales', as well as the financial-market metaphors of bulls versus bears, or the ideas of an 'ecosystem' and the weight of each 'block' on the blockchain, have all enabled not only imagining types of movement or the counting of units in the plural, but also produced the language by which to express the relative sizes and volume ratio of different wealth objects, such as Bitcoin accounts. These idioms reflected a real sense of spatial transformation because each trader was always both a buyer and a seller. Consequently, the existence of topological distance or proximity on the blockchain was ontological, a constant feature of the network (cf. Mol and Law 1994), wherein trading volumes always intensified after a discharge took place.

Digital spatial transformation is nonetheless different than that which takes place during a physical gathering. Such issues as equality, distance and touch – which Canetti emphasized as the core of crowding – gain new traits on the blockchain landscape. Equality, for example, refers to the fact that at least nominally every trader is equal to all others as there are literally no inhibitions or obstacles that may block investors or limit their ability to trade. In the absence of a central/sanctioning authority, the blockchain thus lacks the 'burden' of hierarchical distances people must accept in everyday life when they are subjugated to and interpolated by different 'third parties'. When trade intensified, this nominal cancellation of hierarchies can be seen to *shorten* the distance between peers, as they can operate uninhibited on the virtual platform based on their own investment strategies. This same sense of shortening also highlights an unflinching dependency on mass synchronic action in the bitcoin trading market.

This said, the ever-dynamic transformation of the market also re-creates hierarchies based on the value of one's holdings. Value fluctuations work to scramble the boundaries between traders as they generate and lose wealth objects, which in a closed economy such as the Bitcoin market always influence someone else's holdings. Consequently, wealth hierarchies are re-created within the blockchain (see Roberts 2022; Schneider 2019) in a process that sometimes *increases* the distance between traders, both in terms of the value of their assets and their ability to take or abandon different trade positions. Every modification of such vectors of digital distance influences the distribution of affects online, thus taking crucial part in generating crowding phenomena on the blockchain.

As I claimed above, then, topological transformations on the blockchain are relatively minor when the value fluctuation is minute. But when a powerful whirlpool happens – as was the case in 2017 – it intensifies affective phenomenality on the blockchain and further proliferates the potential for growth or decline in trade volume, respectively, *as a function of value distances* (see also Venonnen 2024). The economic schema is simple. When the value goes up, more sellers rush in, expanding supply. When the value goes down, more buyers attempt to capture the opportunity, expanding demand (much like stock trading). In both cases, if the change upwards or downwards is radical enough, an affective discharge often takes place, *distances-as-volume become shorter*, and crowds are formed both online and offline. The case of the 2017 goldrush was a classic example of how such blockchain crowds simply emerge at the grassroots level with little or no top-down manipulation, which means that every person (or individual) who is involved must recalculate and control their proximity to and distance from all others.

Within this scheme, and simultaneously, every peer is thrust into the wider flux of frenetic trade volumes, emphasizing contingency despite nominal acceptance of the idea that each Bitcoiner is radically disconnected from all the others. Veteran investors know that eventually the fluctuations will stabilize, the distances between investors will consequently widen again and the crowd will dissolve until the next boom-and-bust cycle bursts through the blockchain, causing investors to act synchronically despite their initial relational 'distance'. Blockchain crowds, in effect, *produce themselves* through this ongoing game of value fluctuation, which dynamically provokes distance management between peers.

Distance management can thus be said to occur naturally – or, I should say, outside the control of individual investors. Buying more, whether by rational decision or impulse, condensed holders further into the mass. Sellers are aware that by disposing of some of their bitcoin holding they temporarily *enlarge* the distance between them and the crowd to the extent that they can catapult themselves out and away from that crowd if they liquidate *all* their holdings (and probably make massive profits). Crowd self-organization via distance management, experienced topologically as values and volumes, thus replaces the usual regulatory role of centralized hierarchies, which is premised on the privileged position of a 'third party'.

Distance management is thereby simultaneously subject to the topological transformations of value hierarchies and wealth volumes on the blockchain *and* the idiosyncratic pursuit of individual investment strategies. This duality always impacts trade dynamics at a global scale, generating a space wherein people can congregate to *escape* the normative types of authority they respect (or fear) in everyday life (Baudrillard 1988; Lee 2021; Wiedemann 2014). Crowding on the blockchain is in that double sense a literal force capable of emitting the disciplining power of the collective while also making affective and structural space for *individual* empowerment.

The Power of Bitcoin Crowds

Embassy associates saw themselves as members of a social group whose scope was universal and borderless as much as it was local and restrictive. While referring to the global mass of Bitcoin supporters as a 'community', interlocutors in Tel Aviv also spoke of their own local community as a tangible social milieu. They associated activities on both these scenes with the overall goal of mass adoption, which they believed would dynamically resist counteractive tendencies to centralize the organization and control capital. The vividness of community-centred activities at the local level, in other words, was an essential empowering force in the push towards the Bitcoin universalization at the level of the global community. As Bloom often reminded his audience in public appearances, 'if Bitcoin is ever to become mainstream it must circulate in some way'. He defended this position during an interview I held with him by appealing to economic efficiency:

> The point is that people [must] use bitcoin. There is no other goal. This means that savings will be in bitcoin and salaries will be paid in bitcoin. Now, this will enable decentralization of P2P relationships, so there will be nobody that could force anybody else to do something. As far as I understand this, the end game is that the economy will be more efficient. Today there are many [non-crypto] business initiatives that never even begin [to succeed commercially] because the financial system could not or would not support them. Sometimes it's just too expensive and sometimes the banks block it for different reasons. So as soon as we have money that works [i.e. bitcoin], the economy will be more efficient and there will be more initiatives.

Bloom's response implicitly suggests, however, that macro-level events stemming from the dynamics of Bitcoin global trade and fluctuating values also directly influence the boundaries of the local community. *All power*, as McClelland (1989: 296–97) argues, includes a crowd dimension, and Bitcoin crowds are no different. The meaning of this subtle observation is that crowd movement – via synchronic choices of multiple investors – can under certain conditions dissolve communitarian boundaries. That was the case with BitNation-Pangea, to recall the example I surveyed in Chapter 1. Power is therefore an important heuristic that Bitcoiners in Israel during my fieldwork often misjudged or overlooked, as they over-emphasized their own contribution to the global community while sometimes missing the scale by which the global crowd had indeed shaped the character of their local community in Tel Aviv.

Elias Canetti (1984[1960]) has argued that power is not *the result* of crowd behaviour, nor a manipulation of crowds by demagogues. The exercise of power in any formation – legal/institutional, charismatic or spontaneous (e.g. the result of moral outrage) – is something that *seeks* crowds to fulfil itself, spread out, acquire substance, volume, depth and ground-level traction. For Canetti, then, *the crowd is where power realizes its authoritative potentiality* (Lee 2016: 318). Put otherwise, the crowd is the space for the materialization of different political schemas, which often take the form of emotional substances running through one's veins (Baker 2011; see

Butler 2022). Therefore, the practical realization of political goals *depends* on affective discharges (Hayes 2019), which blur the boundaries of alterity and shorten distances between people at the local level. The formation of a crowd, especially a digital crowd, is undeniably political in the sense that it empowers multitudes to act together (Stage 2013).

The rise of Bitcoin as a global movement was not different, and the surge in value of 2017 exponentially brought it to new levels of crowd formation. This created FOMO, which was contingent on the authority and legitimacy of charismatic big-men/women – a category I borrow from Melanesian and Polynesian political structures – who could artificially mobilize crowds on the blockchain. Mining company bosses, for example, might have tried to influence the pace of value fluctuations in a frenzy of buying and selling (Golumbia 2016; Roberts 2022). Industry influencers likewise used their considerable number of social media followers to support trends and disseminate ideas. Embedded 'in algorithmic universes of suggestion and likeness' (Hayden 2021: 101; see Zuboff 2019) to be effective in the first place, the agency and consequent power of such influencers were pivotal sources of inspiration for a multiplicity of voices that were quickly reciprocating the discourse, including mainstream media coverage of Bitcoin-related affairs. The simultaneous discharge of affects through all these channels triggered crowding.

That said, however, celebrity power is largely suggestive and informal (Stage 2013) rather than coercive (namely, Mazzarella 2017; Tarde 1912). It should therefore be understood as an element in a complex system of communication, not a decisive force. That is also true for the power of Ambassadors to influence crowd dynamics on the ground, which was limited in 2017 as it is restricted now, especially concerning their attempts to link Bitcoin with societal reorganization rather than profiteering. Evidently, some Bitcoiners have achieved celebrity status as 'experts' or 'veterans' (for example, Antonopoulos 2015; Buterin 2017), but they are known mostly among Bitcoin enthusiasts, unable to achieve society-scale exposure. [7]

Crowding phenomena thus still depend on a multiplicity of factors that coexist simultaneously. In 2017, for example, institutional warnings coming from respected economists in Israel, as well as from high-ranking officials in the Israeli financial establishment, were equally limited in their ability to restrict crowding. Even the head of the Israeli tax authority, who in 2017 strongly advised *against* buying bitcoin in a prime-time televised interview, could not single handedly influence hearts and minds. The multitudes, the sprawling crowd, kept swarming regardless of the warnings. The goldrush eventually died out only when the bitcoin value began to plummet, itself a process caused by uncoordinated mass action on the blockchain.

Both media coverage and influencers' pronunciations, for or against Bitcoin, should thus be seen as proxies for the density of the crowd; rather than as tools by which interested stakeholders can manipulate the market (contra Golumbia 2018; see Baudrillard 1985; Borch 2012: 275). The preceding instantiation of discharge at the quasi-magical moment of crowd formation ignites something that from that moment onwards self-organized its volume, speed and mass, expanding and contracting in accordance with market conditions, as well as the changing narratives that accompany ongoing value fluctuations (see Wiedemann 2014).

That is precisely Canetti's (ibid.) intention when he asserts that power *feeds* on the crowd; certain aphorisms, and tropes, and imaginaries, self-perpetuate through the crowd and are being circulated only as long as the crowd exists. When the crowd disperses, political meaning-making often disappears with it, at least at the contextual level of the gathering and its immediate socio-cultural surrounding. Suggestive power – both in the Foucauldian sense of personalized bioadaptive commitments and in the sense of the ability to sanction and enforce others to act in certain ways – *fed* on the crowd that blocked the entrance to the Embassy in 2017 only as long as that crowd was cohesive. That power dissipated when the crowd dissolved about a month later.

There is also another sense of empowerment that comes with the emergence of Bitcoin crowds, as I claim in Chapter 5, which is anchored in prevalent cosmogonic ideas including genesis, confrontation and salvation, all of which are pivotal for the successful implementation of Bitcoin sociality in any context; whether at the Embassy or elsewhere (see Faustino, Faria and Marques 2022). This sense of empowerment has two material manifestations. First, the movement of money on the blockchain endows individuals with the experiential power to prevent others from sanctioning them. Each Bitcoiner is fully and exclusively responsible for their own economic decisions, and transactions are final and irreversible; power here manifests in the form of total control over one's money, along with the fears and inhibitions that come with this lonely position. Second, the affective dynamic linked to wild value fluctuations *ontologically* dismisses the burden generated due to the accumulated history of painful 'stings' each of us carries through life, as Canetti (1984[1960]) called it. It enables people to feel, if only temporarily, that they are free to simply 'get up and go' whenever they wish; this, in contrast to the dystopian possibility of being held hostage by a crisis like that in 2008, which erased fiat savings accounts and even caused some unfortunate investors to jump from roofs.

These forms of empowerment – individual conviction due to suggestion and the overwhelming density of a flowing crowd – are ultimately complementary. Each bitcoin holder, in other words, forms part of the crowd despite their nominal atomization, while the crowd is in a way embodied in each individual. The blockchain, which is a self-sustaining system that regulates itself, thereby cuts distance between people as it simultaneously consolidates individual autonomy. Evidently, every trader maintains total power over their digital wallets. The temporary unification of those who take part in a crowd generates in this way a form of free-flowing political-economic power shared collectively and continuously between fully-autonomous traders. As Christian Borch (2007: 588) has argued, the emotional pull of financial markets 'reflects the generation or emergence of an independent life form'. Borch thus claims that the market itself becomes a living entity, almost literally, because it is ontologically emotive, and thus is felt as a kinetic force pushing and pulling through those making part of it, as if on a rollercoaster. As I claimed above, a pragmatic sense of empowerment thereby becomes a visceral force that surges *within* people, producing crowding phenomena en masse as a factor of synchronic trading activities of multitudes of buyers and sellers (see also Baker 2011; Stage 2013).

Interlocutors in Tel Aviv understood the transformative power of the crowd. Rami once told me that for him, holding bitcoin included an intense expectation, an alertness of the kind acquired when one must manoeuvre through a situation not entirely under his or her control. Roy described this collective immersion in the crowd as being pushed up or down a narrow staircase, here compared to the value of bitcoin. Waves of collective anticipation roiled in reaction to these wild fluctuations, which kept emitting powerful swells that impacted traders across the network. The gushing power of these swells made it important to know how to *drift* with the crowd without getting carried away, as Nissim once pointed out. I now move to briefly discuss this issue.

Drifting with the Crowd

Nissim's 'drifting' denoted participation in a dynamic of power relations that was unrelenting and unpredictable. When discharge caused people to begin buying and selling in large groups – regardless of whether the value went up or down – they were participating in a game of chance that could take them to places they would not normally want to go. Crowd motility might have carved new spaces for interaction between fully contained 'autonomous' individuals, but the resulting intensity, trajectories and changing formations within the crowd could be experienced as tantalizingly dreadful. This was so because discharge and the shortening of value distances do not produce proximity in the sense of a shared collective interest, but rather, they intensify the *collective morphology* on the blockchain. Drifting, in this sense, is dangerous. It is only logical that in such cases everyone would try to sail close to the wind.

'Drifting' also happens in the tightly regulated world of stock exchange trading, wherein large crowds are formed despite their geographical dispersion, sociocultural heterogeneity and diverse economic rationalizations (Borch 2009; Smith 2005). Drifting with crowds on the blockchain is however more perilous, given that trade takes place *outside* the reach of the Hobbesian state; which can be as protectionist as it is coercive. The story of some goldbugs I have met in Tel Aviv suggests that crowd-drifting could at time open an experiential universe across cyberspace, which was consistently transforming through time, wherein normative financial dynamics are launched into the stratosphere of hyper-realism. It thus made *tangible* the prospect of drifting too far or even sinking altogether (Baldwin 2018). Crucially, then, the force of heterogenic and sprawling crowds of bitcoin holders at the global level had to be mitigated by stable, largely homogenous small-scale and demarcated core communities of true believers, where helpless drifters could find refuge. Anchoring oneself in the community was seen as the only way to avoid being swept away by the crowd.

Crowd dynamics in Bitcoin, in short, sustain a perpetual tension felt heuristically as a magnetic attraction or rejection between virtual as well as actual 'peers', who are all players – or *partners* – in a zero-sum game; wherein discharges regularly constitute *interdependency* between total strangers (Pickles 2024; Borch 2007; Smith 2005). Both individually and collectively, the continuous movement of sellers and buyers online – movement in the actual sense of sending money across the web – structures crowd constellations (i.e. exchange en masse), while redefining the situational scope of individual relationships (i.e. P2P exchange) rapidly and unexpectedly. This dynamic stirs up, reflects and intensifies boom-and-bust cycles, *as well as* the structural demands produced by such social institutions as state regulatory bodies, cryptocurrency exchange companies, blockchain mining corporations, cryptocurrency startups, etc. The notion of dynamics, and the demand to 'drift' responsibly, only further elucidated the importance of the 'community' as an island in the stream, where people could *stop* drifting. Even if the boundaries of the community were not always clearly defined, Embassy associates recognized the presence of their colleagues as an opportunity to *rest*. At a public lecture in 2019, Nissim further clarified that point, which will lead me to the conclusion of this chapter:

> Within our community there is a harmonious situation, which gives us power – not physical power but mental power because we are responsible for one another – it is written [in the Bible] that 'all of Israel is responsible to each other' [*kol Yisrael A-revim ze-la-ze*] but this was long gone. Bitcoin is creating the possibility to regenerate this mutual responsibility [*arvut ha-da-dit*], which is in our origins [as a people], on which we were all built, on this we [the People of Israel]

> built our home. But today, if you disagree with the leaders who tell us what to do, [they say] 'he is a traitor', 'he is a bad person', 'he is a leftist' . . . I don't understand that. I understand that if I do something right I will be rewarded, and if I do something wrong I will be punished. It's true that even in the world of Bitcoin there are people [who] have invented new patents to take money from people . . . But we will not let them into our community [because] they do not share our values; we will keep [pursuing] our journey, and we are not tempted by their money or their suggestions that we should deceive and steal.

Conclusion

The Bitcoin crowd carries with it the power to collectively build a utopian political-economic order. Power that is made available at the level of the individual (as a fully autonomous subject) is here collectivized through mass action. During my fieldwork in Tel Aviv, many Ambassadors in fact treated Bitcoin as a literal source of energy that could carry people with it like waves in the ocean. Value fluctuations – which interlocutors saw as part of 'what Bitcoin does' – affected everyone at once, albeit relative to one's holding volumes. Interlocutors consequently had to respond rationally to changing value conditions if they wanted to remain in the gain, while also regulating such effects as thrill or FUD using mundane emotion-management skills. That meant keeping a cool head when the value plummeted, and restraining euphoria when it rocketed to sometimes-unbelievable new heights. Price volatility, in other words, *released* immense socioeconomic, affective and even spiritual forces; to which Bitcoiners had to continuously react, for better or worse, while interacting with others who were doing the same.

Even dedicated maximalists, who paid little attention to the actual fiat-equivalent value of Bitcoin, were affected by these forces. It thus seems to me that the fluctuation itself, which emits energy, is capable of mobilizing affect in its own right. Evidently, those Ambassadors who at times traded in altcoins were often caught up in FOMOs upon mild fluctuations in the fiat-equivalent value of marginal cryptocurrencies, which often remained well under one dollar per unit. The crowd is simply saturated by, and its bursting energy is composed of, the synchronic action of multiple individual traders. The crowd cultivates itself through decentralized mass action, and in the process it necessarily infringes on established economic, financial and even *moral* aphorisms that build instead on the importance of 'centralized' organization and top-down regulation. The prospect of *profiteering*, rather than of profit itself, surges to organize the chaotic dynamic of the crowd, even for those who are motivated to invest in Bitcoin in order to foster social reform; since they too wish to cut their losses when the value falls sharply.

As the blockchain continues to operate, then, it produces crowds from the bottom up – among those who have 'lost the fear of being (digitally) touched' – while structurally conditioning this crowd formation from the top down, as the entire game of purchase and reselling is initially defined by the concrete rules set by Satoshi back in 2008. Financial edgework on the blockchain is thus rationalized at the level of individual decision making, albeit continuously influenced by unpredictable collective trends. Since the blockchain clusters people together and then 'reshuffles the cards', as Yaron had claimed in this interview quoted above, it thus also erases and then reinstates distances between those who congregate on/within it. Blockchain crowds are thereby constituted due to two intrinsic attributions:

(1) *Individuals strengthening mass consensus* – with the double idea of 'trustlessness' and 'decentralization', the blockchain eliminates singular veto decisions, thereby favouring mass action in the determination of value trends. The market opens to a myriad of dispersed users whose participation in the system is voluntary. The relational positioning of all bitcoin holders produces a creative tension between a multiplicity of sellers, buyers, holders and miners, a tension that thus fortifies and benefits the collective rather than any individual user/node (Butler 2022; Hayes 2019; but see Baldwin 2018; Dodd 2018; Faria 2021; Schneider 2019).
(2) *Mass consensus strengthens individuals* – whether the blockchain is heuristically understood to be a living entity or a technical system driven by self-referential or self-maintaining dynamics (Hayes 2019: 15), its elementary units are always reducible to individual 'nodes' and 'peers', whose total control over their own funds is the goal of the entire endeavour. The blockchain might randomly collectivize people into distinct groups whose relational positioning and mass action influence value trends, but it also totalizes the individual agency of each participant, who thereby *becomes* a rationally informed and purportedly 'responsible' owner of their own bank.

These attributions become mutually-inclusive when discharge spreads affects, thus turning the fluctuating financial value of Bitcoin into a measurement (and a driving force) of personal agency. What empowers individuals here also instigates dynamic transitions at the scale of the collective. Fluctuation is the ultimate mobilizing force, whether people seek to maximize it because they want to establish a 'trustless' society or to purchase a new flat. Heterogenic multitudes of supporters, ideologues, traders, investors, entrepreneurs and communities all acquire equal status within the movement of the Bitcoin global crowd, much in the same way as people at a mass gathering suddenly feel a solidarity that abolishes previously established ranks and statuses (McClelland 1989: 168, 307). As I noted, then, the Bitcoin crowd is at once contingent on individual investment strategies and the arbitrary synchronicity of mass action.

It is true that ideological forms of power – or at least pretentions to assume power – preceded the formation of Bitcoin crowds (Golumbia 2018; Zimmer 2017). Satoshi and most other early investors, as I emphasized in Chapter 1, clearly supported libertarian politics and techno-utopian cypherpunk ideals. It is also a truism that the public reach of tweets or posts is initially conditioned by the political and discursive aphorisms of their originators, who position themselves for or against other relevant voices and arguments, thus increasing the impact of their own rhetorical acts in the cacophony of social network marketing threads (Lee 2016). The billionaire businessman Elon Musk has in fact singlehandedly caused huge fluctuations across the cryptocurrency market over the years by tweeting his support for (or disapproval of) this or that cryptocurrency project, while occasionally also selling large quantities of bitcoin through his companies. Such actions can at times destabilize the market (Barber 2021).

But the Bitcoin blockchain remains trustless, and uncensored, regardless of such anomalies. Forms of economic ideology could not restrain the ongoing reproduction of crowds – both on the blockchain and offline – nor could they artificially produce crowds through monetarism or other top-down regulatory decisions, given the absence of institutional enforcement or the sanction power of powerful 'third parties'. As long as it remains legal to buy and sell Bitcoin, the consolidation and motion of crowds will continue to depend on the affective materialization of discharges and the scope of their dissemination, no matter what and who stands behind them. Andrea Brighenti (2014: 38) exemplifies this notion sharply when he describes the self-organization and dynamics of crowds:

> The crowd is not the solid collective which Durkheim described as a new exceptional creature emerging out of the ritual. Nor is it a social group with a shared affiliation or a specific positioning vis-à-vis other groups, which structuralist theorists elected as their topic of choice . . . the crowd should be better conceptualised as an *event*, a nebula-like composition which takes shape at different scales of action and which shapes different territories of interaction – or better, action–reaction complexes. The most visible scale at which this event occurs is the scenery where urban crowds, mediated publics and global masses – as well as those other peculiar entities which are populations, multitudes and peoples – make their appearance.

At the level of firsthand experience, research interlocutors in Tel Aviv could thus be seen to have continuously reacted to crowd-nebula dynamics, which was characterized by sensuous and sensory agitation, a surge of feelings (for example, elation, rage, sadness, etc.) and intense empowerment bursting through people individually and collectively. What holds the nebula together is the ongoing kinetic movement of all the elements in it vis-à-vis one another, suggesting that the dense internal connectedness of crowds and the phenomenon of distance management are always subjected to ongoing changes in scope and intensity. Most Ambassadors in Tel Aviv saw themselves as 'true believers' that contextually experimented with the prescribed egalitarian possibilities of the Bitcoin 'revolution' in their everyday life despite its many internal contradictions; including their fear of overcrowding and 'herd' mentality dominated by cynical influencers who advance the prospects of profiteering over and above the prospect of social change[8]. At the ground level of individual psychology, this also suggests that the very pertinence to a crowd must be verified repeatedly by all participants in real time.

While maximalists like Nissim would probably disagree, this last assertion suggests that the global Bitcoin crowd is entirely 'open', a term Canetti (1984[1960]) used to refer to what he understood as the 'natural' crowd; that is, a crowd that 'grows' uncontained and unhindered. '"Open" is to be understood here in the fullest sense of the word', he argues (ibid.: 16). 'It means open everywhere and in any direction. The open crowd exists so long as it grows; it disintegrates as soon as it stops growing.' 'Closed' crowds, on the contrary, are groups that 'renounce growth and put the stress on permanence' (ibid.: 17). Canetti described these oppositional crowd densities to explain how the apparent fluidity and disorganization of 'open' crowds may paradoxically sometimes lead to stagnation, and the concentration of power in 'closed' crowds might begin to fragment it until it becomes open again. Seen through this wider lens, then, trade dynamics become a decisive element in determining the density of reciprocating peers on the Bitcoin blockchain, and thus in the constant making and unmaking of shapeshifting crowds.

Crowding phenomenality – both affectively and structurally – ultimately forms an augmented space for social action, turning the issue of distance management between closed and open forms of collaboration into one of the most crucial aspects of Bitcoin sociality at any scale; whether the object of observation is the global masses, demarcated communities such as the Embassy, or individual people whose idiosyncratic and self-enclosed bodies make up the wider multitude. During my fieldwork, distance management has thus become a *necessary technique* to be mastered at the level of communitarian organization, enabling Ambassadors to achieve a measure of control during powerful discharges, which at times (temporarily) erased previously set boundaries of alterity between the community and its outsiders. And this, as I will explore in the next chapter, means that the Bitcoin project at large could end up negating or even destroying the libertarian principles it initially set out to protect.

NOTES

1. The time element is also undefined; while the blockchain is programmed to produce exactly 21 million bitcoins, which as I explained above will all be mined by the early 2140s, accumulation and usage of bitcoin as a currency or a store of value can continue as long as nodes exchange bitcoin between them and verify transactions on the blockchain.
2. This crowd phenomenon is sometimes also called 'the Mexican wave' since it gained global popularity during the FIFA World Cap competitions in Mexico in 1986. The wave is nonetheless alleged to have commenced in United States baseball matches in the early 1980s (see Rohrer 2010).
3. From the point of view of Embassy associates, the goldrush was merely one of many boom-and-bust cycles that have accompanied the value fluctuations of bitcoin since at least 2013. 'Bitcoin fluctuates because that is what Bitcoin does', was the sentiment that Ambassadors expressed in various ways and tones. Yet, the goldrush constituted a crowding phenomenon that exceeded anything that interlocutors had seen before. As crowds dwindled in December that year, it was already clear that the Rubicon has been crossed.
4. On the one hand, this informs a negative view of crowds, as with Gustav Le Bon's (1895) claim that unpredictable consolidation risks societal stability. On the other hand, discharge that is the result of value fluctuation works to focus people's attention on the very synchronicity of trading trends, as they normally wish to cut losses or remain in the gain. In that sense, unless a Bitcoin doom scenario occurs (e.g. legal crackdown, in-blockchain manipulation at a huge scale, colossal hack, etc.) – which would cause the decentralized equivalent of a 'run on the bank' – discharge cannot be directed violently out and away from the interiority of the system in which it came into being.
5. Think of the following dilemma, among others: Should an investor replace their stated support of the Bitcoin community – proven through HODLING – with a risk-averse 'diversification' of money into other assets?
6. Another popular tool is a block formation detector, which is visualized as a literal chain of square structures that are quickly being filled with colourful diamonds piling up to the sound of high-pitched 'blings' (e.g. https://chainflyer.bitflyer.jp/). Such visualizations attribute a cogent spatial sense to transactions that could have otherwise been depicted as a series of mathematical calculations or lines of code.
7. Specifically with regard to leaders and influencers in the global Bitcoin scene, their own ability to set trends is also limited for lack of any formal mechanism of crowd control and regulation.
8. According to Canetti (1984[1960]), a crowd that grows too much dissolves, but if the crowd encloses on itself too much, it becomes a 'religious pack' (ibid.: 127–28). The

community in Tel Aviv celebrated a millenarian ethos, not a strictly theological one, as I claimed in Chapter 5, but the dynamics of enclosure could potentially tighten the boundary. While I do not believe that the community in Tel Aviv could become a 'cult' or a 'religion' anytime soon, the integrity of their project indeed depended on their ability to navigate the ongoing expansion and contraction of financial crowds, while simultaneously controlling the boundaries of their community.

CHAPTER 7

NIHILIST SPECTACLES

Blurred Vision

The idea that an existing order is decadent and bound to hell – and that it must be replaced by a new and purified system led by a risk-taking, tradition-shattering cultural avant-garde – is not new. The Italian Futurist movement, which projected moral power on to technology (Adamson 2010) is a particularly relevant comparison to the case of Bitcoin. The artist Filippo Tommaso Marinetti had in fact published the *Futurist Manifesto* on 1 January 1909, almost 100 years to the day before the mining of the Genesis Block that launched Bitcoin as a tradable currency (on 3 January 2009). A poetic glorification of war, danger, misogyny and industrialism, the *Manifesto* makes a clear dividing line between past and future, declaring the present to be 'revolutionary' by virtue of the progressive acquisition of speed, and the future to be a total reinvention of social life emerging from the obliteration of the past:

> We declare that the splendour of the world has been enriched by a new beauty: the beauty of speed. A racing automobile with its bonnet adorned with great tubes like serpents with explosive breath . . . a roaring motor car which seems to run on machine-gun fire, is more beautiful than the Victory of Samothrace.[1] . . . We are on the extreme promontory of the centuries! What is the use of looking behind at the moment when we must open the mysterious shutters of the impossible? Time and Space died yesterday. We are already living in the absolute, since we have already created eternal, omnipresent speed.[2]

Marinetti described 'eternal omnipresent speed' as absolute because it plunges people out and away from where they are standing, no matter how much they resist the thrust. One of the consequences of speeding, which fascinated Marinetti, is the obscuring of forms and outlines, turning external reality indistinct relative to the speeder's own senses. As a political trope, speed first blurs and then leaves behind the nineteenth-century concepts of naturalism, parochialism and romanticism. Seeking new forms of expression and perspectives in the age of accelerated industrialization, Futurist artists thereby experimented with blurred lines in a deliberate attempt to shake off these Old-World burdens. Futurist theatre plays, for example, included scenes in which the actors stepped down from the stage and mingled in the crowd, effectively turning the audience into a part the spectacle. The outcome was a bi-directional revisionism; the confusion that came with breaking the fourth wall did not only turn spectators into unwitting actors, but it also integrated the spectacle into mundane reality. This blurring of boundaries symbolized a rebellion against hierarchy, social control and the received wisdom of past generations. Reality, whether staged or lived in, is here imagined and then enacted as a perpetuated kineticism, a dynamic of constant shapeshifting and boundary crossing that distorts the observer's vision as it advances the Nietzschean idea that modern subjectivities must reject traditional knowledge and be remade again, *ex nihilo*. The *Manifesto* continues:

> Look at us! We are not out of breath; our hearts are not in the least tired. For they are nourished by fire, hatred and speed! Does this surprise you? It is because you do not even remember being alive! Standing on the world's summit, we launch once more our challenge to the stars! Your objections? All right! I know them! Of course! We know just what our beautiful false intelligence affirms: 'We are only the sum and the prolongation of our ancestors', it says. Perhaps! All right! What does it matter? But we will not listen! Take care not to repeat those infamous words! Instead, lift up your head!

Commitment to dynamism was the essence of Futurist programmatic revisionism, which sought to destroy hegemonic forms of authority. This commitment implicitly advocated the experience of multiplicity and instability as rules rather than exception, turning every beholder into the ultimate moral and political judge, and thus relativizing the authenticity of experience. Experience was now being shaped by the totality of a constant drift forward, tumbling everything along the way with crude power. Dynamism could be seen a posteriori as a permanent vector of change, especially in the context of emergent megacities:

> For the dying, for invalids and for prisoners it may be all right. It is, perhaps, some sort of balm for their wounds, the admirable past, at a moment when the future is denied them. But we will have none of it, we, the young, strong and living Futurists! . . . Let the good incendiaries with charred fingers come! Here they are! Heap

> up the fire to the shelves of the libraries! Divert the canals to flood the cellars of the museums! Let the glorious canvases swim ashore! Take the picks and hammers! Undermine the foundation of venerable towns!

Marinetti attributed the power to impact reality to the masses of young men who would rebel against obedience and respectability. The transformation of society was not associated with an individual leader – which is absent from the *Manifesto* – but with the anarchic synergy of *crowds*. It is no wonder that the *Manifesto* was written in the plural, celebrating the restless life-force of multitudes, which, from a bird's-eye view, crystallizes individual participants into an indistinct mass. Identified with speed, rage, revolt, mechanical brutalism and a sense of impatience, Futurists turned the pace of urban crowds into the main principle of modern lifestyles. As Marinetti writes, the future belongs to 'the gliding flight of aeroplanes whose propeller sounds like the flapping of a flag and the applause of enthusiastic crowds.'

Futurism was in that sense a vision of a crowd-society that was nihilistic to the core (Ohana 2016). Marinetti envisioned a new urban future in which the square monumentalism of the nineteenth century, along with its romantic naturalism, would be replaced with the abrasive power of technologies. The awe, inspiration and transcendence associated with classical decorative aesthetics was thus replaced with an image of sophistication, efficiency and dynamism. It is no wonder that the materialist element of the Futuristic movement celebrated electricity in particular – power stations and the electric grid – as literal sources of power that would enable the creation of a New World dominated by a new kind of Man thriving on the ruins of outdated moral codes. These utopian ideals rejected all traditional forms of knowledge and aesthetics, turning instead to an accelerated sense of change as a form of both thrill and salvation.

Embracing speed as a guiding principle for societal reformation thus meant turning distinct façades of everyday sociality into reflections of each other, moving *through* each other too quickly to be identified by their external features. Speed was an architecture of society in the destructive sense, a remoulding of the social landscape. Speed was a symbolic artefact or even an elaborate value system, wherein straight lines and cubes, much like *blocks and chains*, continuously merged in various creative ways until they reshaped objects in the world as curves, turbulences, folds, vortexes and shadows. Speed blurred the landscape, which thus became a uniformity lacking concrete referential parameters of its many parts, an immense homogeneity that in Italy predicted the rise of the Fascist movement.[3] The nihilism of futurism consisted in the mythification of politics, coupled with the drive for spontaneous destruction (Ohana 2016), the idea that the new must dynamically renew itself, and that old truths by default should be eradicated.

While maximalists at the Embassy did not *explicitly* express nihilistic ideas, the framework of their aspired-to revolution was nonetheless based on such typical nihilist features as the epistemological failure of past generations, destruction of hegemonic value systems, radical view of individual freedom, belief in egalitarianism and a sense of cosmic disintegration. These notions perpetuated a sense of instability as much as they pretended to mitigate tensions between peers, businesses, companies, corporations, organizations and other forms of association in the making of a New Economy. Such tensions, along with their nihilist implications, materialized in 2018 when disagreements between some of the most prominent members of the community escalated into full-scale open conflict.

The Fork

In the autumn of 2018, community members began accusing Emil – the administrator of the 30,000-strong 'Israeli Bitcoin' Facebook group and a veteran Embassy associate who was there from the very beginning – of abusing his censorship powers. They complained that he was blocking members who uploaded posts he disagreed with, the subjects of which varied from ideology to financial issues. Moreover, they claimed, Emil was actively silencing legitimate views while trying to promote his own business interests in the group at the expense of free and transparent debate, thereby betraying the unwritten code of conduct of the community. A local Bitcoin blogger summarized this in an article he published on Medium (Aviv 2018):

> By nature of [Israeli Bitcoin] being a crypto [Facebook] group, clashes and disagreements are common. From ICOs [Initial Coin Offering], Bitcoin/Bitcoin Cash [arguments], all the way to shady promotions and referrals.[4] One post about lightning network devolved *[sic]* into a show of ego and eventually the expulsion of [a community member called] Uri W. by the admin of the group who was on the other side of the discussion. This was followed by an almost unanimous uprising of the community against the decision, as Uri was one of the top contributors to the group and the expulsion was unjustified. A few admins protested and were either removed or left of their own volition, another few *[sic]* argued [against the expulsion, claiming] that [if] the community does not have the right to criticize the admin this is not a democracy, but a dictatorship.

Over the course of the next few months things had gotten worse. There had been continuous muting and banning of users without real justification. Those who expressed their thoughts about the management of the group, requesting changes, soon discovered that meta posts were outlawed,[5] and were to be discussed in a separate group. One member exclaimed in response to Emil's admin decisions [that] 'Every time there's a management decision to make, you somehow choose the worst possible one ... The absurdity here is that we're a community gathered to discuss Bitcoin and cryptocurrencies, from a realization that centralized power and decision-making leads to corruption, and yet this community fell to the exact flaws of human nature'.

Following heated discussions online, which also took place behind the scenes in two of the main WhatsApp groups used by Embassy members at the time, prominent Embassy members publicly called on Emil to hand over management of the group to 'the community'. This was to be done by granting other administrators veto powers over *his* decisions. In order to do so, the group management structure would have needed to change, and Emil, as the group creator and hence main administer, refused to enact this change. The opposition in the community organized several 'delegations' in response, all of which were led by Emil's old friend Dani Bloom. I could not attend these meetings, but rumour has it that the debate at times became tense, and voices were raised. After three meetings, negotiations reached a dead end. Emil refused to acknowledge any malpractice, continued to ban people, and scolded those accusing him of 'centralizing power'. Ambassadors and other associates who took part in the controversy became even angrier.

Bloom then decided to write a constitution that would clearly define the rules of debate on the Facebook group. In addition, and more controversially, he and a few others felt that they had to 'fork' the community in order to re-establish free speech and to distance Emil. Rather than duplicating the blockchain, 'forking' in this case was simply used as analogous to splitting. Supporters of the fork claimed that its enactment would be 'a service to the community', and to justify this they sometimes argued that 'the whole community is against Emil'. Once the decision was made among main positioners, Bloom published a short letter accompanied by a six-point manifesto titled *A New Group for the Israeli Bitcoin Community*. It stated that 'the [new] group will not be governed by a single ruler but collaboratively by several administrators who ... act for the community according to a well-defined constitution, protocol, and rules'. Its clauses were:

(1) The group is set up for the benefit of the community and it belongs to community members. It does not belong to any private person, a small group of people, or a centralized body.
(2) The group is dedicated to debates on the many different aspects of Bitcoin, similar technologies, and the rest of the decentralized digital currencies.

(3) Since the term 'community' is not precisely defined and there is no simple way of knowing the wishes of the community, group administrators will be given the authority to act as community delegates for the benefit of the community, in accordance with their common sense.
(4) When a need to take decisions that may influence the characteristics of the group comes about, such as changing the rules or adding and demoting administrators, it is preferred that the decision will be taken among the administrators based on a crude consensus. If a consensus cannot be reached, a vote will take place among the administrators.
(5) The group will aspire to act in accordance with the Bitcoin principles, including openness, transparency, pluralism and lack of censorship, whenever these can reasonably be maintained without damaging the spirit of the debate, the smooth ongoing functioning of the group, and the rules of the State of Israel and the Facebook platform.
(6) This Constitution can be changed only by supermajority.[6]

Bloom published this document on the very Facebook group he now sought to leave, asking those community members who supported the move to sign it. Some did, others not. Most who did sign were active Embassy members or people strongly associated with Bitcoin activism in Israel, who knew the relevant protagonists personally. Within a month, to the surprise of the supporters of the fork, about two thousand followers moved from the original Facebook group to the new one. In a private online chat I had with one of the Ambassadors at the time, he said that this was 'a victory for the community'. Emil remained the 'ruler' of the old group, which kept its original name 'Israeli Bitcoin', while Bloom and a few other veteran Ambassadors became the administrators of the new group. They called it, straightforwardly, 'Bitcoin – The Israeli Community'. Eylon Aviv, the blogger, concluded that:

> The goal is to design a system (ensured by protocol) that ultimately delivers control to the users, from us, the creators of the platform. Even if this takes over the world, I won't have the power to decide what is right and what is wrong. The people who continuously and consistently contribute will be the ones in charge, as long as they serve their community.

For those who collaborated to excommunicate Emil, the entire affair was, however, seen as the perfect exercise of voluntarism and 'openness'. Embassy associate Gili, for example, told me that since ownership and censorship of the 'open-source community' were limited by a commitment to nominal egalitarianism, institutions could be reshaped and reformed quickly as this compares with the relative rigidity of a 'centralized' auditing process in an authority-based system. The fact that Embassy members had no formal ways to scrutinize rebels or punish ‘centralism’ made it possible for them to quickly separate into two groups, set up an alternative forum and keep alive the very idea of a dynamic Bitcoin community free from top-down censorship. They saw their action as the essence of what Bitcoin was all about.

But even digital coins have two sides. While personal animosity continued, Emil remained a member of several WhatsApp groups used by Embassy members. On some occasions he tried to reignite the discussion with his former partners, but they either did not answer or left the group altogether, returning only after Emil himself chose to leave. At one time, a year after the event, Emil challenged the Ambassadors for having ‘given up [the opportunity to evangelize Bitcoin on] a stage of 30,000 people [just] to feed the ego of some of the members’. He argued that it was in fact the community that had compromised Bitcoin values, and that the efforts of the Ambassadors to swell the ranks of the new Facebook group at the expense of the old one – which was still under Emil’s exclusive control – jeopardized the interests of *all* community members in Israel. His engagements were either dismissed or ignored, as the main informal leaders of the Embassy were reluctant to talk with Emil any longer. The fork may have presented the power of collective decision-making – proving that distributed consensus *can* become an instrument of sanction – but it also cracked the integrity of the values that initially legitimated that power.

Shades of Freedom

About a year after the split into two Facebook groups, Emil mentioned this issue in a final series of messages on a WhatsApp group used by Ambassadors regularly both for practical arrangements and exchanging jokes. Clearly hurt and still proclaiming passionate faith in the Bitcoin project, Emil accused his former partners of sacrificing transparency for the sake of self-promotion. Most of the group members remained silent, turning what Emil hoped would be a dialogue into a bitter monologue. Only Nissim eventually answered – quite dismissively though – demonstrating continued animosity. This pushed Emil to leave the WhatsApp group. Here is a part of this exchange, exactly as it appeared online:

> [13:33, 20/09/2019] Emil: Don’t trust, verify — member?
> [13:34, 20/09/2019] Emil: 😉

[13:40, 20/09/2019] Emil: Bitcoin, not the community, not the groups, not the embassy, not the association – bitcoin is what I believe in
[13:41, 20/09/2019] Nissim [writing in Hebrew]: You're a shitcoiner 😂😂😂
[13:42, 20/09/2019] Emil: Your silence and the subject you chose to bring to light, along with those you're hiding under the rug just shows what you believe in
[13:43, 20/09/2019] Emil: Sad, really, that you promote hatred, dishonesty, and lies over the things you pose yourself as promoting
[13:44, 20/09/2019] Emil: Non *[sic]* will speak out because you're afraid, of what? I speak out of love, love for the community and the technology, honesty, and transparency
[13:45, 20/09/2019] Emil: Technology that in itself cannot be corrupted, we here shown *[sic]* that it can be rotten from within, by the oldest trick in the book – divide and conquer
[13:46, 20/09/2019] Emil: You've been posing me as a sole crazy person, dictator, but over the last year you yourself see that despite your attempts to continue throwing blame at me, . . . our entire local community [has become] the laughingstock of the global community
[13:47, 20/09/2019] Emil: Why? What for?
[13:47, 20/09/2019] Emil: You can't and won't answer that, it's enough that the question is there
[13:48, 20/09/2019] Nissim [writing in Hebrew]: You want to know why? Look in the mirror and you'll get the answer.
[13:53, 20/09/2019] Emil: Yes, I am looking, I can. Unlike you, probably. I can because instead of going and talking about this stuff in secret, pumping hate and filth, I stand proud by my actions and words
[13:54, 20/09/2019] Emil: You on the other hand, can't even say what bothers you, you need to tell me 'To find the answer in the mirror' 😂

Emil and his rivals agreed on the meaning of Bitcoin 'values', as they proclaimed allegiance to transparency and decentralized sociality, thus asserting their continuing pertinence to the 'community'. And yet, the conflict brought into visible attention the fact that 'a community' dedicated to the production of individualized forms of freedom still had to find a way to enforce complicity when consensus was not available. It could never do that as long as it discursively accepted many *shades* of freedom, while pragmatically enforcing one colour that was mainly supported by a significant pressure group of elite members and semiformal leaders. It was precisely this criticism that Emil was trying to convey to his former colleagues in the group chat. The game of mirrors that terminated the exchange literally reflected these mutually exclusive versions of freedom. It also exposed the problematic notion of 'liberty' that Emil was allegedly betraying, and it eventually highlighted just how problematic its twin-concept of 'consensus' was, proving it could break down as easily as it could be intensified.

Emil's excommunication was a watershed moment that went far beyond the global conflict among Bitcoiners that had taken place in 2017, which culminated with the establishment of B-Cash (see Chapter 3). That was so due to its more personal nature and its potentially devastating results. In fact, the local conflict that erupted in 2018 between Emil and his former colleagues in the Israeli community threatened to destroy everything that the community had been building and developing since 2011. The split into two different Israeli Bitcoin communities was not merely destabilizing in an organizational sense, but it also cast doubt on the hegemonic idea that a decentralized community can be sustained by voluntarism and dialogue. Instead, the community took in this case a collective act of boundary-making, which was exclusionary and to an extent even violent, as it took one set of rules – which were never institutionalized – and unilaterally replaced it with a rigid 'constitution'. From that moment on, the new constitution came to define the new boundaries of the community. Whether the handling of the conflict between Emil and his former partners meant a tyranny of the majority, as Emil argued, or the collective protection of free speech – as Bloom and his colleagues argued – was a question of perspective that I am still unable to answer.

The case of the fork ultimately suggested that power struggles in the community could turn ugly, and that sometimes pacification demanded a collective organizational response. On the one hand, this meant that the community really could act together cohesively, but on the other it meant that there were political issues that the reliance on trustless technologies simply could not resolve. An innocent-looking motion to 'improve' the management of the Israeli Bitcoin Facebook group thus turned into a fragmentary force that illustrated just how explosive debates about decentralization, collective responsibility, and censorship power may be when the figure of the Sovereign is absent. The fork was a point in time when both individual and collective commitment to idealism was tested empirically and, as I hinted above, it exemplified beyond doubt that power could still be centralized in a 'decentralized community' whose members wholeheartedly declared their belief in freedom of action and speech. And this, as I now discuss, echoed ongoing questions on the scope of authentic speech in peer-to-peer sociality.

Authenticity

As is already clear, authenticity was a fundamental issue that preoccupied Embassy members when they judged whether certain practices were conducive to the cultivation of a community spirit (Swartz 2022). Comparisons with the reality described in *The Matrix* cinematic trilogy were not only prevalent metaphors but concrete emblems used to distinguish the realness of Bitcoin from the illusionary nature of hegemonic currencies. Sometimes people referenced the movie's 'blue and red pill' trope to hint that they rejected conspicuous consumption. These included money forms such as altcoins, ICO campaigns (Swartz 2022), NFTs (non-fungible tokens) and even the act of 'showing off' fortunes gained by trading in bitcoin.[7] The realness of bitcoin, as opposed to those 'matrixial' financial bubbles, was based on its built-in scarcity and decentralized verification system, which enabled people to anchor their aspirations and desires in the real thing, namely Bitcoin. Take, for example, Nissim's understanding of the realness of Bitcoin:

> If we *really* live in our way, with our own money and our own insights, with our own peace of mind, we are healthy. It is a physical and mental health. People take care of their bodies all the time: they run, they do kayaking, bikes, but the health of our mind is equally important. *Bitcoin gives us the possibility to be mentally healthy because we are in control of our lives.* We know where we are and where our money is, we know what we want, nobody can surprise us because we have the best weapon in the world, our money and the ability to use it in the best way we find fit . . . Bitcoin gives us the possibility to acquire self-esteem, freedom and economic ability, and all these things are the basics for mental health. That is [especially] because a healthy person does not wake up with anxiety in the morning. And [because of this] the community is harmonious – if we are all mentally healthy, and we are all able to control our lives in the way we want to lead them, for better or worse, we feel good.

Nissim presented mental and physical health, as well as the ability to be free, as proxies for genuine or authentic living. Acquiring peace of mind through Bitcoin proves, according to this logic, that *resistance* to the commodification of debt or to the profit that banks make when they play with your money, is worthwhile in the long run. If you are your own bank – which means you are free from the appropriation of inflationary and hence illusory money – you can preserve the value of your capital, consolidate your means of existence, even protect your 'work', in Marxist terms. This quite literally heals you because it implies living *correctly*. In that sense, as Nissim told me in a different conversation, 'Bitcoin is not [even] money but echelons of insight.' Ambassador Arik, likewise associated 'insight' with a profound change in his approach to money when he 'got into' Bitcoin, turning away from a short-term 'easy come, easy go' attitude towards a future-oriented savings mode. For him, Bitcoin had not only become a symbol of defiance against the hegemony of fractional-reserve banking, but also the only viable alternative that could secure a substantive future. Other interlocutors have also said that Bitcoin handling helped them to 'open their eyes' and see for the first time what life was really all about (but see Baldwin 2018: 2–3 on Bitcoin's 'hyper-realness').

The appeal of authenticity thus also works to cleanse the community from what are deemed to be corrupting elements (Garrod 2016). As I showed in previous chapters, preoccupation with 'scammers', fraudulent initiatives, pyramid schemes and other types of financial indecency that Ambassadors despised exposed something of an obsession with truth among committed maximalists. Accordingly, abuse of the crypto scene for easy profit was considered loathsome. Bitcoin sociality contained the secrets to salvation and spiritual autonomy, as far as maximalists like Nissim were concerned, and thus could not tolerate their revolution being tainted with anything fake. In 2018, when we spoke about mass adoption, Nissim said:

> Bitcoin naturally dispenses all the rubbish. Those people who only came here to make money [during the goldrush] did not understand the ideology, and so they couldn't take the losses when they came. Because Bitcoin has a wonderful quality – it cleans itself up. All these people who bought bitcoin at high values [in 2017] by now they are already out of the system. I asked people back then, 'Do you know anything on Bitcoin?' and they said, 'Yes, I know everything.' So, these people are idiots. But it's their problem. If he went to the bank, and the bank didn't like him, they would still give him a loan. *But here in Bitcoin every person is their own bank.* If I don't want to interact with you, I say goodbye. Such people leave the community by default.

The contempt Nissim showed towards people who perceived Bitcoin as a mere investment channel resonated with the sense of togetherness and communal intimacy that Embassy associates relished. What remains after the 'fraudsters' are swept aside, then, was seen as passionate, solid and productive, flowing with the might of a righteous mission to create a more egalitarian social system. At the same time, Nissim claimed that Bitcoin 'naturally' filtered out profiteers because they did not truly realize what it meant to 'be your own bank' (see Chapter 3). He thus connected the collective spirit of Bitcoin to the financial autonomy of each of these 'individual' banks, who determined their investment priorities only in relation to the dynamics of the market (Vennonen 2024). Nissim believed he could authentically choose those he associated with precisely because he *was* his own bank, which distinguished him from the 'idiots' whose profit making in fiat meant sending bitcoin *back* into the hierarchical-centralized world.

Authentic participation, or genuine engagement, if you will, in Embassy activities, mostly materialized though patient HODLING. Given that a HODL strategy was nonetheless anchored in future prospects and iconoclastic fantasies, all of which contingent on unknown forces and events, the realness of Bitcoin in a community of followers was contingent if not self-referential; much like those cargo cults Bloom mentioned in Chapter 1. The community, as I have argued, was imagined as the *answer* to such empty appearances, an infrastructure that would replace illusionary money with *genuine* money. This, in turn, would reinforce new types of collaborations that were neither mediated nor hierarchical.

The following example will elucidate this issue further. One afternoon, I sat on a bench outside the Embassy, drinking beer with Nissim, Ariel and Shlomit. Our conversation turned to the ethereality of crypto investment, which involved graphs and numbers and fake news and influencers and memes, to the extent it could pull investors into an entirely virtual world wherein images, brands and trends exploded in one's face constantly (cf. Baldwin 2018). Rather than assume that these aspects of the world of Bitcoin were damaging its alleged authenticity, Nissim and Shlomit agreed that Bitcoin could be a reliable money form precisely because it could be converted to any other value, whether material or abstract. Images of grotesque affluence proclaimed through memes of Lamborghinis and Teslas, or by posting online videos of lush vacations on a beautiful tropical island, were according to them a realization of the metaphors used to describe the solidity and strength of Bitcoin, which Ambassadors commonly compared to iron (*barzel*). Ambassador Ariel went further, drawing comparisons with investment in online gaming. 'The gaming industry proves that people are willing to pay for imaginary worlds', he said. 'Which makes these worlds *real*.' I asked Ariel to elaborate, and he explained:

> Do you know the game Second Life? Where people create avatars and manage their digital profiles with in-built currencies that have real value in US dollars? So, in Second Life you can be the mayor of a city, a rockstar, a prostitute, a physics professor, an astronaut, anything you want to be, actually. It's the same thing with Bitcoin. Bitcoin is a never-ending experience, a continuous thrill that comes with the possibility to imagine yourself as someone else. What am I going to do with all that money I earned in bitcoin [investment]? Maybe I will buy a Ferrari or a Lamborghini? Or maybe I will retire and go to live in a village in Tanzania?

Ariel hinted that experiments with the New Economy were not an exercise in semiotics; rather, the practice of decentralized sociality at the Embassy was *ontological*. Social and personal transformations, which came about when adopters were trying to realize their dreams, were not limited only to social responsibility or distributive justice. Far from the moralizing aspects of Bitcoin and the sense of righteousness that accompanied it when Ambassadors spoke of decentralization, a mundane aspect of ontological comfort that Bitcoin symbolized was intrinsically linked to the ability to make dreams come true or turn holographic fantasies into actual material benefits. Indeed, most Ambassadors regularly took part in capitalist spectacles and middle-class pleasures, ranging from public viewings of Elon Musk's spaceship liftoffs, through live broadcasts of NBA basketball games, to clubbing weekend vacations in Berlin.

My main point here is that the thrill of these spectacles was itself experienced as genuine, satisfactory and rewarding due to the perceived realness of Bitcoin as a money technology. Ariel hinted that the realization of desires and the cultivation of fantasies not only made the prospects of conspicuous consumption *affectively pleasuring* – it also made the authentic expression of any lifestyle choice *ideologically permissible*. This must be examined in light of Guy Debord's critique of capitalist spectacles, to which I now turn.

The Spectacle

In *The Society of the Spectacle* (1994[1967]), neo-Marxist scholar Guy Debord argues that the authenticity, ephemerality and experience of the concrete force of reality have all been substituted with representations. Debord attributes this to the modular commodification of 'appearances', and the economic markets it opens for exploration. Appearance – that is, the desired representation of things, an aesthetic that is culturally acceptable and at times demanded – is thus becoming the most important economic feature of commodities. Commodities always represent something they are not and consequently are quantified regardless of their real value; for example, a bottle of perfume may cost one dollar to produce but sell for one hundred because its desirability can be amplified by evoking imaginaries that have little to do with smell. What is marketed is not the perfume but its image, understood not merely as 'picture' but as an *appearance*, a desire to be seen in a particular way, to overcome real value with symbolic value, to produce a status and an iconicity. The basic premises of his thesis are:

> The concept of the spectacle brings together and explains a wide range of apparently disparate phenomena. Diversities and contrasts among such phenomena are the appearances of the spectacle the appearances of a social organization of appearances that needs to be grasped in its general truth. Understood on its own terms, the spectacle proclaims the predominance of appearances and asserts that

> all human life, which is to say all social life, is mere appearance. But any critique capable of apprehending the spectacle's essential character must expose it as a visible negation of life and as a negation of life that has invented a visual form for itself. (Debord 1994[1967]: Thesis 10)

Appearances, then, and especially digital images that are easy to duplicate and manipulate (think of memes, for example), produce a fabricated, inauthentic experience of social relations. Crucially, Debord argues, in this process *the consumed image itself becomes a relation that mediates between people*, obviating productive dialogue. Any situated encounter is mediated by a collectively oriented exchange of images, which often precedes the content of the interaction itself and therefore guides or frames its meanings a priori. This can also be expressed using typical Bitcoin jargon; in the age of the 'spectacle', authentic experience is mediated by 'third parties'. Every relationship is consequently subsumed in the everlasting reproduction and consumption of images, which communicate false meanings and consequently *alienate* people from the real conditions of power in society (ibid., Thesis 32).

To deviate from the unifying tyranny of the consumed image, Debord advocates a 'return' to genuine experiences. He argues that in contrast to the reproduction of appearances, lived experience emphasizes immediacy, recognizability by another, and direct impact, in any form or shape. Debord argues that even the production of counter-images and other disruptive tools, as well as the insistence on going beyond the economic sphere to enliven traditions and histories, will end up in futility; those subversive claims embedded in such counter-images would themselves be appropriated by the consumed image, commodified, commercialized, and then lost. 'The proletarian revolution', he argues (ibid., Thesis 178), 'is that critique of human geography whereby individuals and communities must construct places and events commensurate with the appropriation, no longer just of their labour, but of their total history.' A continuous critique of the very falsity of the spectacle will enable people to seize the ephemeral unknowability and unpredictability of everyday life, if only momentarily, thereby actively resisting the reifying power of the image.

Debord thereby insists that resistance must negate the idea of the 'spectacle' by way of rejecting commodity fetishism at large, moving away from the Marxist suggestion to redistribute control of the means of production of goods to attempting to influence the means by which illusions, appearances and spectacles are *consumed*. He argues that challenging the 'spectacle' can only be efficient if disruption disobeys the very root of the system of production and consumption of commodified images in late capitalism; that is, resist mass media in all its forms and business models. If it fails to do so, claims Debord, negation itself will become just another aspect of the spectacle, its refraction, which perpetuates the ideological premises prescribed a priori in the transformation of images into simulacrums. It is worth quoting at length Theses 28 and 29, wherein Debord (1994[1967]) explicates this notion:

> (28) The reigning economic system is founded on isolation; at the same time it is a circular process designed to produce isolation. Isolation underpins technology, and technology isolates in its turn; all goods proposed by the spectacular system, from cars to televisions, also serve as weapons for that system as it strives to reinforce the isolation of 'the lonely crowd.' The spectacle is continually rediscovering its own basic assumptions and each time in a more concrete manner.
>
> (29) The origin of the spectacle lies in the world's loss of unity, and its massive expansion in the modern period demonstrates how total this loss has been: the abstract nature of all individual work, as of production in general, finds perfect expression in the spectacle, whose very manner of being concrete is, precisely, abstraction. The spectacle divides the world into two parts, one of which is held up as a self-representation to the world, and is superior to the world. The spectacle is simply the common language that bridges this division. Spectators are linked only by a one-way relationship to the very centre that maintains their isolation from one another. The spectacle thus unites what is separate, but it unites it only in its separateness.

Like Debord, Bitcoiners in Israel created a distinction that turned on the uncovering of the spectrality of the 'centralized' economy, especially with regard to its dependency on debt, thus turning Bitcoin from 'bubble' to 'the solution'. They used the term 'community', both locally and globally, to describe a reality that they perceived as oppositional to the spectrality of spectacles. But as I have been stressing throughout the book, this distinction could not be fully sustained, given that the circulation of spectral images of wealth had the effect of turning all moral economies into refractions of one another.

The global split among Bitcoiners over B-Cash, which I mentioned in Chapter 3, demonstrates that last assertion even better than the fork that took place in Tel Aviv, which I analysed above. That was so because B-Cash publicly incorporated the spectacle of financialization – making money by tapping into the movement of capital itself – into Bitcoin economic and social praxis. This paradoxically reaffirmed the inherent logic of 'centralized' financialization – against which many of the old-guard Bitcoiners were mobilizing in the first place – dividing the entire project into capital-oriented and community-oriented Bitcoin holders. It also generated crowding phenomena within other cryptocurrencies, whose adherents would then invest in either profit or libertarian ideological convictions; seldom managing to capture both edges of this branch simultaneously. The split thus mimetically *reproduced* the logic of capital while simultaneously creating a *new* opposition to this very same logic, in the process of fragmenting it.

Debord's analysis of the spectacle is so important, then, because it gives us tools to analyse the simultaneity of Bitcoin, which is here exposed at once as a continuation of late capitalist logic and its negation. This simultaneity, I suggest, is intrinsic to experiencing the utopian allure of Bitcoin, as it enables supporters in Israel and beyond to distance themselves from the reality of power relations that governs the mundane exchange of cryptocurrencies at large. That is precisely the danger of nihilism, which works to obviate values, but rather than producing concrete solutions end up enhancing the real-world power relations that always continue to ferment in human sociality, whether we want it or not. What could be the implications of such a nihilist collateral in a world where Bitcoin is a dominant financial technology and a key mediator of social relations? Since I have already dealt with some of the millenarian responses to these questions (see Chapter 5), I now move to contemplate their economic facade.

The Bidding Economy

Bitcoin for the Befuddled (Barski and Wilmer 2014) is an intelligent and often funny book, which explains to non-specialists how blockchain technology (and cryptocurrencies more generally) work. It conveys the stated objective of convincing the odd reader to begin using Bitcoin, and, consequently, also supporting the coming into being of an entirely decentralized economic reality. It does so humorously by describing a day in the life of Crowley the Crocodile in the year 2030. As we accompany Crowley's adventures, we realize that his world is dominated by cryptocurrencies, which seem to solve many problems that in the mid-2020s still largely require trusted mediators. This includes a real-time competition between automatic lawn mower machines, the purchase of an apartment using bitcoin and buying a salad from a nice lady called Sophia – who is competing against all other salad makers on the same street. Here is a short excerpt:

> It all starts when Crowley wakes up in the morning. Crowley wears his sleep-optimizing bracelet at night, which uploads his pre-waking vital signs anonymously to the Internet. Using this information, machine-learning systems across the world use bitcoins to bid on the time Crowley's alarm clock should go off, given his physical condition and sleep/wake cycle. The winning bid is the one that lets Crowley sleep the longest. Because Crowley likes to take long, hot showers in the

> morning, he used to run out of hot water. But recently, a resident in his apartment building installed an industrial-grade hot water heater and is now selling hot water to other tenants to help with the cost. A chip in Crowley's hot water faucet automatically dispenses bitcoins directly to a chip in the hot water heater. As Crowley turns the shower knob clockwise, more bitcoins are dispensed and more hot water streams from the shower head. (Barski and Wilmer 2014: n.p.)

Barski and Wilmer thus position Crowley the Crocodile in a near-future that has only become possible due to Satoshi Nakamoto's ingenious technical expertise. Here, every mundane interaction includes some form of cryptocurrency exchange. Lacking any intermediaries, third parties and governmental regulation, the entire economic order has thus been decentralized into a plethora of monetary transactions that derive their legitimacy from the conditions of supply and demand at the time of the interaction. The ever-changing conditions of the market, including the possibility of direct-value transactions between end users (or service providers and their clients), are monitored only by the automatic algorithms of the blockchain. This is a world of fluctuating values wherein economic incentives stand at the heart of every interaction, and thus, strongly impact societal organization. I call these decentralized dynamics 'the bidding economy' because, as Barski and Wilmer also mention, just like bidding it is rooted in a condition of instability and competition, which is balanced out by financial incentives (see Leins 2018). From the moment Crowley wakes up in the morning, in short, he must bid in order to survive.

When Barski and Wilmer envisioned these scenarios in 2014, there were only a handful of altcoins. This may explain why the authors assumed that all of Crowley's bidding practices in 2030 would be done with bitcoin. They assumed that bitcoin would become a dominant currency everywhere, and thus the main medium of exchange in the market. But in the mid-2020s, with thousands of functioning cryptocurrencies, the crypto-bidding economy is in fact already wilder and more vast than they could have imagined. This is so because today different cryptocurrencies can already be used for diverse types of interactions (Dow 2019). Some of these, such as Monero, for example, are more anonymous than others so they are frequently used for transactions that require a high level of secrecy, as with the online purchase of drugs. Increasingly, different kinds of cryptocurrencies are thus used for the purchase of various other goods or services, wherever this is possible (Fantacci 2019). Bitcoin, on the other hand, is now mostly regarded in cryptocurrency circles as a store of value – a way to 'save' money for the future – rather than as means of exchange (for example, Cardoso 2024). In that sense, maybe paradoxically, the dynamics of its use and trade in the market are now more like the ways Barski and Wilder imagined the behaviour of gold or real estate in the fiat economy back in 2014.

But, in principle, this makes no difference. The bidding economy that Crowley must fathom in 2030, whether he pays in bitcoin or in another cryptocurrency, works according to the same dynamic principles, which change rapidly in accordance with the micro-interests of stakeholders at the level of everyday practice. The constant automatic bidding ultimately imitates human behaviour during an auction, or on a stock exchange trading floor, or in a casino. If, in a pre-bidding social world, value was determined by forces competing for the purchase of or trade in a global asset seen as external to actual economic actions – such as the means of production, or resources such as oil, salt, sugar, coffee, diamonds and coal – the bidding crypto-economy turns values into intrinsic properties of the systems that produce them. This means that cryptographic monetary systems produce the values that they need in order to validate themselves. Ideally, the bidding economy therefore determines its own parameters as part of its ongoing dynamic, including the conditions for its own transformation.

An example from Crowley's reality elucidates this dynamic quite well. If a pizza truck happened to pass by Crowley's house while another was cruising around the same area, the bidding dynamic would force the prices down in an instant. If, on the other hand, the truck owners heard through their industrial spy network that their only competitor had unfortunately driven over a bag of nails and gotten a flat tire, they would be able to *increase* the price in an instant. The pizza, in short, does not have a fixed price; its value fluctuates in accordance with the micro-adjustments of events taking place in the vicinity. Value, albeit abstract and quickly fluctuating, here becomes a material token in and of itself.

This state of affairs could even take a more cynical turn. Let us consider Sofia, from whom Crowley buys salad. Crowley's digital wallet chose Sophia's bid partly because it was the cheapest in the neighbourhood and partly because Crowley has already eaten her salad before and marked digitally that he liked it very much. But Sofia is not merely a law-abiding housewife who happened to have some leftover salad. In a nihilist, accelerationist economic environment of the kind she lives in, Sofia is also likely to be the head of a local salad cartel whose soldiers have brutally suppressed all competition in the area. While Crowley is under the impression he is bidding for the optimized-value dinner option around, he is in fact operating in a centralized market premised on radical oppression rather than autonomy or free choice.

As I hinted, it is possible to link these bidding practices with the earlier epistemic shift from an economy based on the stabilization of value to one based on constant fluctuation (Malherbe et al. 2019). With the decoupling of the dollar from the gold standard in 1971 and the emergence of the credit economy (see Chapter 2 and Chapter 4) – i.e., the fractional-reserve banking framework that Embassy associates viewed as their nemesis – the logic of capital accumulation already acquired the characteristic of Crowley's bidding-economic model (albeit Crowley's version excludes the possibility of credit). Contemporary remittance commissions are a good equivalent. If my employer in the newly-established Federal Balkan Republic pays my fixed salary to an Israeli bank, to use an implausible case study, I must get involved in several levels of negotiation – or bidding – that will eventually determine the final value that will be deposited into my account. First, I must negotiate with my bank the value of the exact commissions for receiving that money. Second, I must follow the changing values of currencies in the international financial markets in order to maximize the amount that will be deposited in my account after the money has been converted from Federal Balkan pounds to NIS. Every minor difference in the ratio – a difference that keeps updating as a function of the ongoing trade in foreign currency values across the world – means a fluctuation of hundreds or even thousands of NIS in the final calculation, up or down, given that the basic salary is measured in thousands of Federal Balkan pounds. I therefore must 'bid' on the value of the transaction in accordance with the exchange rate of the day and try to get the best deal I can. The crypto-economy of the 2030s is not the antithesis of contemporary trends, but their hyper-real extension.

The bidding economy in a cryptocurrency-dominated future thus means a world lacking in stable values. Rather, prices and rewards are calculated within approximate statistical margins of whatever people are willing to pay for whatever commodity or service at the time and place of the exchange. The bidding economy is potentially infinite in scale because, as I stressed above, multiple cryptocurrencies are being used simultaneously for various activities at all times. A world mediated by blockchain technology is a world in which betting on values is built into the very operational logic of financial infrastructure. It is a hyper-bidding world in which all cryptocurrencies are in constant flux vis-à-vis all other cryptocurrencies, given the number of transactions at any moment. The notion of constantly updating prices produces a radical capitalist marketplace wherein no value is ever fixed. This capricious environment represents a market radicalized to its limits and purified into its essence; it is about expanding uncertainty from the realm of financialization into everyday life (cf. Leins 2018).

This is where the Futurist nihilist perspectives again can be compared with the reality of a Bitcoin-dominated economy. The lack of human autonomy in Futurist imaginaries resulted from the absolutism of machine control. As in the Italian Futurist vision, smoothly functioning computers, perfectly designed code, mathematical precision and speed are all essential for the instantiation of a 'decentralized and trustless' bidding economy. In this economy, people defer power and authority to machines, which *automatically* run and manage society. Human beings serve the machines, monitor them, so that those same people will not have to employ ethical decision-making processes to impose value judgements on others in their social surroundings. The winning alarm clock bidder described above is punished because her algorithms failed to detect Crowley's hangover. And Crowley can sell a house without the slightest interest in the tenants renting it at the time. The only thing that matters is who owns the house at the time of the transaction, even if it happened to be Sofia, the salad gangster.

The bidding economy, moreover, has no history. This is because every new transaction deletes alternatives that were viable until the moment it was enacted. The new transaction is then integrated into the chain of blocks that goes back to Genesis, which is the only history permitted – undoubtedly a muted history lacking pluralism, divergent voices or the ability to protest. In such social reality, as in Plato's cave parable or Debord's notion of the spectacle, a constant mythologizing of 'freedom' is necessary to sustain a flawed moral order premised on exploitation and self-deception. I am not suggesting that this is the situation now, but rather, warning that it could come about once the bidding economy is sufficiently expansive.

Conclusion

Futurism assigned masses and crowds with new powers at the expense of the old elites, thereby breaking up hierarchies but also leaving behind a void of meaninglessness. Parallels with sociality at the Embassy in the twenty-first century are self-evident. C*reatio ex nihilo* – the genesis of a New Economy, which interlocutors associated with the mining of the first bitcoin block – was taken as the point of origin of their political revisionism. Here, the streets of a *new metropolis* were transmuted into *cyberspace*, while the electric grid was replaced with decentralized ledgers. Given the zeitgeist of the day, political power here moves from industry to finance. Anti-historicism – that is, the rejection of traditionalism as well as alternative perspectives – is also a common feature. Embassy members, much like the Italian Futurists before them, were explicitly engaged in the reinvention of moral imaginaries, seeking to replace 'old-fashioned' norms, which they argued subjected individuals to various stages of decay. They hoped, as I explained throughout the book, that techno-social assemblages would destroy established conventions and doctrines, replacing them with an entirely new sensibility that would also reform not only the structure and statute of economic institutions but also some of the central values on which late-modern Western society is still based (for example, nationalism).

Yet, as was the case in the Futurist movement, Bitcoin sociality in Israel sometimes reproduced rather than destroyed previous hierarchical systems. As the fork I described above suggests, striving to decentralize society could turn into a centralist force in its own right (Nelms et al. 2018). Since they partly rely on aspirations for a grand new start – which entails a positive approach to destruction – forms of distributed consensus of the kind that made the Facebook fork possible can in that sense emit a nihilist sentiment that might sweep through the masses. That was certainly what happened with the Italian Futurist fascination with speed, vitality, and dynamism (through technological accelerationism). It ended up sanctifying an impossibly-perfect Brave New World, and thus the co-optation of these Futurist ideals to the Fascist movement (Ohana 2016). Radical philosophy transformed into radical politics, which in this case were used by vicious leaders to sustain a full-scale dictatorship that took part in a devastating global war. This should raise questions among Bitcoiners also outside Israel, concerning the influential role of various 'experts' on trading dynamics (Golumbia 2018), as well as the potential implications of the continuing centralization of money on the blockchain (Dodd 2018; Nelms et al. 2018).

The case of the fork that divided the community in two should thus be seen as an alarm bell. Competing views produced a social conflict that decentralization could not solve. As I emphasized above, that has already happened at a much larger scale with the global Bitcoin Cash split in 2017 (see Chapter 3), when the so-called 'CEO type' that interlocutors inimically mentioned in their conversation with Brian (see Chapter 4) tried to take control from the 'communalist' type. In the terms I used in Chapter 3 concerning individualism, all this suggests that an ongoing struggle between Individual A and Individual B over financial policies and social norms – within and outside the world of Bitcoin supporters – might well determine Bitcoin's future development. If a Randian-leaning Individual A prevails, I allow myself to guess, some of the romantic notions that stood at the very heart of the intentional community I encountered in Israel might well twist into the nightmare of Crowley's bidding economy, along with the kinds of crowd loneliness it potentiates.

During my fieldwork, Embassy associates were generally oblivious to the authoritarian implications of crowding and to the possible replacement of their own idealism with a nihilist economic stance. When crowding is used as an instrument of monetary circulation, it can, although not necessarily, lead to socioeconomic disasters (Borch 2012; cf. Canetti 1984; McClelland 1989). It is this blind-spot I wish to emphasize, not merely at the level of analytic criticism but also as a friendly advice to my Bitcoiner friends. After all, interlocutors in Tel Aviv only associated a measure of nihilism with traders and profiteers, thus positioning themselves on the other end of the financial abyss as authentic, genuine, and well-meaning. Most interlocutors thus located their Bitcoin activism at the forefront of a global ethical turn, and hence as the ultimate mirror image of the rational, self-interested and egocentric Randian individual. They chose to ignore, in other words, some of the potentially damaging results of their own reliance on informal decision-making mechanisms, thereby also whitewashing the ontological insecurity one is likely to acquire when living in a world that is fully subjected to arbitrary crowd movements; such as the world of Crowly the crocodile and its relentless bidding. By embracing a communalist version of the bidding economy they might have avoided the dangers of centralized sovereignty, but also inevitably denied its protections and guarantees.

One of the main problems with the idea that Bitcoin is the answer to commodification, alienation and empty appearances, then, is its chaotic boom-and-bust cycles.[8] A distinction between genuine and stimulatory experiences creates a hierarchy of preferred economic realities: Bitcoin stands at the top in its communalist form, side by side with rare metals such as gold; then comes Bitcoin as a profit-making device, which is half-tolerated; followed by some 'serious' cryptocurrency projects, which have gained the trust of the public; and lowest are located all forms of state-sanctioned money. This is precisely the reality of the spectacle. Continuing Debord's logic, the critical argument would be that this hierarchy merely ranks different sets of *appearances,* which advance imaginaries of distinct political economies and idiosyncratic experiences of authenticity while effectively supporting different grades, forms and levels of inequality, centralization, and hierarchic social structures. The grim conclusion is that Bitcoin, being an aesthetic as much as a commodity, must be continuously endorsed by communities in ever more spectacular ways, reproducing its aura and the image of self-liberation, regardless of the mundane character of its liberating potentialities or whether this liberation is possible in the first place.

That is ultimately the reason that a millenarian-nihilistic rejection of the past and the embrace of crisis can foment violent reactionary forces. When a group of influential crypto investors decides to set up a project that would significantly influence the market, no moral commitment or ideological argumentation can prevent them from doing so. The endemic possibility to fragment communities by splitting blockchains thus works against the stability required for any type of future-oriented planning. If values continuously fluctuate, and if at any moment every blockchain can be spliced and reignited as a new 'coin' with new rules and values, economic reality will become inherently hostile. The very instability of the market would always come at someone else's expense, in other words, and at the collective rather than individual level. Although a nominal egalitarianism accompanies the emergent DeFi financial sector in the structural sense – a zero-sum game in which horizontal collaboration rather than vertical positioning determines success (see Shapiro 2022) – it has the potential to produce immense financial and political inequalities; wherein some accumulate enormous wealth and some struggle to survive. If this sounds familiar as compares with the contemporary world economy, it should ring a bell among those who aspire to reform this economy[9].

In this chapter I have therefore come a full circle to confront with some of the problems that accompanied the quest for Liberty at the Bitcoin Embassy in Tel Aviv. A liminal space in which the New Economy was supposed to be generated at the level of grassroots activity, the Embassy gave way to what we all must recognize as a remarkable experiment; which to a great extent, at least while I was there, could be regarded a success. Yet, sociality at the Embassy enabled associates to subvert political structures and moral standards without having to recognize some of the potentially autocratic implications of their actions. The fork, which I described above, was in that sense a cleavage or a peep hole through which we as observers can gaze through and see deeper. It demonstrated precisely how the dynamic of nihilistic iconoclasm can turn 'inwards', fragmenting the decentralized community rather than shattering political structures in the 'centralized' economy. This meant that under the right circumstances, the Embassy *could* become a proto-nihilist space. Since I remain sympathetic to the Bitcoin project and the people who sustain it in Israel and abroad, I hope that this assertion will motivate communalist-leaning Bitcoiners to set up proper arbitrage mechanisms that could tackle such potentially restrictive processes.

NOTES

1. The Winged Victory of Samothrace is a second-century BCE Hellenistic marble statue on display at the Louvre.
2. The *Futurist Manifesto* is available here: https://genius.com/F-t-marinetti-the-futurist-manifesto-annotated. Accessed 11.08.2025.
3. Futuristic art in fact came to define Fascist infatuation with power and sporadic violence, which ended up choking even those collectivist forms of freedom that Futurist visionaries pretended to generate in the first place.
4. In the financial market, 'Initial Public Offering' (or 'IPOs') is a strategy to recruit funds from private investors. The term is used to describe the first time that a company sells some of its shares to the public. 'Initial Coin Offering', or 'ICOs', were a passing fashion in the emergent cryptocurrency market between 2017 and 2018, which attempted to replicate this process. At the time, usually unknown crypto companies offered cryptographic 'coins' for sale, claiming that the funds recruited

will enable the developers to add new features to their projects. Investors could potentially earn large sums in case the 'coin' they purchased cheaply surged in value. This trend nonetheless died out when investors realized that many, if not most, ICO recruitment campaigns were outright fraudulent.

5. 'Meta posts' are posts dealing with the platform itself rather than with the subject for which it was constructed.
6. The precise number that constituted a supermajority was not stated.
7. 'ICO' is an acronym standing for 'Initial Coin Offering' (see note 4 of this chapter). NFTs were a later trend, which came into the picture in 2020, providing tokens that work like a permanent digital signature that could be used to evaluate the price of digital commodities based on the history of their circulation between buyers and sellers on the blockchain (see Shapiro 2025; Swartz 2022).
8. Golumbia (2018) argues that these cycles are in fact manipulations by 'whales'. Butler (2022) provides a more nuanced critique, arguing that some cycles are the result of coordinated action, and some not. From a mathematical point of view, it verges on the fantastic to affect the blockchain in a way that will undermine the credibility of verification or bypass the requirement for a distributed mass consensus (Antonopolous 2015).
9. As Dodd (2018) has noted, 'whales' on the blockchain hold massive fortunes and thus have unproportional ability to influence the market.

CONCLUSION

The One(s) and the Many

In this book, I have explored the tension between individual-oriented and community-oriented political philosophies in the everyday praxis of Bitcoin. During my fieldwork in Tel Aviv, this tension emerged from the normative tendency to perceive relations between individuals and communities or even crowds in terms of encompassment. On the one hand, there were collective trends, social processes and materials that could only be reckoned in the plural, and thus as phenomena that always *contained* singular perspectives; these were phenomena that worked on individuals from the outside, such as FOMO. On the other hand, however, there were idiosyncrasies and atomic units that followed their own internal logic. 'Individual banks' constituted a counterforce to the overwhelming power of collective pressures or structured limitations that confined people from the outside because they were also seen as self-referential, self-sustaining and ultimately autonomous in the sense that such individuals were free to refuse collective trends at any given moment, even able to simply detach themselves from the social collective altogether if they wished (Dumont 1986; see MacFarlane 1993: 17–19).

According to this discourse, individuals were thus unable to singlehandedly influence collective trends at all, albeit in their personalized capacity as sellers or buyers who even then had to choose specific strategies from a given pool of possibilities (such as HODL). They were, however, able to fully control their own lives based on the supposed financial independence provided through the accumulation of Bitcoin. In that sense, the people I met in Tel Aviv were continuously living between idioms of 'ones' and idioms of 'many', directing their political, economic, moral and spiritual convictions to mitigate the sometimes-contradictory social demands that came with these respective measurements.

Interlocutors often emphasized explicitly that the entire effort in Bitcoin was to enhance the force of individual perspectives while maintaining a measure of collective cohesion rich with symbolic and moral content. This idea was initially counterintuitive to me, as I stated in the Introduction. An emphasis on trustless automation as a condition of liberation, much like the idea that decentralization constitutes independence, did not at first seem to differ from techno-social concepts of the libertarian kind that emphasize *individual autonomy* as a basic civil freedom (Hughes 1993; see Levy 1993). I was thus surprised to discover early on in my fieldwork that Embassy members spoke about themselves in the plural as a 'community', both globally and locally. At the global level, they saw themselves as promoters of a revolutionary idea that would transform the world, and at the local level they saw themselves as an intentional community, whose members were committed to alternative moral standards. Early adopters, or 'true believers', were thus said to have generated the value of bitcoin *ex nihilo* through time, both by exchanging bitcoins between them regardless of its monetary value, and by contributing technically to sustain the blockchain protocols. I observed that this communitarian solidarity was the core dynamic of bitcoin's survival as a viable alternative to fiat currency.

Especially during public meetings, which ranged from business to play to ritual, it appeared that the community materialized the fantasies of societal reorganization that interlocutors were promoting. The passion people put into debates on the New Economy was genuine, and, as this manifested generically in the activities at the Embassy, it also inspired a dynamic of sharing and collaboration. As I demonstrated, much like techno-utopian communities and social movements before them (Turner 2006), sociality at the Embassy included alliances and rivalries, rumours and gossip, endless arguments and occasional falling-outs between members. Precisely because these everyday tensions were common, members experienced an overarching notion of communalist *Geist*, or at the very least a holistic mutuality and a sense of higher purpose that encompassed those who saw themselves as carriers (and sometimes as promoters) of the Bitcoin spirit.

The innovation here was the demarcation of a social sphere where masses could expand almost unfettered as they were simultaneously *collapsing* into the individuality of any community member. In realistic terms, this simultaneity meant that those who were part of the Bitcoin Embassy always imagined themselves as free from any binding collective definition, while also claiming the critical importance of community life as a vector of meaningful living. Here lay the potential for elegant disruption or creative distortion, which contrasted the image of Bitcoin as providing the foundation for a nihilistic social order premised on individuated 'nodes' constantly alienating one another as they fetishize capital. As an infrastructure supporting a collective ethos of egalitarian reciprocity, 'P2P' network design accentuated a tension between the one and the many, and in that sense superseded personal encapsulation. Interlocutors were in fact busy reinventing what it even meant to sustain a 'community' as they engaged 'peerage' as an organizing life principle. They were not trying to fit ready-made models of sociality into new technological and theoretical structures. As they managed financial transactions on the blockchain they annulled the paradox of a money system that was exclusive and inclusive simultaneously (Nelms et al. 2018), creating instead a sophisticated social space that turned these aspects from dead-ends into generative forces. To that end, Ambassadors often claimed that Bitcoin's ability to change societal conventions at a wider scope must begin with a change of individual perspective and the incorporation of a new course of action; wherein 'one' could (paradoxically, still) trust the 'many' by engaging economically and politically with 'trustless' technologies.

Embassy members ultimately established a community of practice through two main forms of collaboration. First, they worked together. Ambassadors divided the shifts between them on a voluntary basis but were seldom alone, as people would often pop in for a coffee or beer. Those who lived nearby and did not have another job – like Nissim, who had moved from the Jerusalem area to Tel Aviv so he could be more involved – would arrive daily to help with ongoing tasks. 'Work' included proselytizing the Bitcoin social message, explaining how to use the ATM, organizing events, and taking care of such mundane functions as cleaning the space or answering the phone. Secondly, Embassy members regularly hung out just for fun, and they dedicated much time to different forms of play. They held lively onsite meetings, chatted online – especially on the Israeli Bitcoin Facebook group that they established – and regularly attended drinking nights, parties, lectures and picnics. This, as Bloom claimed, was supposed to functionally strengthen relations between them, but it went deeper to constitute a space in which the community could actually imagine together and design how the future decentralized reality which they promoted would eventually look.

Those in the Embassy who were convinced that Bitcoin was an unprecedented historical innovation at the economic level also envisioned it as a political instigator of liberty. Structurally inverting Marxist theory – which assumed deterministic transition from a capitalist class system to a communalist-egalitarian system through mass unionization – Embassy members perceived the achievement of collective freedom as the necessary result of the mass liberation of *individuals*. At a global scale, this theory acquired gigantic dimensions. A mass of liberated individuals constituted a super-entity, wherein individuals were able to move in relation to other individuals more or less freely based on their own interests, while still adhering to a well-defined collective ethos. This differed from collectivist social movements like Marxism through structural decentralization, which ensured that masses could still be organized globally without forcing rules or leadership upon adopters. Paradoxically, the unifying factor was the anarchic power of crowds, which could be anchored inside each 'individual' Bitcoin adopter while eliminating conventional proxies for respectability and privilege, including awe, polity and deferment.

Dynamics of crowding, as I observed both at the Embassy and in the wider world of Bitcoin enthusiasts (largely accessed online), reflected in that sense an interesting phenomenon. On the one hand, it was a direct offspring of *modernist* social movements, whose ideological and empirical boundaries encompassed the many individuals who took part in them. But on the other hand, it was made up from a collection of fully autonomous individuals. This imaginary of autonomy was seen to *supersede* and sometimes eliminate the authority of institutions that direct, guide or limit individual freedom of choice (MacFarlane 1993; see Brighenti 2014; Lee 2016). At the Embassy this duality generated a vortex towards ostensibly 'new' social and economic order, which derived its legitimacy both from the consensual moral authority of the collective (or the 'many') in its 'networked' manifestation *and* from the self-defined moral authority of individuals (or 'ones'), who dissociated themselves from any type of institutional power (namely, Mol and Law 1994).

Community in a Crowd

With the exception of close-knit religious orders (Cohn 2004), modern-day egalitarian communities typically lack ideological unity (Andelson 2002). Their success should thus be measured in the robustness of their decision-making mechanism rather than in levels of commitment on one hand, or chronological longevity on the other (Rubin, Willis and Ludwig 2019; *contra* Kanter 1972). Sociologist Jonathan Andelson (2002: 137) argued that communitarian boundaries are in fact shaped by real-life emotional tides, alternating between political-economic contexts and ideological diversification recurring through time (see Bateson 1958), more than the ideologies that attempt to predefine these boundaries.

Although Embassy members were not an intentional community in the traditional sense, and despite the emphasis they put on voluntary collaboration between freestanding individuals, their community was similarly agile. Alongside the morality of open-source sociality, the community encompassed (and usually tolerated, despite the incident of the fork I analysed in Chapter 7) diverse standpoints, moral convictions, and methods of investment, which enabled diehard Bitcoin purists and half-convinced risk-averse investors to collaborate as part of a fully decentralized political system. This becomes possible because discharge on the blockchain temporarily reduces distances between people virtually and physically. In Chapter 6 I described this as a force pulling 'peers' into anecdotal reciprocity unaffected by the interests of any perceived collective entity or even individual faith. People sell and buy frantically when the blockchain fluctuates not because they 'believe' that the banking system is just about to collapse, on one hand, or because they altruistically support the general libertarian cause, on the other. They simply feel an urge to preserve the value of their money, which is the crux of the entire game. The fact that interlocutors attempted to constitute a similar dynamic offline factually extends this practice also into the level of communitarian organization.

Several contemporary authors (Borch 2012; Brighetti 2014; Lee 2016; Mazzarella 2017; Hayden 2021) have argued that crowding phenomenality represents a meaningful historical shift in the scope and character of mass political participation. While the major social movements of the twentieth century highlighted a collectivist ethos as the *sine qua non* of large-scale social mobilization – a sociopolitical unity that encompassed and at times even annulled forms of individual agency – twenty-first-century reliance on decentralized organization elicits new forms of social collaboration between a multiplicity of interconnected, yet self-contained, individual subjects. As these developments are reported in the popular media, however, online crowding continues to be a destabilizing phenomenon, a factual social force that is increasingly turning things upside-down and inside-out. This stance makes crowds idiomatically problematic, as they increasingly come to be identified with new forms of revolutionary or iconoclastic behaviour.

But the analytical point, I believe, is somewhat wider. Borch and Knudsen (2013) go beyond the allure of stability, legality and social order to argue that in the last two decades the morphology of *global masses online* have become an indispensable aspect of personalized conduct, even *offline*. This is a remarkably astute observation. Think of the financial crisis of 2008 – which coincided with the birth of Bitcoin – or the events associated with the Arab Spring of 2011. Think also of later manifestations of crowd behaviour such as the storming of the US Capitol in January 2021, on the one hand, and the strict lockdown measures used during much of 2020 in many countries to contain the Covid-19 pandemic. All these could only make part of our everyday reality at such scales because of massive online dynamism, accelerated information flow, and well-developed social mobilization networks. Borch and Knudsen (2013: 111) have identified three domains in which this ongoing crowd dynamics becomes a significant social force in the current hyper-globalized world, all of which also represent new forms of what they identify as typically *postmodern crowds*. 'The first', they argue,

> is the political domain, with protesting and occupying crowds (Occupy Wall Street, Los Indignados, etc.) that express explicit political protest. The second manifestation of postmodern crowds appears within the broad field of sports, leisure, and consumption, where collective energy is focused on high-profile brands, fan communities and event crowds (whether as sports events, festivals, markets, or the like). Finally, a third form of postmodern crowding, which traverses the other two, relates to new digital social media where crowding is produced around certain agendas, issues, and hot topics.

In all these instances, it is the creation of new forms of differentiation – vis-à-vis modern forms of alterity – that define the relevance of digital crowds to everyday politics (Hayden 2021). Seen in this light, it thus becomes clear that the exchange of Bitcoin also takes part in the constitution of new modes of alterity and differentiation at a global scope (Shapiro 2024). The global crowd of Bitcoin adopters exemplify in that sense a shift towards the formation of new kinds of social movements, which uphold entirely new dynamics of human association in cyberspace. These crowds sprawl regardless of common moral imperatives that might limit their growth, or the decisive weight of governmental policies in setting up societal priorities.

The Israeli Bitcoin community could be seen as a product of such crowd dynamics, as it was established on the very conviction that people could suddenly feel closer to total strangers regardless of the geographical distance between them, through Bitcoin. This phenomenon took place primarily through the synchronicity of mass action on the blockchain and the need for consensus at a large scale, which inspired the boom-and-bust sociality I documented at both local and global registers. As most interlocutors at the Embassy saw it, this sociality was entirely pragmatic; that is, directed towards the achievement of concrete goals. At the same time, however, they embraced its deeper emotional dimension and its moral horizon, which focused on grassroots governmentality at the level of collective management . Together, this sociality was seen to generate a new world.

Whether crowd dynamics online would eventually inspire revolution or mobilization towards the kind of permanent resistance promoted by Brian (see Chapter 4), is still to be tested.

Either way, Bitcoiners in Tel Aviv successfully developed communitarian cohesion that did not rely on higher organizational or moral authority to which individuals had to obey. They consciously attempted to draw a new kind of social map, as a famous Borgesian allegory holds, which covers the entire territory that it purports to model. An experiential individualism divorced from the scrutinizing power of the collective, in short, is not merely a process that inspires the formation of chaotic crowds. In Tel Aviv the very same force was explicitly tailored to the task of building new moral economies at the level of vernacular communitarian organization. As Bloom, Nissim and many other interlocutors have argued over time, this same force would eventually integrate a massive social movement in its global scope, which was simultaneously rooted in local habits and traditions – all the way down to the whims, desires and eccentricities of the individual subjects that comprised its central building blocks everywhere.

It is here that the community and the crowd finally fuse, theoretically as well as practically. Embassy members perceived their community as living proof that 'decentralization' could work despite the dominance of a 'centralized' logic in society at large, while adhering to the idea that mass global adoption would be the ultimate extrapolation of mass-crowd dynamism. Articulating millenarian aphorisms and ideas about personal autonomy, thus created a direct link not only with the Bitcoin global crowd, but also with mainstream economic activity. By examining a tentative solution to the conundrum of 'fragmented holism' – as I called it in passing in Chapter 4 – Embassy associates actively confronted the popular scepticism concerning the viability of Bitcoin as an alternative financial infrastructure. Their praxis can help rephrase some of the main critiques that are still directed towards the Bitcoin project.

Reformulating Critiques

The Futurist recruitment of 'cheering' crowds (Marinetti 1909) towards social and political revisionism unleashed mobs and gangs as much as it produced free-thinking publics. It was so successful that different political factions in Europe at the end of the nineteenth century and the early twentieth century explicitly embraced and legitimated crowd violence as a political tool. The spell of 'revolution' was tied in the popular imagination from the 1920s onwards to unruly and inherently untameable crowds (Beck and Kewell 2014). From the Red and White Terror campaigns of the Russian Revolution to the Italian Black Shirts and the German Brown Shirts, street crowds emitted brute force. Until the 1970s, more or less, different writers, thinkers, journalists and politicians – including Canetti (ibid.) – consequently deemed crowd morphology chaotic, and hence potentially dangerous. While radical reformers such as the Futurists craved that form of chaos as a means to destroy the old, mainstream conservative voices claimed that crowds were a societal risk, a force to be suppressed and controlled. Beck and Kewell (2014: 111–28) convincingly argue (ibid.: 127) that 'by the 1920s there was a consensus . . . that crowds, mobs, and other forms of spontaneous political gatherings and movements represented one of the principal threats to modern society, its stability and sustainability'.

Over the past decade, diverse critics of the Bitcoin project have taken a similar, if updated, approach, claiming that Bitcoiners have been living a postmodern form of false consciousness, which threatened to turn them into a decentralized mafia. These ideas have signposted crowding phenomena on the blockchain as a dangerous dispersion of anarchic powers, echoing contemporary rhetoric on efficient 'crowd control' in cities, or common perceptions on the irrationality of conspiracy theories and the opportunism of those who spread them online. This logic holds Bitcoiners at large as a random aggregation of cynical investors lacking creativity, direction or morality (Golumbia 2016). Views of Bitcoin as a tax evasion scheme, on the one hand, or a 'financial sect' on the other – both still prevalent – designate Bitcoiners as a criminal mob in the first instance, and as a dogmatic flock of worshipers in the second. In both cases the critique focuses on bitcoin's value fluctuations vis-à-vis the soft power of centralized organizations on the blockchain (Schneider 2019), which involve frenetic boom-and-bust cycles that often serve the interests of 'whales' and key industries (such as the blockchain mining industry; cf. Calvão 2018). Bitcoin investors across the globe are in that sense associated with a Wild West image of lawlessness and a 'grab what you can' mentality, wherein the strongest prevail, especially as fantastic gains and devastating losses are at stake.

This same reading also forms the backdrop of the analytical discrepancy between decentralization and trustlessness among cryptocurrency promoters, which scholars have correctly emphasized (Faustino 2019; Faustino, Faria and Marques 2022; Swartz 2017). One pivotal argument assumes a logical failure (Nelms et al. 2018), a paradox (Dodd 2018) that is untenable to Bitcoiners. The working assumption here is that cryptocurrencies are a 'fragile money technology' (Faria 2021: 86) due to their highly volatile markets and speculative nature. To overcome this fragility, supporters either deceive themselves with delusional hopes or deceive *others* in pursuit of easy profits (Golumbia 2018). Such critiques turn cryptocurrencies into an empty vessel (Faustino, Faria and Marques 2022), which is either ineffective as money or mimetic as an asset. They thereby also assume that users' influence on the market is inherently limited, if not irrelevant. Nigel Dodd (2018), as discussed, argues that Bitcoin *cannot* in fact fulfil its prescribed goals as a money technology as long as Bitcoiners see it as a 'thing' rather than a social process (see Simmel 2004), and David Golumbia (2016) portrays Bitcoin not only as a cult for a one-eyed king, but also as a full-fledged right-wing conspiracy.

Such critical readings have however missed the *digital crowding aspects* of Bitcoin. Online crowding phenomena disperse people in ways that severely limit the ability of industry leaders to gain power. Crowding cannot therefore be seen as a prelude to organized mobbing. Boom-and-bust cycles – magnified by social and traditional media – produce a collective effervescence (albeit different in nature to the famous Durkheimian example; see Hayden 2021: 102), which can be exciting and 'harmonious' as much as it can be hostile or competitive. The intensification of trading on the blockchain simply flares up, and with it is extended across the crowd of global investors a measure of independence from external considerations.

Bitcoiners experience the dynamics of global trading as ineffable tangibility, an immersive thrill and a sense of comfort in the anonymity of masses, echoing Canetti's ideas about distance shortening in a public event. This visceral tangibility is also quantifiable; a frenzy of buying and selling that follows a discharge always produces value fluctuations, which investors understand as the material objectification of market dynamics that undergirds the distribution of bitcoins across the blockchain. In this socio-economic realm, it is crowding that produces the ability (and sometimes urgency) to exercise one's own will; namely, to remain in the gain, avoid losing, outsmart the market, etc. (see Borch 2012; Smith 2005).

The critical point is, therefore, not the alleged misrecognition of logical conundrums, but the strange, counterintuitive positionality of Bitcoin traders, miners, evangelists and other fellow travellers (see Maurer, Nelms and Swartz 2013) in the contemporary capitalist moment: they embrace hyper-capitalist value formations caused by online crowding phenomena but at the same time they promote anti-capitalist moral idioms, including collaborative action and the egalitarian ethos of 'open source' sharing. It is this positionality, which seem to be strongly linked to postmodern liminal spaces, that I suggest we begin exploring more critically.

Liminality and Cosmogony

Embassy associates understood the world of Bitcoin as an entire cosmos. It included a 'big bang' in the form of Satoshi's Genesis Block, time-capsules hidden in hack-proof wallets, topological space-time curves on the blockchain, trajectories of money that close distances and habitable 'ecosystems' at varied sizes and scales. This was a universe continuously shaped by new affective supernovas in times of discharge and perilous lines of flight that suddenly sucked you into black holes. It was a cosmos populated by Bitcoiners themselves, of course, but also by a multiplicity of extra-human life-forms such as bots, NFTs, crypto-cats and Dogecoins.[1] It was a new frontier in cyberspace, where the sun shone even when it was pitch dark, thus creating a permanent twilight-zone where one could always see clearly the glowing trajectories of shooting coins on their way to the moon. It was a space that Ambassadors were eager to explore.

For maximalists, Bitcoin was and still is much more than a form of money. It comes close to a kind of life force perpetually reproduced by the physical bodies that make up the structure of the blockchain – CPUs, databases, hard drives and so on – all of which are seen to generate a near-metaphysical substance that interlocutors could nevertheless experience physically as emotional responses to market dynamics (see Borch 2009). It was not the value of Bitcoin as money that proved its utility, but its circulation as a life-giving force to the community of adopters. The handling and distribution of bitcoin as money was thus seen to emit a higher value to Bitcoin as a new organizational infrastructure, giving rise to a sense of collective responsibility *as well as* of cohesive (or integral) individuality. Embassy associates thereby promoted the vision of an egalitarian community – to which they dedicated much of their time, energy and financial resources – only because they were able to experience 'in the body' that a bitcoin-based New Economy successfully integrated these two levels of economic practice.

All this was possible because the Embassy space itself occupied a liminal, or liminoid, to be precise, space. Since the Embassy was not here nor there, thus accommodating both types of economic practice simultaneously, it blended elements of the old and the new into a single framework. This liminoid positionality enabled Ambassadors to generate a cosmogonic counter-theory to prevalent neoliberal aphorisms about markets, freedom, governance and hierarchy. Choosing to extend some free-market hyper-capitalist notions of state, money and individuality – while also producing a viable critique of these same notions, as well as other hyper-capitalist realities (such as the spectacle) – interlocutors eclectically formed a pragmatic model for sociality that they claimed could resolve contemporary moral, economic and political conundrums at the level of grassroots activity. Activism at the Embassy thereby enabled interlocutors to commit themselves to the New Economy, while also intermediating between utopian visions and normative social frameworks of value. This became a path for self-improvement and ultimately a getaway strategy from an anticipated disaster.

Ironically, this pragmatism in the middle must have been a crucial element in the ultimate commercialization of Bitcoin, for better or worse. While Satoshi's initial call to action certainly was influenced by strong libertarian convictions, it also managed to attract wider crowds because it highlighted the total singularity of each individual Bitcoiner *regardless* of their ideological convictions. Trustlessness and decentralization were sufficient to build a movement that at least in Israel blurred political distinctions between right- and left-wing politics. A focus on individual freedom also entailed large-scale synchronicity despite the often chaotic and unpredictable flows of information, appearances and 'values' online, both on the blockchain and in designated forums. Bitcoin substantiated in this sense post-political sensibilities, which no longer considered authoritative 'mediation' or tropes of civil and national stability (for example 'our shared values', the Nation as a family, etc.) as forces capable of restraining collective organization from below. Grassroots efforts to build a New Economy were premised on this stance because they constructed an environment where world-making cosmologies could emerge and prosper.

Bitcoin and the World to Come

True believers in the Embassy were well versed in the technical, economic and often also the philosophical aspects of money policies at a global scale. They saw Bitcoin as a solution to some of the most daunting problems that these contemporary money policies and power structures entailed. The novelty of Bitcoin, according to them, was not in its capacity to substitute social 'trust' with 'trustless' machines. Rather, its novelty was in the creation of a self-referential collective autonomy – that is, a dynamic social entity that held itself together from within as it kept morphing and sprawling, constituting a sense of self-perpetuation dedicated only to the maintenance of its own self-generating dynamic. It is this dynamic, as lived by Embassy associates, that I have sought to describe and explain in this book. While I am not entirely convinced that they were right in their fetishist admiration of the role of 'individual banks' in the emergent construction of a new world, I can appreciate their courage to take risks and do things differently.

The ethnography of the Embassy taught me that contemporary crowds across the virtual-actual divide have a self-generative morphology. Under certain conditions a gush of energy may direct crowds towards high cliffs, from which they will jump into the abyss of economic death. During my fieldwork at the Embassy, three people confessed in separate heart-to-heart conversations that in case Bitcoin crashed one day, they would prefer to 'go down with the ship' and lose all their savings than to cash out and fully return to the 'centralized' world. All-out nihilism, as I claimed in Chapter 7, is one of the potential consequences of a world without a Sovereign. In such a world, the blockchain could become an organic entity that serves itself, sustaining its life-giving force not in relation to the 'centralized' values of the mainstream economy but in vacuity, which could guzzle *all* forms of value. As in Plato's cave parable, a constant mythologizing of 'freedom' would then have to legitimate the story of Bitcoin as the bringer of salvation, pushing to the side or entirely erasing other possibilities for redemption and collective deliverance. A decentralized bidding economy that is sufficiently expansive would be subject to the rules framed by those with the most stake in it, which means that techno-utopians of the alt-right brand could replace Ambassadors' romantic striving towards Liberté with authoritarian oppression (cf. Tsavelis 2024; also Agamben 1998).

The millenarian expectation of the fall of banks thus misrecognizes, intentionally or not, that 'substitution' can easily turn into a spectacle of destruction, which would shatter communities and grassroots economies in a world divided by far greater hierarchies than the ones that the desired financial meltdown is supposed to eliminate. Embassy members' disdain for the 'CEO type' – as it came up in their conversation with Brian – exposed their rejection of corporatism and a sensitivity to class hierarchy. However, this same attitude might turn out to be a realistic nightmare if the new leaderless Bitcoin communities in a post-crisis world decide to collectively exploit the multitude of individuals who have just lost everything. Even if crowds do advance towards a specific 'goal', as Bloom would have it, they are still formed merely for the sake of their own forming, subject to pulsating discharges that are never fully controlled by any of its members. The formation of Bitcoin crowds could indeed engage individuals politically and economically in moral associations that would redeem the wrongs of their predecessors. While providing the thrill of financial edgework, however, this same process of forming could also generate unpredictability, instability, aggression and fraud.

A century before I walked into the Embassy, the popular utopian fixation with innovative technologies and unprecedentedly high velocities inadvertently ended up inspiring oppressive political regimes, leading from the joy of speed and urban freedom celebrated in Futurist artefacts and theatre shows to the sacrificial ethics of Fascism and Stalinism. A continuous growth of the global crowd of Bitcoin adopters might consist not merely in shifting moralities at a cross-cultural scale, but also in the instantiation of new forms of nihilistic political philosophies, which could lead to mass alienation far exceeding Marx's worst nightmare. The questions interlocutors in Tel Aviv asked themselves, at times remarkably similar to Futurist ruminations about a splendid modernist future, position a fish-eye lens in front of the problems we are now facing worldwide at this turbulent stage of late modernism. They invite us to look not only at our distorted image in this fish-eyed mirror, but also at what is happening behind our backs, along with the perhaps unrecognized dangers that might lurk there (Baudrillard 1988).

Going beyond the heuristic 'community', which denotes more-or-less stable boundaries that separate between insiders and outsiders, the lenses of intensification, affect and discharge that together form crowds might provide a meta-analytic framework through which such heuristics can be juxtaposed and compared. An affective vortex that intensifies during mass action is thus tantamount to other algorithmically monitored digital crowding phenomena. These include spontaneous mass raids into a public space as part of a *Pokemon Go!* game (Vanolo 2018), 'flash mob' activism and virtual 'swarming' phenomena of other kinds (Baker 2011; Hayden 2021; Lee 2016; Wiedemann 2014). These spaces of crowd action reflect real-world social structures and moral convictions. They arise in-between virtual and actual spaces – i.e., through the intrinsic liminality that characterizes the fusion of digital and analogue domains. These domains 'in between' should be scrutinized and debated more seriously if we wish to better understand emergent contemporary crowd-based cosmologies and modes of organization. Critically examining postmodern crowds would in that sense become an important scholarly and popular task, as societies across the globe begin to come to terms with a post-truth public sphere whose shapeshifting boundaries are now more than ever determined through the spectacular circulation of capital.

The fact that Embassy members developed a subversive sociality without, on the one hand, turning to radical individualist withdrawal, or to the extremism of revolutionary anti-statism on the other, is nonetheless an important and encouraging lesson. Where violent resistance failed – think, for example, of the riots that accompanied economic conferences and G-forum meetings at the turn of the century, whose political force evaporated as soon as public shock softened – Bitcoin communities in Israel and beyond successfully now work out new forms of grassroots engagement from below. These forms of engagement may produce a lasting impact even if they do not revolutionize the system. Interlocutors in Tel Aviv have in that sense opened a door through which we could begin contemplating peaceful solutions to growing frustrations in an age of technological hyper-acceleration and axial changes in power structures, not only regarding geopolitical arrangements in a conflicted world-system but also concerning the rapidly changing relationships between citizens, corporations, and states.

NOTE

1. I expanded on Dogecoin in Chapter 1. Crypto-cats were an early version of NFTs sold online with an encrypted proof of authenticity and a registered pedigree that would enable owners to resell them later for more money, as collectors sought to accumulate entire series/families of 'cats'.

REFERENCES

Abramson, Allen, and Martin Holbraad. 2014. 'Introduction: The Cosmological Frame in Anthropology', in Allen Abramson and Martin Holbraad (eds.), *Framing Cosmologies: The Anthropology of Worlds*. Manchester: University of Manchester Press, pp. 1–30.

Adamson, Walter L. 2010. 'How Avant-Gardes End – and Begin: Italian Futurism in Historical Perspective', *New Literary History* 41(4): 855–74. https://doi.org/10.1353/nlh.2010.0038.

Agamben, Giorgio. 1998. *Homo Sacer: Sovereign Power and Bare Life*. Stanford, CA: Stanford University Press.

Andelson, Jonathan. 2002. 'Coming Together and Breaking Apart: Sociogenesis and Schismogenesis in Intentional Communities', in Susan Love Brown (ed.), *Intentional Community: An Anthropological Perspective*. Albany, NY: State University of New York Press, pp. 131–51.

Anderson, Benedict. 2016[1983]. *Imagined Communities: Reflections on the Origin and Spread of Nationalism*. London: Verso.

Antonopoulos, Andreas M. 2015. *Mastering Bitcoin: Unlocking Digital Cryptocurrencies*. Sebastopol, CA: O'Reilly.

Antonopoulos, Andreas M. and David A. Harding. 2024. *Mastering Bitcoin: Programming the Open Blockchain*, third edition. Beijing: O'Reilly.

Asad, Talal. 2018. *Secular Translations: Nation-State, Modern Self, and Calculative Reason*. New York: Columbia University Press.

Asad, Talal. 2020. 'Thinking About Religion Through Wittgenstein', *Critical Times* 3(3): 403–42. https://doi.org/10.1215/26410478-8662304.

Atzori, Marcella. 2017. 'Blockchain Technology and Decentralized Government: Is the State Still Necessary?', *Journal of Governance and Regulation* 6(1): 45–62.

Aviv, Eylon. 2018. 'The Forking of the Israeli Bitcoin Community Group, and Why Should You Care', *Altcoin Magazine*. Retrieved 11 May 2023 from https://medium.com/thecapital/the-forking-of-the-israeli-bitcoin-community-group-and-why-should-you-care-406baad558f2.

Back, Adam. 2002[1997]. 'Hashcash – Amortizable Publicly Auditable Cost-Functions'. Retrieved 3 February 2019 from http://www.hashcash.org/papers/amortizable.pdf.

Baker, Stephanie Alice. 2011. 'The Mediated Crowd: New Social Media and New Forms of Rioting', *Sociological Research Online* 16(4): article no. 21. Retrieved 14 July 2025 from http://www.socresonline.org.uk/16/4/21.html.

Baldwin, Jon. 2018. 'In Digital We Trust: Bitcoin Discourse, Digital Currencies, and Decentralized Network Fetishism', *Palgrave Communications* 4(14): 1–10. https://doi.org/10.1057/s41599-018-0065-0.

Barber, Gregory. 2021. 'When Musk Tweets About Crypto, Its Eloncoin All the Way Down', *Wired Magazine*, 17 May. Retrieved 23 July 2021 from https://www.wired.com/story/elon-musk-dogecoin-bitcoin-tweets-prices/.

Barbrook, Richard, and Andy Cameron. 1996. 'The Californian ideology', *Science as Culture* 6(1): 44–72. http://doi.org/10.1080/09505439609526455.

Barlow, John Perry. 1990. 'Crime and Puzzlement', *Electronic Frontier Foundation*. Retrieved 1 March 2025 from https://www.eff.org/pages/crime-and-puzzlement.

Barlow, John Perry. 1996. 'A Declaration of the Independence of Cyberspace', *Electronic Frontier Foundation*. Retrieved 21 June 2020 from https://www.eff.org/cyberspace-independence.

Barry, Andrew, and Nigel Thrift. 2007. 'Gabriel Tarde: Imitation, Invention and Economy', *Economy and Society* 36(4): 509–25. https://doi.org/10.1080/03085140701589497.

Barski, Conrad, and Chris Wilmer. 2014. *Bitcoin for the Befuddled*. San Francisco, CA: No Starch Press.

Bateson, Gregory. 1958[1936]. *Naven, a Survey of the Problems Suggested by a Composite Picture of the Culture of a New Guinea Tribe Drawn from Three Points of View*. Stanford, CA: Stanford University Press.

Baudrillard, Jean. 1985. 'The Masses: The Implosion of the Social in the Media', trans. M. Marie, *New Literary History* 16(3): 577–89.

Baudrillard, Jean. 1988. *America by Jean Baudrillard Translated by Chris Turner*, second edition. London: Verso.

Beck, Matthias, and Beth Kewell. 2014. *Risk: A Study of Its Origins, History and Politics*. Fords, NJ: World Scientific Publishing.

Benkler, Yochai, and Helen Nissenbaum. 2006. 'Commons-Based Peer Production and Virtue', *The Journal of Political Philosophy* 14(4): 394–419.

Berlin, Isaiah. 1958. *Two Concepts of Liberty*. Oxford: Clarendon Press.

Béteille, André. 1986. 'Individualism and Equality', *Current Anthropology* 27(2): 121–34.

Bookchin, Murray. 1982. *The Ecology of Freedom: The Emergence and Dissolution of Hierarchy*. Palo Alto, CA: Cheshire Books.

Borch, Christian. 2007. 'Crowds and Economic Life: Bringing an Old Figure Back In', *Economy and Society* 36(4): 549–57. https://doi.org/10.1080/03085140701589448 .

Borch, Christian. 2009. 'Body to Body: On the Political Anatomy of Crowds', *Sociological Theory* 27(3): 271–89.

Borch, Christian. 2012. *The Politics of Crowds: An Alternative History of Sociology*. Cambridge: Cambridge University Press.

Borch, Christian, and Britta Knudsen. 2013. 'Postmodern Crowds: Reinventing Crowd Thinking', *Distinktion: Scandinavian Journal of Social Theory* 14(2): 109–13. https://doi.org/10.1080/1600910X.2013.821012.

Brighenti, Andrea Mubi. 2010. 'Tarde Canetti and Deleuze on Crowds and Packs', *Journal of Classical Sociology* 10(4): 291–314.

Brighenti, Andrea Mubi. 2014. *The Ambiguous Multiplicities: Materials, Episteme and Politics of Cluttered Social Formation*. New York: Palgrave Macmillan.

Brunton, Finn. 2019. *Digital Cash: The Unknown History of the Anarchists, Utopians, and Technologists Who Created Cryptocurrency*. Princeton, NJ: Princeton University Press.

Buterin, Vitalik. 2015a. 'Superrationality and DAOs', *Ethereum Foundation Blog*, 23 January. Retrieved 28 February 2021 from https://blog.ethereum.org/2015/01/23/superrationality-daos/.

Buterin, Vitalik. 2015b. 'Visions, Part 2: The Problem of Trust', *Ethereum Foundation Blog*, 27 April. Retrieved 17 May 2021 from https://blog.ethereum.org/2015/04/27/visions-part-2-the-problem-of-trust.

Buterin, Vitalik. 2017. 'The Meaning of Decentralization', *Vitalik Buterin*, 6 February. Retrieved 11 September 2023 from https://medium.com/@VitalikButerin/the-meaning-of-decentralization-a0c92b76a274.

Butler, Simon. 2022. 'The Philosophy of Bitcoin and the Question of Money', *Theory, Culture & Society* 39(5): 81–102. https://doi.org/10.1177/02632764211049826.

Calvão, Filipe. 2018. 'Crypto-Miners: Digital Labor and the Power of Blockchain Technology', *Economic Anthropology* 6(1): 123–34.

Canetti, Elias. 1984[1960]. *Crowds and Power*. New York: Farrar, Straus and Giroux.

Caradonna, Toni. 2020. 'Blockchain and Society', *Informatik Spektrum* 43: 40–52.

Cardoso, Campos, Bruno. 2024. 'Towards Hyperbitcoinization: Bitcoin Maximalism as Speculative Fiction', in Matan Shapiro (ed.), *Crypto Crowds: Singularities and Multiplicities on the Blockchain*. New York: Berghahn Books, pp. 23–39.

Chaum, David. 1985. 'Security Without Identification: Transaction Systems to Make Big Brother Obsolete', *Communications of the ACM* 28(10): 1030–44.

Cohn, Norman. 2001[1993]. *Cosmos, Chaos, and the World to Come*, second edition. New Haven, CT: Yale University Press.

Cohn, Norman. 2004[1957]. *The Pursuit of the Millennium: Revolutionary Millenarians and Mystical Anarchists of the Middle Ages*. London: Pimlico.

Dai, Wei. 1998. 'B-money', Retrieved 5 February 2019 from http://www.weidai.com/bmoney.txt.

De Filippi, Primavera. 2018. 'Citizenship in the Era of Blockchain-Based Virtual Nations', in Rainer Bauböck (ed.), *Debating Transformations of National Citizenship*. Springer Open Access, pp. 267–77.

Debord, Guy. 1994[1967]. *The Society of the Spectacle*. New York: Zone Books.

Delanty, Gerard. 2018[2003]. *Community*. London: Routledge.

Diffie, Whitfield, and Martin E. Hellman. 1976. 'New Directions in Cryptography', *IEEE Transaction on Information Theory* 22(6): 644–54. https://doi.org/10.1109/TIT.1976.1055638.

Dodd, Nigel. 2018. 'The Social Life of Bitcoin', *Theory, Culture & Society* 35(3): 35–56.

Dow, Sheila. 2019. 'Monetary Reform, Central Banks, and Digital Currencies', *International Journal of Political Economy* 48(2): 153–73.

Dumont, Louis. 1972. *Homo Hierarchicus: The Caste System and its Implications*. London: Weidenfeld and Nicolson (published in French in 1966, first translated into English in 1970).

Dumont, Louis. 1977. *From Mandeville to Marx: The Genesis and Triumph of Economic Ideology*. Chicago, IL: University of Chicago Press (published as *Homo aequalis* in French in 1977).

Dumont, Louis. 1986. *Essays on Individualism: Modern Ideology in Anthropological Perspective*. Chicago: University of Chicago Press (published in French in 1983).

DuPont, Quinn. 2019. *Cryptocurrencies and Blockchain*. London: Polity Press.

Durkheim, Emile. 1995[1912]. *The Elementary Forms of Religious Life*, trans. K. E. Fields. New York: The Free Press.

Fantacci, Luca. 2019. 'Cryptocurrencies and the Denationalization of Money', *International Journal of Political Economy* 48(2): 105–26.

Faria, Inês. 2019. 'Trust, Reputation and Ambiguous Freedoms: Financial Institutions and Subversive Libertarians Navigating Blockchain, Markets, and Regulation', *Journal of Cultural Economy* 12(2): 119–32.

Faria, Inês. 2021. 'The Market, the Regulator, and the Government: Making a Blockchain Ecosystem in the Netherlands', *Finance and Society* 7(1): 40–56.

Faria, Inês. 2022. 'When Tales of Money Fail: The Importance of Price, Trust, and Sociality for Cryptocurrency Users', *Journal of Cultural Economy* 15(1): 81–92. https://doi.org/10.1080/17530350.2021.1974070.

Faustino, Sandra. 2019. 'How Metaphors Matter: An Ethnography of Blockchain-Based Re-Descriptions of the World', *Journal of Cultural Economy* 12(6): 478–90. https://doi.org/10.1080/17530350.2019.1629330.

Faustino, Sandra, Inês Faria and Rafael Marques. 2022. 'The Myths and Legends of King Satoshi and the Knights of Blockchain', *Journal of Cultural Economy* 15(1): 67–80. https://doi.org/10.1080/17530350.2021.1921830.

Giesler, Markus, and Mali Pohlmann. 2003a. 'The Anthropology of File Sharing: Consuming Napster as a Gift', in Punam Anand Keller and Dennis W. Rook (eds.), *NA – Advances in Consumer Research* Vol. 30. Valdosta, GA: Association for Consumer Research: pp. 273–79.

Giesler, Markus, and Mali Pohlmann. 2003b. 'The Social Form of Napster: Cultivating the Paradox of Consumer Emancipation', in Punam Anand Keller and Dennis W. Rook (eds.), *NA – Advances in Consumer Research* Vol. 30. Valdosta, GA: Association for Consumer Research, pp. 94–100.

Goddard, Victoria. 2016. 'Work and Livelihoods: An Introduction', in Susana Narotzky and Victoria Goddard (eds.), *Work and Livelihoods: History, Ethnography and Models in Times of Crisis*. Abingdon: Routledge, pp. 1–29. https://doi.org/10.4324/9781315747804.

Golumbia, David. 2016. *The Politics of Bitcoin: Software as Right-Wing Extremism*. Minneapolis, MN: University of Minnesota Press.

Golumbia, David. 2018. 'Zealots of the Blockchain: The True Believers of the Bitcoin Cult', *The Baffler* 38: 102–11.

Graeber, David. 2001. *Toward an Anthropological Theory of Value: The False Coin of Our Own Dreams*. New York: Palgrave MacMillan.

Graeber, David. 2011. *Debt: The First 5,000 Years*. New York: Melvillehouse.

Greenfeld, Taro Karl. 2000. 'Meet the Napster', *Time Magazine*, 2 October. Retrieved 18 July 2024 from https://content.time.com/time/subscriber/article/0,33009,998068,00.html.

Greenfield, Adam. 2018. *Radical Technologies: The Design of Everyday Life*. London: Verso.

Handelman, Don. 1998[1992]. *Models and Mirrors: Towards an Anthropology of Public Events*. London: Berghahn Books.

Handelman, Don. 2021. 'Passages to Play: Paradox and Process', in Don Handelman, Matan Shapiro and Jackie Feldman (eds), *Moebius Anthropology: Essays on the Forming of Form*. New York and Oxford: Berghahn Books, pp. 151–70.

Harris, Robin, ed. 1997. *The Collected Speeches of Margaret Thatcher*. New York: Harper Collins.

Hayden, Cori. 2021. 'From Connection to Contagion', *Journal of the Royal Anthropological Institute* (N.S.) 27: 95–107.

Hayek, Friedrich A. 1958[1948]. *Individualism and Economic Order: A Critical Analysis of Socialist Economics and a Plea for the Preservation of 'True Individualism'*. London: Routledge.

Hayes, Adam. 2019. 'The Socio-Technological Lives of Bitcoin', *Theory, Culture & Society* 36(4): 49–72. https://doi.org/10.1177/0263276419826218.

Hebdige, Dick. 1979. *Subculture: The Meaning of Style*. London: Routledge.

Holbraad, Martin. 2014. 'Revolución o muerte: Self-Sacrifice and the Ontology of Cuban Revolution', *Ethnos* 79(3): 365–87. https://doi.org/10.1080/00141844.2013.794149.

Hughes, Eric. 1993. 'A Cypherpunk's Manifesto'. Retrieved 28 February 2019 from https://www.activism.net/cypherpunk/manifesto.html.

Huizinga, Johan. 2000[1939]. *Homo Ludens: A Study of the Play-Element in Culture*. Boston, MA: Beacon Press.

Humayun, Mariam, and Russell Belk. 2017. 'In Ones and Zeroes We trust? Money, Religion & Bitcoin', in Ayelet Gneezy, Vladas Griskevcius and Patti Williams (eds.), *NA – Advances in Consumer Research* 45. Duluth, MN: Association for Consumer Research, pp. 677–78.

Humayun, Mariam, and Russell Belk. 2018. 'Satoshi is Dead. Long Live Satoshi: The Curious Case of Bitcoin's Creator', *Consumer Culture Theory* 19: 19–35.

Ingham, Geoffrey. 2004. 'The Nature of Money', *Economic Sociology: European Economic Newsletter* 5(2): 18–28.

Ingham, Geoffrey. 2020. *Money*. Cambridge: Polity Press.

Kalb, Don. 2017. 'Regimes of Value and Worthlessness: How Two Subaltern Stories Speak', in Susana Narotzky and Victoria Goddard (eds.), *Work and Livelihoods: History, Ethnography and Models in Times of Crisis*. Abingdon: Routledge, pp. 123–36.

Kanter, Rosabeth Moss. 1972. *Commitment and Community: Communes and Utopias in Sociological Perspective*. Cambridge, MA: Harvard University Press.

Kapferer, Bruce. 2010. 'The Aporia of Power: Crisis and the Emergence of the Corporate State', *Social Analysis* 54(1): 125–51.

Kapferer, Bruce. 2024. 'Introduction: Liminality: Structure/Anti-structure and Egalitarian Dynamics', in Bruce Kapferer and Marina Gold (eds.), *Egalitarian Dynamics: Liminality, and Victor Turner's Contribution to the Understanding of Socio-Historical Process*. New York and Oxford: Berghahn Press.

King, Timothy, and Dimitrios Koutmos. 2021. 'Herding and Feedback Trading in Cryptocurrency Markets', *Annals of Operations Research* 300(1): 79–96. https://doi.org/10.1007/s10479-020-03874-4.

Kroker, Arthur, and Michael A. Weinstein. 1994. *Data Trash: The Theory of the Virtual Class*. Montreal: New World Perspectives.

Kupfer, Joseph H. 2007. 'When Waiting is Weightless: The Virtue of Patience', *The Journal of Value Inquiry* 41: 265–80.

Laidlaw, James. 2013. *The Subject of Virtue: An Anthropology of Ethics and Freedom*. New York: Cambridge University Press.

Land, Nick. 2018. 'Crypto-Current: An Introduction to Bitcoin and Philosophy', *Šum* 10(2). Retrieved 11 September 2023 from http://sumrevija.si/en/sum10-2-nick-land-crypto-current-an-introduction-to-bitcoin-and-philosophy/.

Lash, Scott. 2012. 'Deforming the Figure: Topology and the Social Imaginary', *Theory, Culture & Society* 29(4/5): 261–87.

Latour, Bruno et al. 2012. '"The Whole is Always Smaller than its Parts": A Digital Test of Gabriel Tardes' Monads', *The British Journal of Sociology* 63(4): 590–615.

Lattas, Andrew. 2007. 'Cargo Cults and the Politics of Alterity: A Review Article', *Anthropological Forum* 17(2): 149–61. https://doi.org/10.1080/00664670701438407.

Lazarus, Robert. 2022. 'Circulating Cassettes of Ceremony: Indigenous Peer-to-Peer Networks in Arnhem Land', *Media, Culture & Society* 44(1): 141–60. https://doi.org/10.1177/01634437211045543.

Le Bon, Gustave. 1895. *The Crowd: A Study of the Popular Mind*. Mineola, NY: Dover Publications, Inc. (first published in French as Psychologie des Foules).

Lee, Raymond L.M. 2016. 'Do Online Crowds Really Exist? Proximity, Connectivity and Collectivity', *Distinktion: Journal of Social Theory* 18(1): 82–94. https://doi.org/10.1080/1600910X.2016.1218903.

Lee, Raymond L.M. 2021. 'Collectivity, Connectivity and Control: Reframing Mass Society in the Digital Era', *International Review of Sociology* 31(3): 1–18. https://doi.org/10.1080/03906701.2021.1913546.

Leins, Stefan. 2018. *Stories of Capitalism: Inside the Role of Financial Analysts*. Chicago, IL: University of Chicago Press.

Levy, Stephen. 1993. 'Crypto Rebels', *Wired Magazine*, 1 February. Retrieved 17 January 2023 from https://www.wired.com/1993/02/crypto-rebels/.

Luhrmann, T.M. 2012. 'A Hyperreal God and Modern Belief: Toward and Anthropological Theory of Mind', *Current Anthropology* 53(4): 371–95.

Lyng, Stephen. (ed.). 2005. *Edgework: The Sociology of Risk-taking*. London: Routledge.

MacFarlane, Alan. 'Louis Dumont and the Origins of Individualism', *Cambridge Anthropology* 16(1): 1–28.

Maddox, Alexia, et al. 2016. 'Constructive Activism in the Dark Web: Cryptomarkets and Illicit Drugs in the Digital "demimonde"', *Information, Communication & Society* 19(1): 1–16.

Malherbe, Léo, et al. 2019. 'Cryptocurrencies and Blockchain: Opportunities and Limits of a Mew Monetary Regime', *International Journal of Political Economy* 48(2): 127–52.

Maurer, Bill, Taylor Nelms and Lana Swartz. 2013. '"When Perhaps the Real Problem is Money Itself!": The Practical Materiality of Bitcoin', *Social Semiotics* 23(2): 261–77.

Mauss, Marcel. 1990[1925]. *The Gift: The Form and Reasons for Exchange in Archaic Societies*, trans. W.D. Halls. New York: Norton.

May, Timothy. 1988. *The Crypto Anarchist Manifesto*. Retrieved 1 March 2025 from https://theanarchistlibrary.org/library/timothy-c-may-crypto-anarchist-manifesto.

May, Timothy. 1992. 'Libertaria in Cyberspace', *Satoshi Nakamoto Institute*. Retrieved 6 February 2019 from https://nakamotoinstitute.org/libertariain-cyberspace/.

May, Timothy. 1994. 'The Cyphernomicon: Cypherpunks FAQ and More, Version 0.666,1994-09-10'. Retrieved 24 March 2025 from http://www.kreps.org/hackers/overheads/11cyphernervs.pdf.

Mazzarella, William. 2010. 'The Myth of the Multitude, or, Who's Afraid of the Crowd?', *Critical Inquiry* 36(4): 697–727.

Mazzarella, William. 2017. *The Mana of Mass Society*. Chicago, IL: University of Chicago Press.

McClelland, John. 1989. *The Crowd and the Mob: From Plato to Canetti*. London: Unwin Hyman.

Menger, Carl. 2009[1892]. *On the Origins of Money*. Auburn, AL: Ludwig von Mises Institute. Retrieved 11 November 2023 from https://mises.org/library/book/origins-money.

Mol, Annemarie, and John Law. 1994. 'Regions, Networks and Fluids: Anaemia and Social Topology', *Social Studies of Science* 24(4): 641–71. https://doi.org/10.1177/030631279402400.

Nakamoto, Satoshi. 2008a. 'Bitcoin: A Peer-to-Peer Electronic Cash System'. Retrieved 3 July 2021 from https://bitcoin.org/bitcoin.pdf.

Nakamoto, Satoshi. 2008b. 'Bitcoin P2P e-Cash Paper. Email Correspondence'. Retrieved 1 March 2025 from https://www.mail-archive.com/cryptography@metzdowd.com/msg09971.html.

Narotzky, Susana. 2012. 'Europe in Crisis: Grassroots Economies and the Anthropological Turn', *Etnográfica* 16(3): 627–38. https://doi.org/10.4000/etnografica.2145.

Narotzky, Susana, and Niko Besnier. 2014. 'Crisis, Value, and Hope: Rethinking the Economy: An Introduction to Supplement 9', *Current Anthropology* 55(Supplement 9): S1–S16. https://doi.org/10.1086/676327.

Navaro-Yashin, Yael. 2007. 'Make-Believe Papers, Legal Forms and the Counterfeit: Affective Interactions Between Documents and People in Britain and Cyprus', *Anthropological Theory* 7(1): 79–98. https://doi.org/10.1177/1463499607074294.

Nelms, Taylor C. et al. 2018. 'Social Payments: Innovation, Trust, Bitcoin, and the Sharing Economy', *Theory, Culture and Society* 35(3): 13–33.

Ohana, David. 2016. *The Nihilist Order: The Intellectual Roots of Totalitarianism*. Consolidated paperback edition. Brighton: Sussex Academic Press.

Pianalto, Matthew. 2014. 'In Defence of Patience', in Dane R. Gordon and David B. Suits (eds.), *Epictetus: His Continuing Influence and Contemporary Relevance*. Rochester, NY: RIT Press, pp. 89–104.

Pickering, Andrew. 2011. *The Cybernetic Brain: Sketches of Another Future*. Chicago, IL: University of Chicago Press.

Pickles, Anthony J. 2024. 'Gambling Crowds as Crypto-Oracles? Bridging the Real and the Blockchain through Utopian Markets and Oracular Shenanigans', in Matan Shapiro (ed.), *Crypto Crowds: Singularities and Multiplicities on the Blockchain*. New York: Berghahn, pp. 66–83.

Pittman, Holly. 2018. 'Administrative Role of Seal Imagery in the Early Bronze Age: Mesopotamian and Iranian Traders on the Plateau', in M. America, et al. (eds.), *Seals and Sealing in the Ancient World: Case Studies from the Near East, Egypt, the Aegean, and South Asia*. Cambridge: Cambridge University Press, pp. 13–35. https://doi.org/10.1017/9781108160186.004.

Popper, Nathaniel. 2015. *Digital Gold: The Untold Story of Bitcoin*. New York: Penguin Books.

Rand, Ayn. 1957. *Atlas Shrugged*. New York: Random House.

Richard, Analiese, and Daromir Rudnyckyj. 2009. 'Economies of Affect', *Journal of the Royal Anthropological Institute* 15(1): 57–77. https://doi.org/10.1111/j.1467-9655.2008.01530.x.

Rio, Knut, and Olaf Smedal. 2008. 'Totalization and Detotalization: Alternatives to Hierarchy and Individualism', *Anthropological Theory* 8(3): 233–54.

Roberts, Siobhan. 2022. 'How "Trustless" is Bitcoin, Really?' *New York Times,* 6 June. Retrieved 9 September 2023 from https://www.nytimes.com/2022/06/06/science/bitcoin-nakamoto-blackburn-crypto.html.

Rohrer, Finlo. 2010. 'Who Invented the Mexican Wave?', *BBC Magazine*, 16 October. Retrieved 9 August 2025 from http://news.bbc.co.uk/2/hi/8742454.stm.

Rubin, Zach, Don Willis, and Mayana Ludwig. 2019. 'Measuring Success in Intentional Communities: A Critical Evaluation of Commitment and Longevity Theories', *Sociological Spectrum* 39(3): 181–93. https://doi.org/10.1080/02732173.2019.1645063.

Schneider, Nathan. 2019. 'Decentralisation: An Incomplete Ambition', *Journal of Cultural Economy* 12(4): 265–85. https://doi.org/10.1080/17530350.2019.1589553.

Schrempp, Gregory. 2016. *The Science of Myths and Vice Versa.* Chicago, IL: University of Chicago Press.

Scott, Brett. 2014. 'Vision of a Techno-Leviathan: The Politics of the Bitcoin Blockchain', *Current Anthropology* (*E-International Relations.* Open Access online) 37(3): 395–428.

Shapiro, Matan. 2019. 'Dynamics of Movement: Intensity, Ritualized Play and the Cosmology of Kinship Relations in Northeast Brazil', *Anthropological Theory* 20(2): 193–220. https://doi.org/10.1177/1463499619844102.

Shapiro, Matan. 2022. 'Crypto-Egalitarian Life: Ideational and Materialist Approaches to Bitcoin', *Social Analysis: The International Journal of Anthropology* 66(3) special issue (Bjørn Enge Bertelsen, Bruce Kapferer and Knut Rio [eds.], 'Egalitarian Life: Ethnographic Perspectives on Political Experimentation'): 62–82. https://doi:10.3167/sa.2022.660304.

Shapiro, Matan. 2024. 'Introduction', in Matan Shapiro (ed.), *Crypto Crowds: Singularities and Multiplicities on the Blockchain.* London: Berghahn Books, pp. 1–22.

Shapiro, Matan. 2025. 'Playtime: Monitoring and Surveillance in NFT Sociality', in Vita Peacock, et al. (eds.), *Rhythm and Vigilance: Ethnographies of Surveillance and Time.* Bristol: Bristol University Press, pp. 178–95.

Shapiro, Matan, and Hanna Skartveit. 2025. 'Cosmic Crisis: Bitcoin and the Future Economic Collapse', in Diana Espírito Santo and Ruy Llera Blanes (eds.), *Temporal Explorations in the Anthropology of Religion: History, Cosmology and Spirits.* London: Bloomsbury Academic, pp. 147–68.

Simmel, Georg. 2004[1900]. *The Philosophy of Money* (third enlarged edition), ed. D. Frisby, trans. D. Frisby and T. Bottomore. London: Routledge.

Smith, Charles W. 2005. 'Financial Edgeworkers: Trading in Market Currents', in Stephen Lyng (ed.), *Edgework: The Sociology of Risk-taking.* London: Routledge, pp. 187–200.

Smith, Graeme. 2007. 'Margaret Thatcher's Christian Faith: A Case Study in Political Theology', *The Journal of Religious Ethics* 35(2): 233–57.

Stage, Carsten. 2013. 'The Online Crowd: A Contradiction in Terms? On the Potentials of Gustave Le Bon's Crowd Psychology in an Analysis of Affective Blogging', *Distinktion: Scandinavian Journal of Social Theory* 14(2): 211–26. https://doi.org/10.1080/1600910X.2013.773261.

Strahilevitz, Lior. 2002. 'Charismatic Code, Social Norms, and the Emergence of Cooperation on the File-Swapping Networks', *U Chicago Law & Economics, Olin Working Paper* No. 162. http://doi.org/10.2139/ssrn.329700.

Strathern, Marilyn. 1996. 'Cutting the Network', *The Journal of the Royal Anthropological Institute* 2(3): 517–35.

Swartz, Lana. 2017. 'Blockchain Dreams: Imagining Techno-Economic Alternatives After Bitcoin', in Manuel Castells (ed.), *Another Economy is Possible: Culture and Economy in a Time of Crisis*. Cambridge: Polity Press, pp. 82–105.

Swartz, Lana. 2018. 'What Was Bitcoin, What Will it Be? The Technoeconomic Imaginaries of a New Money Technology', *Cultural Studies* 32(4): 623–50.

Swartz, Lana. 2020. *New Money: How Payment Became Social Media*. New Haven, CT: Yale University Press.

Swartz, Lana. 2021. 'Bitcoin as a Meme and a Future', *Noema*, 11 February. Retrieved 17 May 2022 from https://www.noemamag.com/bitcoin-as-a-meme-and-a-future/.

Swartz, Lana. 2022. 'Theorizing the 2017 Blockchain ICO Bubble as a Network Scam', *New Media & Society* 24(7): 1695–713. https://doi.org/10.1177/14614448221099224.

Szabo, Nick. 1997. 'The Idea of Smart Contracts'. Retrieved 15 May 2023 from https://nakamotoinstitute.org/the-idea-of-smartcontracts/.

Szabo, Nick. 2002. 'Shelling Out: The Origins of Money'. Satoshi Nakamoto Institute. Retrieved 17 June 2022 from https://nakamotoinstitute.org/shelling-out/.

Taddeo, Mariarosaria, and Antonino Vaccaro. 2011. 'Analyzing Peer-to-Peer Technology Using Information Ethics', *The Information Society* 27(2): 105–12. https://doi.org/10.1080/01972243.2011.548698.

Tarde, Gabriel. 1903. *The Laws of Imitation*, trans. E.C. Parsons. New York: Henry Holt and Company.

Tarde, Gabriel. 1912. *Penal Philosophy*. Boston, MA: Brown and Little Company.

Thatcher, Margaret. 1987. 'Interview for "*Woman's Own*" ("No Such Thing as Society")', Interviewer: Douglas Keay. Retrieved 1 April 2021 from https://www.margaretthatcher.org/document/106689.

Thatcher, Margaret. 1997[1977]. 'The Ian Macleod Memorial Lecture', in Robin Harris (ed.), *The Collected Speeches of Margaret Thatcher*. New York: Harper Collins, pp. 58–69.

Tönnies, Ferdinand, and José Harris. 2001[1887]. *Community and Civil Society*. Cambridge: Cambridge University Press.

Tsavelis, Dimitrios. 2024. 'The Sociality of the Blockchain and the Appification of Money Affordances of a New Paradigm for Crowds', in Matan Shapiro (ed.), *Crypto Crowds: Singularities and Multiplicities on the Blockchain*. London: Berghahn Books, pp. 40–65.

Tuddenham, Mitchell. 2024. 'Unstructured Simplicity: The Peer-to-Peer Collective and Concurrent Formations of Cryptocommunities', in Matan Shapiro (ed.), *Crypto Crowds: Singularities and Multiplicities on the Blockchain*. London: Berghahn Books, pp. 111–33.

Turner, Fred. 2006. *From Counterculture to Cyberculture: Stewart Brand, the Whole Earth Network, and the Rise of Digital Utopianism*. Chicago, IL: University of Chicago Press.

Turner, Victor. 1969. *The Ritual Process: Structure and Anti-Structure*. Ithaca, NY: Cornell University Press.

Turner Victor. 1974. *Liminal to Liminoid, in Play, Flow, and Ritual: An Essay in Comparative Symbology*. Rice Institute Pamphlet – Rice University Studies, 60, no. 3: 53–92. Retrieved 31 October 2025 from https://hdl.handle.net/1911/63159.

Vanolo, Alberto. 2018. 'Cities and the Politics of Gamification', *Cities* 74: 320–26.

Vennonen, Anna. 2024. 'Affective Processes in Cryptocurrency Markets: An Exploration with Crowd Theory', in Matan Shapiro (ed.), *Crypto Crowds: Singularities and Multiplicities on the Blockchain*. London: Berghahn Books, pp. 84–110.

Vidan, Gili, and Vili Lehdonvirta. 2019. 'Mine the Gap: Bitcoin and the Maintenance of Trustlessness', *New Media & Society* 21(1): 42–59.

Weber, Max. 1921. *Economy and Society: An Outline of Interpretive Sociology* (2 vols.). Berkeley, CA: University of California Press.

Weber, Max. 2002 [1930]. The Protestant Ethic and the Spirit of Capitalism, trans. T. Parsons. London: George Allen & Unwin Ltd (first published in German in 1905).

Wiedemann, Carolin. 2014. 'Between Swarm, Network, and Multitude: Anonymous and the Infrastructures of the Common', *Distinktion: Journal of Social Theory* 15(3): 309–26. https://doi.org/10.1080/1600910X.2014.895768.

Wiener, Anna. 2018. 'The Complicated Legacy of Stewart Brand's "Whole Earth Catalogue"', *The New Yorker*, 16 November. Retrieved 9 January 2023 from https://www.newyorker.com/news/letter-from-silicon-valley/the-complicated-legacy-of-stewart-brands-whole-earth-catalog.

Wiener, Anna. 2020. *Uncanny Valley: A Memoir*. New York: MCD Books.

Zelizer, Viviana A. 2005. *The Purchase of Intimacy*. Princeton, NJ: Princeton University Press.

Zimmer, Zac. 2017. 'Bitcoin and Potosí Silver: Historical Perspectives on Cryptocurrency', *Technology and Culture* 58(2): 307–34.

Zuboff, Shoshana. 2019. *The Age of Surveillance Capitalism: The Fight for a Human Future at the New Frontier of Power*. New York: Public Affairs.

INDEX

www.ingramcontent.com/pod-product-compliance
Lightning Source LLC
LaVergne TN
LVHW012000100226
R19193800001B/R191938PG831182LVX00003B/5